THE CRUSADERS

RÉGINE PERNOUD

THE
CRUSADERS

Translated by
Enid Grant

IGNATIUS PRESS   SAN FRANCISCO

Orignal French edition: *Les Croisés*,
published by Librairie Hachette, Paris, © 1959

First English edition © 1963, Oliver and Boyd, Ltd.
Edinburgh and London
All rights reserved
Reprinted by permission.

First American edition
©1962, Martin Secker and Warburg, Ltd
G. P. Putnam's Sons, New York

Cover art: Jean Baptiste Mauzaisse (1784–1844)
King Louis VII takes the standard at Saint-Denis in the presence of
Queen Eleanor of Aquitaine and receives the pilgrim's staff
from the hands of Pope Eugenius III
before leaving for the Second Crusade in 1147.
Chateaux de Versailles et de Trianon, Versailles, France
Réunion des Musées Nationaux/Art Resource, N.Y.

Cover design by Riz Boncan Marsella

Published in 2003 by Ignatius Press, San Francisco
ISBN 978-0-89870-949-0
Library of Congress control number 2002112063
Printed in the United States of America

CONTENTS

MAPS

TRANSLATOR'S PREFACE

This book is a translation of *Les Croisés* by Mlle. Régine Pernoud, published by Librairie Hachette. Three maps selected by the author have been included in addition to the original text.

The work of translating this book was always interesting because Mlle. Pernoud has taken a directly human point of view as she describes how ordinary people responded to the great challenge of the Crusades.

She has made a lively assessment of a cross-section of the Crusaders, tracing the lives of churchmen, barons, ladies, merchants, and artificers, in times of peace and war, on their journeys and in the towns and castles of the Holy Land.

The story is unfolded as a revelation of human strengths and weaknesses—love, greed, ambition, piety, courage— thrown into sharp relief by the immensity of their setting.

The narrative is made vivid and extremely telling by the many passages of contemporary prose and verse which have been chosen as illustration. Here I should like to express my gratitude to Dr. G. F. Cunningham for his delightful verse translations of the medieval French poems in the original text.

E. G.

INTRODUCTION

For many years the Crusades have held a particular attraction for historians. The names of René Grousset, Jean Richard, and Claude Cahen spring readily to mind. Making systematic use of Arab as well as Western sources, they have taken us a stage farther in our knowledge of the Latin kingdoms of the East. An important contribution has been made by Runciman and by Stevenson, and an admirable synthesis, *The History of the Crusades*, has been published by the University of Pennsylvania.

The Crusades represent one of the peaks of achievement of the medieval world, for they are an exploit unique in its kind, being neither migration nor colonization, but a movement of volunteers who came from all the races of Europe, independent alike of regular resources and of centralized authority. For us today they are indeed an amazing spectacle, and one that leads us on to conjecture about the men who took part in them.

It is from this angle alone that we propose to look at the Crusades. The actual events are now sufficiently well known for us to be able to refer to sources that have been proven reliable—thanks to the labor of the historians mentioned above—and thus attempt a better understanding of the men who lived through them. What were their modes of life, their outlook, their customs, their mentality? How did they solve their material problems of equipment, provisioning, tactics? What was their driving force? What was it that stirred them to action, to battle, and to love? It was this ancestor of ours, this Crusader, who built Chartres and Amiens, who brought forth from the soil whole new towns, who forged our language, who thought up the concepts of courtly love and the search for the Holy Grail. There are many things about this man that astonish us. In the course of an adventure that lasted for two centuries he astonished himself too, and this led to such a large number of chronicles, letters, and contemporary accounts that he is revealed to us in a much more brilliant light than if he had been confined to his ordinary existence as a peasant in Picardy or a baron in Languedoc.

Several excellent books are available that give a complete picture of the political and military history of the Crusades. They supply an outline of the essential facts in a form both pleasant and easy to read. There is, for example, Paul Rousset's notable book *Histoire des Croisades* (Payot, 1957), or there is the shorter study *Les Croisades* contributed by René Grousset to the series "*Que sais-je?*" (Presses Universitaires, 1944). Perhaps, however, it will be useful to the reader to give here a brief résumé of the chief events of the period.

It would be contrary to the principles of historical research to go on using the old classifications, which, according to Paul Rousset, "enumerate Crusades like the wonders of the world". There was certainly a "first" Crusade, but, after that, appeals and departures followed one another in a rhythm that varied but never ceased until the end of the thirteenth century. By that time the term *Crusade* had become a misnomer, since it was applied to the struggle against the might of the Turks rather than to the effort to retake Jerusalem.

The object of the appeal launched by Pope Urban II at the Council of Clermont in 1095 was in fact the reconquest of the Holy Land, and this was the simple intention behind the Crusaders' vow. After the thirteenth century the high ideal became a little blurred, and the expeditions of the four-teenth century could not, in all honesty, be called Crusades. It seems more correct to take as our point of departure the history of the Latin kingdoms overseas rather than that of the various armed groups that came to their aid during the twelfth and thirteenth centuries.

For the First Crusade, four different groups met outside the walls of Constantinople. There were, first, the northern French and the men of Lorraine under the leadership of God-frey of Bouillon and his brother Baldwin of Boulogne; sec-ond, an army of Frenchmen from the country between the Seine and the Loire, together with men from the north of Italy, under Hugh of Vermandois (brother of the reigning King of France, Phillip I), Stephen of Blois, and Robert Curthose (son of William the Conqueror); thirdly, men from the Midi under the count of Toulouse, Raymond of Saint Giles; and finally, there were Normans from Sicily led by Bohemond of Tarento and his nephew Tancred. (Bohe-mond was a son of the Norman Robert Guiscard, who had conquered Sicily and part of southern Italy.)

After a preliminary victory over the Turks at Dorylaeum (July 1, 1097), the Crusaders reached the walls of Antioch and took it after a terrible siege that lasted for eight months (October 20, 1097, to June 28, 1098). The credit for the capture of the town was due to Bohemond, and he managed to induce the other crusading leaders to hand it over to him, thus founding for himself and his descendants the principal-ity of Antioch, which survived until 1268. This, incidentally, caused friction with the Byzantine Empire, which had once possessed Antioch and northern Syria and had expected to have these territories returned by the Crusaders.

During the siege of Antioch an Armenian prince, Thoros, appealed for help to the Crusaders. Baldwin of Boulogne went to his aid and relieved the province of Edessa. Later he allowed Thoros to be killed in a riot and made himself the sole ruler of Edessa, taking the title of count. This county of Edessa in Cilicia lasted until 1144, when it was retaken by Zengi, the atabeg, or governor, of Mosul.

On Friday, July 15, 1099, three years after their departure, the Crusaders made themselves masters of Jerusalem. A week later, on July 22, Godfrey of Bouillon, chosen as ruler by his companions to ensure the safeguarding of their conquest, took the title Advocate of the Holy Sepulchre.

The count of Toulouse, Raymond of Saint Giles, then undertook the conquest of the Tripoli district, which was important because of its geographical position, being the link between the principality of Antioch in northern Syria and the kingdom of Jerusalem. With the help of a Genoese fleet he captured in turn Tortosa (1102) and Giblet (1104), then laid siege to Tripoli, which was taken after his death by his son Bertrand, on July 12, 1109. Tripoli was the last of the domains that the Crusaders won for themselves overseas. The region, together with the title of count, remained in the hands of the descendants of Raymond of Saint Giles until 1187, when Tripoli passed under the control of the princes of Antioch. It was finally conquered by the Mameluke Turks in 1289.

The overseas possessions of the Crusaders were thus made up of four distinct fiefs: the principality of Antioch, the county of Edessa, the county of Tripoli, and the kingdom of Jerusalem.

The history of the Crusades revolves around the kingdom of Jerusalem. After Godfrey died in 1100, his brother Baldwin succeeded him and took the title of king. He imposed a more united organization on Frankish Syria and extended its boundaries by occupying Transjordan and by establishing a military post on the Gulf of Akaba on the Red Sea.

He was succeeded in 1118 by his cousin Baldwin of Bourg, who took the title of Baldwin II and directed his efforts, although without success, against Aleppo and Damascus, two towns still held by the Muslims. The daughter of Baldwin II, Melisende, had married Count Fulk of Anjou. In 1131 he succeeded his father-in-law and established friendly relations both with the Byzantines and with the Muslims of Damascus. Unfortunately, Fulk died in 1143, leaving Melisende to act as regent for his young son, Baldwin III. It was at this time that the governors of Aleppo and Mosul (Zengi, followed by his son, Nur ed-din) took the opportunity to seize Edessa (1144–46). An expedition to which the name of Second Crusade is given set out to help the Holy Land. It was badly led and failed in an attempt to take Damascus by siege (1148). Nur ed-din rounded off his victory by stripping the principality of Antioch of all its possessions beyond the Orontes; then he united Syria for the Muslims by seizing Damascus (1154). Baldwin III marked the beginning of his personal rule by retaliating and took Ascalon from the Egyptians (August 19, 1153). He married Theodora, niece of the Byzantine Emperor Manuel Comnenus, in 1158. Amalric, Baldwin's brother, who succeeded him in 1162, followed a policy of friendship with Egypt, which felt itself threatened by the power of Nur ed-din. Then in 1171 the youthful Saladin, Nur ed-din's lieutenant, deposed the last descendant of the Fatimite dynasty in Egypt; soon he captured Damascus (1174) and Aleppo (1183) and thus, by uniting Egypt and Syria, the two halves of the Muslim world, effectively encircled the Frankish states.

Amalric died in 1174. His son, the leper King Baldwin IV, displayed in spite of his terrible disease an activity that kept Saladin at bay and even carried the Franks to victory at Montgisard (November 25, 1177), one of the most brilliant military achievements of the Crusades. But the incapacity of his successor, Guy of Lusignan, the Poitevin baron who married Baldwin's sister Sybilla, led to the downfall of the kingdom. At the battle of the Horns of Hattin (July 4, 1187) the crusading army was utterly defeated by Saladin, who then proceeded to take all the Frankish towns one after another. Acre fell on July 10, Jaffa and Beirut on August 6, and finally Jerusalem itself on October 2, 1187.

It seemed now as if the Frankish occupation of Syria was at an end. In the kingdom of Jerusalem the Crusaders held only Tyre; in the principality of Antioch only the town of Antioch and the stronghold of Margat; and in the County of Tripoli only Tripoli, Tortosa, and Krak des Chevaliers.

However, Conrad of Montferrat, newly arrived in Syria from Piedmont, proved himself an energetic defender of Tyre. He forced Saladin's men to withdraw, and soon afterward the Franks began the siege of Acre, which fell into their hands two years later (August 1189 to July 12, 1191), thanks to help brought by the kings of France and England, Philip Augustus and Richard Cœur de Lion in the Third Crusade. The peace concluded with Saladin on September 3, 1192, left to the Franks the coast of Palestine from Tyre to Jaffa and allowed them to travel freely to Jerusalem on pilgrimage.

From now onward Acre became the capital of the "kingdom of Jerusalem", while another Frankish kingdom was established in Cyprus, conquered from the Byzantines by Richard Cœur de Lion. In succession, Henry of Champagne (1192–97), Amalric of Lusignan (1197–1205), and John of Brienne (1210–25) bore the title of "King of Jerusalem". It was held next by Frederick II, King of Sicily, who disembarked at Acre in 1228. In the meantime, an expedition of men coming mainly from Picardy, Flanders, and Champagne had been turned against Byzantium by the guile of the Venetians, and in 1204 these Crusaders made themselves masters of the empire. Their leader, Baldwin of Flanders, became the first ruler of the Latin empire of Constantinople, which lasted until 1261, when a Greek Emperor, Michael Paleologus, was restored to the throne.

Frederick II, by the Treaty of Jaffa in 1229, had gained the restitution of the three holy towns of Bethlehem, Nazareth, and Jerusalem, but his presence in Palestine was in itself the cause of a civil war, which broke out immediately after he left. Between 1229 and 1243 the history of Frankish Syria is a tale of battles between the Franks and the Imperialists, or representatives of the Germanic Emperor. In 1244 Jerusalem was finally retaken by the Turks. Four years later, the King of France, Louis IX, went on crusade and led his armies into Egypt, a country often attacked, particularly by John of Brienne, during the first half of the thirteenth century. The King seized Damietta, but he was surrounded by the Egyptians and taken prisoner. He was forced to surrender and spent the next four years in Syria (1250–54) restoring discipline, repairing the coastal fortresses, and prolonging by several years the survival of a kingdom damaged as much by internal anarchy as by the assaults of the Muslim forces. The Mameluke Turks, under the leadership of the Sultan Baibars (1260–77), united under their own power Egypt and the whole of Syria (Aleppo, Damascus, and Jerusalem). Baibars seized the principal strongholds one by one—Caesarea (1265), Jaffa (1268), Antioch (1268), then Krak des Chevaliers (1271). After him the Sultan Qalaoun took Tripoli (1289), and his son and successor, Al-Ashraf, by the capture of Acre (May 28, 1291), brought to an end the existence of the Frankish kingdom of Syria.

NONVIOLENCE AND NONRESISTANCE

Günther, bishop of Bamberg, arranged to make a pilgrimage to the Holy Land and eventually found himself at the head of more than twelve thousand of the faithful of his own and neighboring dioceses—"barons and princes, rich men and poor". This enormous crowd managed to travel fairly easily and in the spring of 1065 arrived in Palestine. As the pilgrims neared Jerusalem, the thought of celebrating the approaching feast of Easter in the Holy City helped them to forget their weariness.

On Good Friday they were between Caesarea and Ramleh, barely two days' march from their journey's end, when they were suddenly attacked by a group of Bedouins. A hail of arrows fell on the exhausted crowds; ironically enough, their only refuge was the wagons that carried the sick people and the women and children, hastily converted into barricades. Most of the pilgrims had come unarmed; a few "felt compelled to defend themselves", as the chronicle puts it; others carried the spirit of pilgrimage to the point of martyrdom and refused to offer any resistance. At one moment a priest induced them all to throw aside their weapons and to fall on their knees in prayer. Then they decided to beg the Arabs for a truce. The massacre apparently dragged on from Good Friday until Easter Day and probably ended only because the attackers were short of arrows, or tired of killing, or because the spoils were not worth the trouble.

All those who set off for the Holy Land were aware of the perils of the journey. The fate of Bishop Günther and his

German pilgrims was well known on account of the large numbers involved and the long duration of the massacre, but it was not an isolated case. Death at the hands of marauders was hardly worse than being offered for sale in the slave markets of Syria or Egypt. This, for many, was the end of the pilgrimage; others escaped after being ransomed or stripped of their belongings by various exactions. The Byzantine guardians of the Holy Places collected heavy tolls from the Western pilgrims, and the chroniclers tell of many poor people left without the means to return home and forced to live on the charity of the tiny Christian communities in Palestine.

About the year 1056 Lietbert, bishop of Cambrai, and his company were so thoroughly fleeced in Cyprus that they were able to travel only as far as Laodicea. There they met the bishop of Laon, Hélinand, on his way back from the Holy Land. He painted such a black picture of the difficulties awaiting them in Jerusalem that the pilgrims decided to go back home. Another victim was Geraud, abbot of Saint-Florent-lès-Saumur, who was seized by Saracens outside Jerusalem, tortured, and put to death. Pope Victor II had met Lietbert's Flemish party on their return, and their unsuccessful pilgrimage had at least the effect of making him write to the Eastern Empress Theodora asking her to put an end to the system of exactions that the Byzantine guardians of the Holy Places levied on the pilgrims. Apart from this, he was powerless to improve the situation.

In spite of the hazards, pilgrimages to the Holy Land continued. Nothing could stop Christians from turning their thoughts and their steps toward the land where the gospel was first preached and where the Savior of mankind had lived his life on earth. Similar pilgrimages in our day, even though they attract considerably more people now than they did fifty or even twenty years ago, give only a slight idea of the enthusiasm that they could arouse in the medieval Christian. A man of those days knew all about Palestine before ever he set foot in it. His heart and mind alike had been sustained since earliest childhood by Holy Scripture, and from Jacob's Well to the journeys of Saint Paul he knew every name and every landmark in the country. The psalms he sang, the sermons he heard, the daily liturgy governing the rhythm of the year and of his whole existence—all told him of the Holy Land.

The act of pilgrimage is an important part of the Christian life. It can be traced back to the early days of Christianity and was known before that as a custom of the Jews. In the Middle Ages the idea became very highly developed—more so, perhaps, than at any other time except our own, when unexpectedly enough, French students set off in thousands every year for Chartres, and crowds of people from every nation make for Lourdes or Fatima. For a Christian, pilgrimage is not a ritual act as it is for a Muslim. It has not even, properly speaking, a place in the liturgy. It does, however, resolve into action one of the vital ideas of Christianity—that is the idea of transition, of the Easter transformation. At this point it is bound up with that most essential part of Christian life—the need to strive after another way of living, to deny one's own personality in order to follow Someone else. This idea, in the space of one era of Christian civilization, changed to a surprising extent the face of the Western world by establishing the great roads of pilgrimage and raising churches at every stage on the route. In addition to this, although of secondary importance, there is the idea of atonement, of penitence, that is connected with pilgrimage. For instance, on three separate occasions the journey to Jerusalem was imposed as an act of penitence on Fulk Nerra, the terrible count of Anjou, and whether he would or no, he was forced to perform it.

Finally, in the psychological makeup of medieval people there was an inherent and strongly felt need for truth in a concrete form—the need to see and to touch everything for oneself. The author of an account of the pilgrimage of Saint Willibald, who visited Palestine in the eighth century, describes himself as "one who has seen with his own eyes". Thousands of texts could be quoted to show that it was a specific characteristic of the feudal age to attach a spiritual validity to a solid object. This was the outward expression of a mental state formed by the use of the sacraments—those tangible signs of an invisible reality—and molded by the Gospels. In a sense, pilgrimage is the literal translation into everyday life of one of the most frequent of Christ's injunctions; "Arise and walk", he said to those whom he healed, and "Come, take up your cross" to those who wished to follow him. A man brought up on such teachings was conditioned to translate into action any message he received; it was impossible for him to remain passive, particularly if he was a contemplative. Hence that observation which has become a commonplace in studies of Christian spirituality, that all the truly great contemplatives have been men of action, like Saint Bernard, and the great mystics, like Saint Teresa of Avila, people of an amazing practical ability.

That the cult of relics, which is itself inherent in the Christian tradition, flourished so widely in the Middle Ages is due to this same compulsion to touch and to see. It is understandable that this should be so in an age that insisted that some physical sign should accompany each transaction. Thus the taking over of an estate was marked by the *traditio*, the giving of a sod of earth or a truss of straw as a symbol of the whole; the conclusion of a bargain was indicated by a handshake, and so on. The *idea* behind the Crusades has often been a subject for discussion. In fact, nothing could have been less like an idea or an ideology than the compulsion that drew the awakened West toward the Holy Land. The attraction was, in fact, a positive reality—it was the land itself, the place where our Lord had lived. Guibert of Nogent gets to the heart of things when he says that the Crusader set himself the task of winning back the earthly Jerusalem in order to enjoy the celestial Jerusalem that it represents. In feudal times, when all rights and duties and all social relations were governed by the idea of a fief, of a tangible possession, it would seem only right that the land of our Lord should be the fief of Christendom; the reverse would seem an injustice.

Pilgrimages to the Holy Land, like those to Rome, had been customary since the early days of Christianity. From the year 333 comes an account by a man of Aquitaine describing the stages of his journey, first to Constantinople, then to Jerusalem, from his home in Bordeaux. Saint Jerome's choice of Jerusalem as the place for working on his version of Holy Scripture had the result of encouraging the building of churches, monasteries, and hostels for pilgrims— there were about three hundred of these in Jerusalem in the fourth century.

During the early centuries of Christianity the relations between the eastern and western parts of Europe were close, and it must not be forgotten that although Rome was the religious center, there were no fewer than eight Greek and five Syrian Popes during the seventh and eighth centuries. Egypt, Syria, and North Africa saw the rise of differing forms of monasticism, and Christianity flourished there even though heresy caused frequent divisions.

This state of affairs was to be altered completely in fewer than fifty years. From the moment when Muhammad's followers began to spread his teaching by means of the "holy war", these centers of Christian life were overwhelmed one by one. Archaeologists can trace the advance of the Muslims through Palestine, Syria, Egypt, and North Africa by the trail of buildings which they left in ruins. The first to fall, in A.D. 638, was the Church of the Holy Sepulchre, which had been raised by Constantine.

Once this advance was halted, first by the failure of the assault on Constantinople in 718 and then by the battle of Poitiers in 732, a more peaceful approach became possible. It was to be seen first in the friendly relations developed between Charlemagne and Haroun al-Rashid, the famous caliph of Baghdad. If the historian Ekkehard can be believed, the latter "gave up in favor of Charlemagne his dominion over those places that had been sanctified by the mystery of the Redemption". The acknowledgment of this right of protection over the pilgrims who might venture to Palestine and the communities that might be established there is clearly the basis of the Emperor's popularity as a hero of the *chansons de geste*. It is certain, however, that by the year 808 at least one monastery on the Mount of Olives and one nunnery near the Church of the Holy Sepulchre had been reestablished, and a hostel and a basilica had been built at the "field of blood" (Haceldama). In spite of terrible difficulties pilgrimages still continued (that of the Anglo-Saxon Willibald mentioned above had begun in 722 and was to last seven years), but they were accomplished under the most precarious conditions. Although physical safety was better assured than in the past, the pilgrim was now faced with a multiplicity of dues. Bernard the Monk, for example, who made his journey between 866 and 870, was imprisoned in Cairo for nonpayment of the city's entrance tax in spite of a pass which had been given to him at Bari by the Saracens themselves.

Also, pilgrims were at the mercy of the whim of such a ruler as the sadistic Caliph Hakim. In 1009 he began without warning to persecute both Christians and Jews and to destroy all the churches and monasteries in Palestine, a savage act that aroused great feeling among the peoples of the West. He is said also to have forced Christians to wear round their necks a copper cross weighing ten pounds, while Jews had to carry a calf's head made of wood. These repressive measures gave rise to a series of tales in which it is difficult to distinguish history from legend. A hint of them is found in the stories of William of Tyre, a twelfth-century historian who used his sources with care. He gives an example of how the memory of this time of persecution still lingered a hundred years after. The right of providing the branches that were carried in procession to the Holy Sepulchre on Palm Sunday belonged to a certain family in Jerusalem. It was said that an ancestor of this family had offered his own life for others of the Christian community by taking upon himself the blame for an act of profanation of a mosque of which they were accused. As he went to his death, he had asked those who were saved by his sacrifice to care for the members of his family. So it was decided that the profits made at this feast should go each year to his descendants.

Persecution ended suddenly in A.D. 1020, and the Byzantines were able in 1048 to rebuild the Church of the Holy Sepulchre. In 1080, in spite of the arrival of the Turks, the Hospital of Saint John was founded. However, reports on the state of the Holy Land and the dangers which Christians ran there brought back by pilgrims such as those who escaped from the expedition led by Bishop Günther were far from reassuring. Pilgrims usually organized themselves in groups-not only for security, but for other reasons shared nowadays by those who journey by train to Lourdes. This foreshadowed the time when Christendom, conscious of itself and aware of its greater strength in face of the Muslims, began to query the lengths to which nonviolence should be carried and to dream of substituting for peaceful pilgrimage a more effective action for the recovery of a land the loss of which it could not accept as irreparable. After four hundred years of nonviolence, eleventh-century Christians who had already tested their weapons against the Muslims in Spain and the Mediterranean began to wonder whether it was not time to oppose the "holy war" with a "righteous war".

PART ONE

THE MEN

CHAPTER I

THE POPE OF THE FIRST CRUSADE

In the Middle Ages our Lady of Le Puy was revered as much as our Lady of Lourdes is today. People of all classes were drawn on pilgrimage to her shrine in its strange setting of volcanic rocks at the heart of France. Serfs, monks, lords, and prelates mingled in an endless succession, barefoot and carrying candles. Here, in the fervor of this throng, in the new cathedral with its great porch, its cloister, and its annexes where the pilgrims were given shelter, the *Salve Regina*, long known as the hymn of Le Puy, was first heard, and here it is still intoned by the priest at the conclusion of the Mass.

One day in August 1095, the ever-present crowd watched some unusual preparations. A hole was being made with picks in one of the walls of the building. It was gradually enlarged and finally became a new entrance to the cathedral, magnificently draped with heavy curtains of scarlet wool. The reason for this unusual activity was not far to seek—the Pope, the head of Christendom, was expected at Le Puy. He had recently crossed the Alps—probably by the usual route through the Col de Genèvre, Pavia, Turin, the Col de Suse, Briançon, and Grenoble—then had gone to Valence and consecrated the newly built cathedral there on August 5. Now he was traveling toward Le Puy by way of Romans-sur-Isère and Tournon, where he had crossed the Rhône, and the hills of

Vivarais. In honor of this important pilgrim Adhémar of Monteil, bishop of Le Puy, had caused the new doorway to be made. It would be sealed again immediately after the Pope had entered, for it was felt that no lesser person should tread where the Vicar of Christ had passed through.

On August 15 Pope Urban II celebrated a solemn Mass at Le Puy before a crowd even greater than usual. This was on the Feast of the Assumption, the principal feastday of the year at this shrine dedicated to the Virgin.

In the eleventh century the Pope, the head of Christendom, certainly did not enjoy the somewhat remote prestige that is accorded to the Sovereign Pontiff in our day. It was not at all out of the ordinary for him to travel, particularly to France, and everyone then could experience in his own district a little of that feeling approaching familiarity that is today [1959] the privilege of the Romans alone. For people of those days, seeing the Sovereign Pontiff did not mean seeing him in all the circumstance of pomp, crowned with the tiara and raised upon the Sedia. When they gathered on the roads, after his approach had been announced, they saw him on horseback or carried on a litter, in a procession of prelates and lay lords. His journeys made him known to Christians everywhere.

The fact that Urban II was a man of France enhanced his popularity. His speech and the fine features of a man of Champagne endeared him to the crowds on that Feast of the Assumption, and the tales told about him were all to his credit. He had been one of those monks whom a recent predecessor, the energetic Gregory VII, had withdrawn from the cloister to bring new life to the clergy and to revive the somewhat corrupt episcopate. They were to cooperate in the Pope's vigorous program of reform, standing firm against both lay and ecclesiastical powers, even against the Emperor himself,

in the fight against the traffic in benefices, against simoniac
clergy, and against the nepotism indulged in by the rulers of
the time, who set their favorites at the head of abbeys or
ecclesiastical provinces.

As a young man, Urban had been known as Odo of
Châtillon. He had been trained by Saint Bruno himself,
founder of the Carthusian order. Almost immediately after
his election as Pope he was obliged to enter the lists against
the Emperor Henry IV and the antipope, Guibert, his nominee, against the King of England, William Rufus, son of the
Conqueror, and against the King of France. The situation
was almost hopeless; he was forced to flee from Rome and
could rely on only five loyal bishops in the whole of Germany. Then gradually he began to recover his rights. He was
even able to return to Rome. The antipope had retreated to
Ravenna, and his followers, under imperial protection, now
held only the castle of Sant'Angelo and the actual sanctuary
of Saint Peter. In May 1095 the Pope had been able to hold
a council at Piacenza, where he effectively demonstrated that
he was, in fact, the head of Christendom. It was a surprising
thing that this man who had found his vocation in the peace
and renunciation of the cloister should have developed there
the fighting qualities of a successful leader.

While the crowd slowly scattered after the day's final ceremonies, Urban II held a long discussion with the bishop of
Le Puy, Adhémar of Monteil, the son of that count of Val-
entinois who held the castle of Montélimar. He had been a
knight before taking holy orders and was a man of fine character, respected and trusted by the Pope. In the days that
followed, monks or clerics were sent off in all directions as
messengers in the service of the bishop. They carried pontifical letters calling every abbot and bishop loyal to Urban
to a general council to be held at Clermont on the day of

the second Feast of Saint Martin, Sunday, November 18. Lay barons as well as members of the clergy were invited to its closing ceremony.

Urban II left Le Puy two days later for La Chaise-Dieu, where he was received by Durand, bishop of Clermont. On August 18 he dedicated the church there. It must, have been a happy day for this former monk to meet on this occasion three of his Cluniac friends—Hugh, bishop of Grenoble; Audebert of Montmorillon, bishop of Bourges; and Durand himself. Hugh was later canonized as Saint Hugh of Châteauneuf. He was the man who helped Saint Bruno to establish his new order in the valley of La Grande Chartreuse. These four men had all been members of the order of Cluny, which had raised to its highest pitch Catholicism's inherent feeling for splendor. The phrase "a man of perfect beauty" was the greatest commendation that the succeeding abbot could find when he wished to praise Saint Mayeul.

On the following October 25, before going to Clermont, Pope Urban II consecrated the high altar of the immense basilica at Cluny. This church was the largest in Christendom, bigger even than Saint Peter's in Rome, and it was embellished with all the glories of Romanesque art. The Pope held frequent discussions there with high-ranking clergy— including Géraud of Cardhaillac, bishop of Cahors, who will be encountered again later in Cyprus and Jerusalem—in order to settle the agenda to be followed at the Council. One of these men, Durand, bishop of Clermont, died on November 18, the very day the Council assembled, and its first business was the solemnization of his funeral.

Urban went on from La Chaise-Dieu to Saint-Gilles du Gard. He arrived on September 1, the feastday of the abbey's patron saint, when crowds of pilgrims were attracted there by the ceremonies. It is very likely that the count of Toulouse,

Raymond of Saint Giles, was among them. He was one of the most powerful vassals of the King of France, overlord of vast and wealthy lands in the south. If he was indeed present during the ten days of the Pope's stay, he probably had many talks with him while the ceremonies and processions outside followed their ordered course.

"More than two hundred and fifty episcopal crosses", wrote Bernold the chronicler with a journalistic touch when he described the scene in the cathedral at Clermont on Saint Martin's Day in 1095. Two hundred and fifty high dignitaries of the Church—bishops and mitred abbots—were among those who walked in procession to the chant of the *Veni Creator*. A huge crowd of onlookers had been attracted to Clermont, far too many to be easily accommodated even in that great cathedral, in spite of its size, its narthex, and its choir, which had an ambulatory with chapels radiating from it—this cathedral was one of the first buildings designed in this manner. The building in which the Council was held was not the present cathedral. It was replaced by one of Gothic design, further adorned, centuries later, by the towers and spires of Viollet-le-Duc. By way of contrast, the church of Notre-Dame du Port, the foundations of which had then just been laid, still stands today. There were no less than fifty-four churches in eleventh-century Clermont.

This assembly was both impressive and significant, for it was a gathering of the faithful flock around their shepherd. For many, their attendance there implied considerable courage. Pibo, bishop of Toul, now very old and infirm, had journeyed halfway across France to be there. He was a Saxon by birth and had previously been chancellor to the Emperor Henry IV. His mere presence at the Council was a protest against his powerful master and the latter's nominee, the antipope. Many bishops from the north of France had come, as if to demonstrate their loyalty to the See of Saint Peter in defiance of the Holy Empire. Among them were Lambert of Arras, Gerard of Thérouanne, and Gervin of Amiens, and the abbots of Saint Waast, Anchin, and Saint Bertin. From dioceses and abbeys within the Holy Roman Empire had come Poppo, bishop of Metz; Abbot Martin of Saint Denis du Mont; Richer, bishop of Verdun (represented by his legate); and many more.

John of Orleans and Hugh of Senlis were two bishops who came from the royal domain of France, although their King had quarrelled with the Pope. From Normandy ventured Gilbert, bishop of Evreux; Serlon, bishop of Séez; and Abbot Goutard of Jumièges, who died from old age and sickness during the course of the Council. These came from territories administered by Odo of Conteville, full brother of William the Conqueror, a man who had fought thirty years before at the Battle of Hastings and has his place on the Bayeux tapestry. He had acted as a viceroy for his brother and had been given the title of earl of Kent.

Another important group were the representatives from Spain: Berengar of Rosanes, bishop of Tarragon; Peter of Audouque, bishop of Pampeluna (Pamplona); Bernard of Sédirac, a former Cluniac monk who had been sent by Saint Hugh to Spain to become abbot of Sahugun, the "Spanish Cluny", and afterward archbishop of Toledo; also Dalmace, bishop of Compostella, another former monk of Cluny. The name of each of these bishoprics was a reminder of victories over the Moors. It was exactly ten years since Alphonso VI of Castille had retaken Toledo, and in 1092 the hero of the *Reconquista*, Roderigo Diaz the Cid Campeador, had established a new Christian state around Valencia. The great enterprise undertaken in Spain against Islam, and so strongly supported by

Cluny, was now beginning to bear fruit. Finally, the clergy of Auvergne, Aquitaine, and Languedoc were, naturally, well represented behind Adhémar of Monteil.

The atmosphere of the Council was stirring. Exciting ideas were at work like leaven, and ardent discussions were inspired by Gregory VII's reforms. Robert of Molesmes was there, the man who, in living illustration of Saint Bernard's work, was to found the Cistercian order, the spread and influence of which were to become enormous within the Church.

Meetings took place with full solemnity. Ecclesiastical justice was the first matter dealt with; quarrels were settled—such as that between the great canonist, Yvo, bishop of Chartres, and Geoffrey, abbot of La Trinité de Vendôme; previous sanctions against the sale of sacraments by simoniac clerics were renewed; decrees were issued on the taking of Communion in the two kinds which was usual at the time; the dates of Ember Days were determined; and, incidentally, men in holy orders were forbidden to frequent taverns.

In particular the Pope gave the full weight of his authority to the renewal of the right of sanctuary. This was the right which granted safety from pursuit to any criminal who could reach a monastery, a church, or indeed any holy place; even the wayside crosses were to become places of sanctuary, and a person clinging to one of them was not to be harmed. Another important decision was made that strengthened the idea of the truce of God and widened its scope. Every Christian over the age of twelve had to vow to observe its ordinances—it was forbidden to carry on private warfare during the whole of Lent, from Advent until the octave of the Epiphany; on each feastday of our Lord, of the Virgin Mary, and of the apostles; and finally during the whole time between Wednesday night and Monday morning.

It is with astonishment that one records another decree of this Council, one completely at odds with the most elementary rules of diplomacy. In the very heart of the realm of France this Pope, so long harried and not yet able to make himself master of all his own domains, dared to summon the King himself to appear before him like a common criminal. Philip I was publicly found guilty of adultery, having put aside his lawful wife and taken the wife of one of his vassals, Fulk le Réchin. When he was summoned by the spiritual power to renounce this illicit union, he refused to come before the Council and was solemnly excommunicated.

When one considers that the Pope had in mind a great project for which he intended to seek support among the vassals of that same King, this excommunication is in itself enough to indicate the mental climate of the time. It is obvious that political considerations were not the dominating factor.

The Council ended on November 27. Laymen were admitted to the closing ceremony, so the crowds which gathered in the morning were even greater than on previous days. The meeting was held in the open air at the Champ-Herm (probably the Place Champet), where a raised platform had been erected for the Pope and important churchmen. Only a few people there had any idea of the startling appeal that would be made before the Council closed. Adhémar of Monteil, quiet and self-assured, was one of them, while Raymond of Saint Giles, now many miles away, had in his usual hotheaded and excitable fashion already dispatched messengers to announce his support of the Holy Father's proposals.

Urban's speech has been reported by several chroniclers, but probably Fulcher of Chartres was the only one of them who heard it in person. His account is likely to be the most accurate impression of what was said. He writes:

Well-beloved brothers,

The heavy demands of the times have forced me, Urban, by the grace of God the wearer of the pontifical tiara and Pontiff of the whole earth, to come before you, the servants of God, as a messenger to reveal the divine will. . . .

Although, children of God, you have made a solemn promise to keep peace among yourselves and faithfully uphold the rights of the Church, you must now, fortified anew by the grace of our Lord, show the strength of your zeal in the performance of a precious task which concerns all of you no less than it concerns the Lord. It is imperative that you bring to your brothers in the East the help so often promised and so urgently needed. They have been attacked, as many of you know, by Turks and Arabs, who have spread into imperial territories as far as that part of the Mediterranean which is known as the Arm of Saint George[1] and who are penetrating ever farther into the lands of these Christians, whom they have defeated seven times in battle, killing or capturing many of them. Churches have been destroyed and the countryside laid waste. If you do not make a stand against the enemy now, the tide of their advance will overwhelm many more faithful servants of God.

Therefore, I beg and beseech you—and not I alone, but our Lord begs and beseeches you as heralds of Christ—rich and poor alike make haste to drive this evil race from the places where our brothers live and bring a very present help to the worshippers of Christ. I speak in my own person to you who stand here. I will send the news to those who are far off, but it is the voice of Christ which commands your obedience.

---

[1] The Hellespont.

It was at this point in the Pope's speech that there appeared for the first time in the Church's history the promise of an "indulgence". The word, like the thing it stood for, has since played so important a role that it is as well to consider its meaning.

It often happens, even today, that a phrase such as "three hundred days" or "seven years and seven times forty days" of indulgence is found at the end of a prayer or invocation. Some people understand by this that the mere fact of saying that prayer or invocation will earn for them the remission of so much time in Purgatory. In fact, the sort of tariff mentioned is a clear reminder of those medieval customs that flourished in Urban's time. A believer who made his confession, expressed regret for his fault, and obtained pardon for it undertook at the same time to do the penance given him by the priest. The punishment was proportionate to the crime, and it is still one of the conditions—called *satisfaction* by theologians—of absolution, but it has now become much less spectacular. In the Middle Ages such penances consisted generally of long periods of fasting, and sometimes even, as in the case of Fulk Nerra, pilgrimage to the Holy Land was imposed.

In proclaiming the indulgence Urban II offered remission of all penances for their sins to those who "took the cross":

> If anyone who sets out should lose his life either on the way, by land or by sea, or in battle against the infidels, his sins shall be pardoned from that moment. This I grant by right of the gift of God's power to me.

The Pope declared that everything belonging to the Crusaders would be put under his own protection during their absence and would be as safe from harm as the property of the Church. Then he ended his speech with this exhortation:

May those men who have been occupied in the wicked struggle of private warfare against their fellow Christians now take up arms against the infidel and help to bring this long-delayed campaign to a victorious end. May those who have been brigands now become soldiers, and those who have fought against their own families now fight as they should—against barbarians. Let those who have served for mercenaries' pay now earn an everlasting reward, and let those who have dissipated their body and soul now gather their strength to win a double prize. What more is there to say? On the one hand, there are people in great distress—on the other, there are those who live in plenty; over there are the enemies of God—here are his friends. Join us without delay! Let those who are going settle up their affairs and collect what they will need to pay their expenses, so that when the winter is over and the spring comes they may set off joyfully under the guidance of our Lord.

Robert the Monk, in his version, suggests that the Pope drew a comparison between the wealth of the Orient and the poverty of the Western world, but Fulcher of Chartres, who, let us remember, provides the best source for what happened at the Council, makes no allusion to this. According to him, the Pope promised only heavenly riches. In fact, at that time the Western world displayed evident signs of prosperity. New buildings, churches, and even whole towns were rising; fairs and markets were being organized, and the movement for the freeing of towns from feudal control had begun at least thirty years before.

What the Pope was seeking at this meeting of important representatives of Christianity was nothing less than an expeditionary force against Islam. His astounding request was greeted with immense enthusiasm. The shout of "*Deus lo volt!*" (God wills it!) that rang out over the meadow at

Clermont echoed across the Christian world. The sound was
heard from Sicily to distant Scandinavia and aroused a strength
of feeling that was beyond even the Pope's expectation, and
that lasted for more than two centuries before it finally died
away.

This drive against the Turks was a project that had no real
precedent, and so the necessary organization had to be worked
out from the beginning. Urban II had probably considered
this in his conversations with Adhémar of Monteil; he may
also have been able to draw upon Raymond of Saint Giles'
experience as a knight. Possibly ideas for the planning of the
enterprise were taken from the Spanish *Reconquista* or the
Norman seizure of Sicily. Some years earlier, in 1063, an
"international" force composed of men from Italy, Provence,
Languedoc, Burgundy, and Aquitaine had attacked and taken
the stronghold of Barbastro in Spain, and many people saw
in this force a forerunner of the Crusades. But no one at the
time missed the essential significance of the appeal made at
the Council of Clermont and its release of a whole series of
actions unparalleled in their far-reaching effect.

The pilgrimages to the Holy Land form the only true precedent to the Crusades. The historian Paul Rousset has firmly
established the link between these pilgrim journeys and the
armed pilgrimage that the crusading movement was to become. The words "crusade" and "crusader", which seem so
natural to us, were not in use at the time. When they used
the phrase "take the cross", they were merely making a literal application of the words of the Gospel. The application
consisted, at Clermont and at later gatherings, of cutting a
small cross out of cloth and applying it then to one's shoulder. This was an outward sign of the taking of the vow to go
to Jerusalem "for the sake of true religion; not for honor or
riches but in order to free the Church of God", as Urban II

had said. The name "crusader", *crucesignatus*, is used only occasionally and then only as an epithet.

Words such as "pilgrimage", "the expedition to Jerusalem", "the road to Jerusalem", "the way to the Sepulchre", or "to our Lord" [2] were used to describe the journey. Those who set out were known as *"la gent Notre Seigneur"* (our Lord's men), or *"Hierosolymitani"* (Jerusalem farers), the term for pilgrims to Jerusalem. They were distinguished by the cross, symbol of forgiveness, of suffering that atones, and reminder of the One that was raised on the hill of Golgotha in the land they intended to recapture; They were "armed with the sign of the cross", and after its recapture the True Cross was carried as a standard before the armies going into battle. The Crusaders' war song was a liturgical chant, the *Vexilla Regis prodeunt*, composed four centuries earlier by Fortunatus, a bishop who was also a poet, and normally sung at Vespers on Good Friday and on feastdays of the Cross.

By a strange transposition of modern thought into a bygone age some historians of our day have suggested that the root causes of the crusading movement were economic and similar to those of colonialism. In fact it was precisely because the Latin kingdoms had no impulse toward colonization, and no colonists, that they had such a precarious existence The overwhelming majority of those who went on crusade had no other idea than to return home once their vow was accomplished.

Jean Richard, a present-day authority on the history of the Crusades, writes, "A Crusade is often thought of as an expedition of landless knights and broken peasantry. Some people have wished to link this exodus with an economic

---

[2] *Hierosolymitana expeditio, peregrinatio, iter Hierosolymitanum, via sepulchri Domini.*

crisis resulting from the introduction of a perfected method of harnessing, which caused widespread unemployment. It was unfortunate for the kingdom of Jerusalem that these adventurers were not numerous enough!" [3]

Adhémar of Monteil was the first to rise. He moved toward the Pope and "with a radiant face", as Baudry of Bourgueil describes him, begged permission to take the cross. To an uproar of applause, Urban II blessed the little crosses snipped out of some cloth that had been brought. Soon he was hemmed in by a crowd of spectators, all demanding to be marked with the cross of Christ. Some reporters of the scene, their judgment overcome by their enthusiasm, have suggested that the cardinals present cut up their red robes to supply crosses, forgetting that in those days the cardinals did not wear scarlet. [4]

Messengers arrived the next day, November 28, from Raymond of Saint Giles, announcing his intention of joining the Crusade. A final meeting of the Council was held to appoint a spiritual head of the expedition, and it was felt that the bishop of Le Puy, Adhémar of Monteil, the first man to take the cross, was the only possible choice. Various details of organization remained to be settled. The date of departure was fixed for August 15 in the following year, 1096, and certain qualifications were laid down regarding those who wished to take the cross. Since the taking of a vow was involved, recruits must first seek the advice of their priests; monks had to have permission from their bishop or abbot, while minors and married women needed the consent of

---

[3] *Le Royaume latin de Jérusalem* (Paris, 1953) p. 29.
[4] The wearing of the scarlet robe was instituted by Pope Paul II in 1464. The Pope in earlier times is often shown dressed in a red cloak. The white soutane was not worn until the sixteenth century (Saint Pius V).

those who were responsible for them. The armies were to assemble at Constantinople, the capital of the Eastern Empire, a mighty citadel which stood firm against the rising tide of Islamic conquest.

Urban II left Clermont on December 2 and continued his journey. He visited various towns in southern France, preaching the Crusade and dedicating the host of churches that were springing up in this most fruitful period of the life of France, when both its romanesque art and the *chansons de geste* began to blossom. On December 7 the church of Saint Flour was dedicated; this was followed by the consecration of the abbey church of Saint Geraud at Aurillac. The Pope solemnly consecrated the cathedral of Saint Stephen at Limoges on December 29, and the abbey church of Saint Savior in the same town on the next day; then came the consecration of the high altar in the abbey of Saint Savior at Charroux on January 10 and of another altar in the monastery of Saint Hilary at Poitiers on its feastday, January 13. He made almost a grand tour of the district, moving from Angers to Marmoutiers, then to Bordeaux and Toulouse. Here on May 28, 1096, he consecrated the collegiate church of Saint Sernin in the presence of Raymond of Saint Giles. Then he dedicated the cathedrals of Maguelonne and Nîmes, and on July 15 the altar of the new church of Saint Giles du Gard. Urban went on to Villeneuve-lès-Avignon, Apt, and Forcalquier before he crossed the Alps to reach Milan in August 1096.

By this time, the Crusaders had already begun to move along their various paths toward the meeting places appointed by the Pope.

CHAPTER II

THE POOR

"It was not a ruler who conquered this country, but a people." These words were used in the thirteenth century by Balian of Sidon, a Frankish baron of the Holy Land, while protesting against an attempted usurpation of the Emperor Frederick II. Certainly the popular element in the First Crusade was very noticeable. For proof of this one need only compare the narrative of what took place at Clermont with the version given less than a hundred years later by William of Tyre, a writer whom we have already quoted and whose integrity as a historian stands very high:

> The pilgrims who journeyed to Jerusalem came from many different countries. Among them was a man from the bishopric of Amiens in the kingdom of France. He was Peter the Hermit, who had been living a solitary life in the woods. He was a little man and looked a poor, stunted creature, but wonderfully endowed with a great heart and bright spirit, with wisdom and forthright speech. When he reached the gates of Jerusalem, he paid his tax and entered the city. . . .
>
> He heard it said that the patriarch of the city was a man of fine character and great holiness: Simeon was his name. Peter thought he would go and inquire of him about the condition of the Church, and of the clergy and the people. So

he went and asked about these things, as he had intended. The patriarch, judging Peter by his words and the expression of his face, realized that here was a man of good sense who feared the Lord, and he began to relate to him at leisure all the ills that afflicted Christianity.

While Peter listened to what this good man told him, he was unable to restrain his heavy sighs and great tears of pity, asking again and again whether it was not possible to do something about this state of affairs. The patriarch replied: Brother Peter, our Lord has had sighs and tears and prayers in plenty from us, if he cared to heed them. But, since our Lord in his justice keeps us so long in misery, we must understand that our sins are not yet forgiven and that we are still at fault. However, there are some people called Franks, from beyond the mountains, who have a great reputation here for their active Christianity, and for this God has given them peace and great power.

If these people took pity on us and prayed and planned on our behalf, we might look forward with confidence to receiving help from them through the grace of God. It is quite clear that the Greeks and the empire of Constantinople, who are our neighbors and like kindred to us, can give us neither aid nor advice, for they have been completely destroyed and cannot even defend themselves.

To this Peter replied: All that you tell me of my native land is true. By Christ's mercy, faith in our Lord is held in higher regard there than in the other lands through which I have traveled since I left my own country. I am sure that if my people knew of the misery and servitude in which you live, God and their own good hearts would prompt them to advise and help you. My advice to you now is to send letters immediately to the Pope and the Church of Rome, and to the lords and rulers and kindred of the West, telling them of your great need. Then for the sake of God and of the faith in Jesus Christ they will bring you help to the glory of God and the good of their own souls. As you are not wealthy people and cannot face great expense, if you think I am worthy to carry so great a message I will take it myself. I will do it gladly for the love of God and the remission of my sins. I promise that I will faithfully bear your message to them, if our Lord God leads me there.

The patriarch rejoiced greatly when he heard these words. He sent for the most important men in the Christian community, both priests and laymen, and told them of Peter's goodness and of the offer he had made. They were extremely pleased and thanked him for it. The letter was written without delay, sealed with their seal, and given into his keeping.

Then follows an account of a dream that came to Peter while he slept in the Church of the Holy Sepulchre. Our Lord appeared to him and told him to go to the Pope in Rome and beg him to undertake the reconquest of the Holy Land.

William of Tyre's account was written about the year 1170. Thus, less than a hundred years after it happened, a strange confusion had arisen in men's minds over the origins of the Crusade. The part played by the Pope, the Vicar of Christ, Christ on this earth, had been minimized. In the eyes of the world his personality and his actions had been pushed into the background by those of Peter the Hermit. Thus it became Peter who set in motion the whole train of events after his pilgrimage to Palestine had shown him the woeful state of the holy places and the enslavement of the Syrian Christians. It was believed that Peter, inspired by a vision, had gone to see the Pope, and even, according to some accounts, that the Pope did not preach the Crusade at Clermont until after Peter had led his army into Syria. Stories such as these were repeated by some of the most careful and well-informed of writers. Until today, in what may be called the folklore of history, Peter the Hermit has held his place as the foremost personality of the First Crusade.

But who in fact was Peter the Hermit?

The historian Guibert of Nogent, who wrote between the years 1099 and 1108, knew him. He describes him as a little man riding a donkey across Picardy and the country around Amiens and preaching the Crusade with extraordinary success:

> I have seen towns and villages crowded to listen to his preaching. I cannot remember anyone else who was given such a remarkable reception—the crowds surrounded him; he was overwhelmed with gifts and acclaimed as a saint. He was most generous in giving these gifts away again—some went to prostitutes for whom he arranged legal marriages. His great personal authority enabled him to spread peace and good fellowship wherever he went. All that he said and did seemed to be inspired by some divine power.

There has been no lack of great preachers in the annals of Christianity, from Saint Ambrose and Saint John Chrysostom to Saint Vincent Ferrier and Archbishop Fulton Sheen, but few indeed have won so early a place in legend. Charlemagne himself did not develop into an epic hero until three centuries after his death, but in fifty years or less this little man on his donkey was immortalized as the hero of the great epic of the West. What indeed has not been written about him? It was not enough that the credit for kindling the blaze of this adventure should go to him; he was also said to be of noble birth, a distinguished scholar, the mentor of the princes Godfrey and Baldwin of Bouillon, and a valiant fighter. Spain, Germany, Hungary, even Syria claimed to be the land of his birth. Only the Church has held aloof; this astonishing man has not been canonized.

The historian sees him as one preacher among many, although he was more successful than most. We can imagine him as resembling his contemporary, that pilgrim painted on the vaulted roof of the crypt at Tavant, wearing his rope-girdled tunic and his pointed hood. Guibert of Nogent says that Peter dressed in a woolen tunic, with a hood of home-spun and a long cloak that flapped at his heels, and that he went barefoot, without hose or breeches. He was certainly short; the Greeks called him by a diminutive form of his name, Coucoupetre—Peterkin. In the Crusaders' songs he is endowed with a gray beard, but his beard was as false, historically speaking, as that of the great Emperor himself. His donkey, on the other hand, had his place in truth as well as in legend. Guibert tells how some of Peter's listeners pulled hairs from its coat by way of gaining holy relics.

Whatever one may think of all this, there is no denying that Peter the Hermit possessed the power to sway those eager crowds. The existence of his power is the one certainty that can be gathered from the pile of literature that obscured this little man until the scholar Hagenmayer was able to uncover him. We shall understand it better if we consider for a moment the significance of preaching in the Middle Ages.

At that time, a preacher was not a man addressing a seated congregation within the shelter of four walls. Rather did he resemble a Sunday morning orator in Hyde Park, or even more the Abbé Pierre in the Place du Panthéon. He could preach anywhere. It was not necessary to be in church—a crossroads, a square, or a marketplace would do as well. Fairgrounds were as popular with itinerant preachers as they were with wandering minstrels, and the crowds would flock around them as they will nowadays around hawkers and strolling musicians. The people in these crowds were responsive; they were prepared to argue, to criticize, to heckle, or to applaud. The People's Crusade was an event that typifies the enormous power a gifted speaker can exercise over men who are ready to go into action.

The number of ordinary folk who went on ahead of the barons was the outstanding characteristic of the First Crusade. It was a popular movement before it became a Crusade of knights. Guibert of Nogent has a much-quoted description of peasants shoeing their oxen and piling their wives and children and their few possessions onto carts. This sort of picture catches the imagination, for nothing like it had ever happened before. There are any number of stories of flight, of migration, of conquest, but this movement of unimportant people setting off to win back a beloved country is unique in history. Even revolutions have not been so sustained by the populace. It is this fact that explains Peter the Hermit. It has been said that he was a personification of the people. This is not so. What has happened is that his Crusade has surpassed all others in its appeal to the popular imagination. In an age when warfare was the prerogative of the feudal knight, it is astounding to see settled villagers transformed into warriors. It is this that has taken hold of the fancy and turned fact into legend.

His successful preaching put Peter at the head of the first expedition. On February 11, 1096, a group of French barons met in Paris and in the presence of King Philip nominated his brother, Hugh of Vermandois, head of the French Crusaders. By March the little man on the donkey had already left Lorraine, leading his followers.

He probably went by Namur, Liège, and Aix-la-Chapelle. Then on Holy Saturday, April 12, 1096, he camped outside Cologne, joining other preachers who had been transformed,

like himself, into captains of war. Walter the Penniless—a
significant name—was there with his eight companions, also
Gautier de Poissy, William, Simon, Matthew, and others
whose names are now unknown.

The importance of these bands has often been discussed.
The chroniclers traditionally estimated their numbers at sixty
thousand, and this figure was accepted without question until recently, when a total of fifteen to twenty thousand was
suggested. In any case, even if we knew the exact numbers at
any given moment, they would not teach us much, for they
certainly did not remain stable. While some people must have
fallen by the wayside, it is also probable that the bands tended
to "snowball" as they went, for the preaching never ceased.
A canon called Frumold, the treasurer of Cologne Cathedral, was said to have waited three months for Peter so that
he could join him on his arrival. When he took the cross he
donated all his belongings to the monastery of Brauweiler,
but three marks of fine gold and ten of silver were returned
to him by the abbot, Albert, so that he could buy his equipment. Frumold made a vow that, if he returned from the
Holy Land, he would become a monk at Brauweiler, and
this in fact he did.

Walter the Penniless appears to have journeyed separately.
He and his party made their way across Hungary without
incident, but in Bulgaria they pillaged the countryside around
Belgrade, seizing necessities that had been refused them, and
brought bitter reprisals down upon their heads. Some of them
escaped, and eventually, about July 20, led by Walter, reached
Constantinople by way of Nish, Sofia, and Adrianople.

Peter the Hermit rested for about a week in Cologne and
left there on April 19 or 20. With his company he followed
the course of the Rhine and the Neckar toward Ulm There
is no record of their journey through Germany, Bavaria, and

Hungary. Their troubles began toward the end of June, when they reached Semlin, although Coloman, King of Hungary, had given a kindly welcome to these pitiful warriors, who had such slight resources for their difficult march. Considering the disparate elements of this mob, which included as many stragglers, old people, women, and children as able-bodied men, the wonder is that unrest had not broken out even sooner. Peter's authority over them all must have been considerable, but undoubtedly lack of discipline provoked these troubles with the Hungarian people. Peter decided to hasten the march.

It was probably on June 26 that they moved off toward Belgrade, crossing the Save by boats and improvised rafts. The distance of forty-seven leagues between Belgrade and Nish was covered in seven days. Then, about July 3 or 4 came those incidents of pillage and massacre that Albert of Aix records. Some of the pilgrims had quarreled with the Bulgars, and in revenge they set fire as they left to a row of mills standing in a line along the river near the Morava bridge. The governor of Nish set off in pursuit and attacked the rear guard, taking many prisoners and making off with the chest, which held such funds as the Crusaders possessed.

Peter, however, reassembled the scattered members of his expedition, and they continued on their way, reaching Sofia on July 8. Just before this, they had camped at Bela-Pelanka, where the first envoys from Alexius Comnenus, Emperor of Constantinople, had reached them. In the hope of preventing further troubles over the search for food, the Emperor forbade the Crusaders to remain in the same place for more than three days.

They then traveled the twenty-nine or thirty leagues from Sofia to Philippopolis, where they arrived on July 14; another thirty-one leagues took them to Adrianople by July 23, and here they were again met by officials bearing messages of welcome and goodwill from the Emperor. On August 1, 1096 Peter the Hermit and his followers arrived at Constantinople. Their journey from the Rhineland to the Bosphorus had thus taken them a little over three months.

The Emperor's daughter, Anna Comnena, has described these events, showing herself to be a reliable historian, although she has a southern tendency toward exaggeration and a distinct liking for literary effect:

> People ablaze with holy enthusiasm surged around Coucoupetre, leading their horses and carrying arms and provisions. The streets swarmed with men whose faces bore an expression of good humor and shone with the desire to obey the will of God. These Celtic warriors were accompanied by an enormous crowd of ordinary fellows and their women and children, each wearing a cross of red on one shoulder. Their number was more than the sands of the sea and the stars of the sky. They had streamed out from every country, flooding into the Greek Empire through Dacia.... They formed a throng of men and women such as had never before been known in the memory of man.

They certainly made a very strong impression both on the Byzantine officials and the imperial court and on the ordinary population of Constantinople. Anna Comnena describes the steps taken to deal with the situation:

> The Emperor ordered some of his commanders to go out and meet the Crusaders in peace and to help them by all means in their power to find provisions. At the same time, the officers were to shepherd them very carefully, keeping the column moving in an orderly manner, using force if necessary but without going so far as a pitched battle.

This passage gives a very good idea of the Emperor's equivocal attitude, in which, apparently, there was a good deal of reserve. It must be remembered that Peter had been preceded by Walter the Penniless, and before him a troop of Crusaders from Lombardy had arrived. The Emperor Alexius had therefore acquired a certain amount of experience of these difficult guests, which reinforced his natural caution.

His daughter Anna states that he advised Peter to stay in Constantinople until the crusading barons arrived and that the disaster that befell his company was the result of Peter's own impatience. Other writers, however, hold a different view. The Anonymous Historian of the First Crusade, who is generally accurate in his statements, alleges that it was the Emperor, anxious, and with good reason, to get rid of these people, who hastened the departure. "The Christians behaved very badly, stealing lead from the church roofs, so that the Emperor was annoyed and gave orders that they were to cross the Bosphorus."

The imperial fleet took the Crusaders on August 5 to the shore of Asia Minor, where they began at once to lay waste the countryside. Peter the Hermit set up his headquarters in the fortress of Civetot on the Gulf of Nicomedia. This was the place that had been assigned to them. It was near a town that Anna Comnena calls Helenopolis—known today as Hersek.

Albert of Aix, a chronicler writing during the first half of the twelfth century, is generally well informed, although he had no personal experience of the events he describes. He states that the Emperor took responsibility for their provisioning and that on his orders merchants came "in ships loaded with foodstuffs—grain, wine, oil, barley, and cheese. They sold all these things to the pilgrims at a fair price, and they gave good measure." Nevertheless the Crusaders, undeterred, and indeed encouraged, by the fact that they were now in enemy territory, began to rob the local inhabitants. Furthermore, racial differences between the Lombards, Germans, and French, all thrown together in the camp, caused grave troubles.

Toward the end of September a group of Germans seized the castle of Xerigordon four days' march from Nish; most unwisely they remained there. When the Turks heard of it, they besieged the place in force, and after several days of terrible suffering, the Crusaders—who had been completely without water—were driven to surrender. This incident served as a grim forewarning of the complete disaster that in a few weeks' time was to overtake the People's Crusade.

Peter the Hermit went back to Constantinople to arrange supplies and perhaps to ask for the officers without whom his ill-assorted followers remained an impotent mass. While he was away, most of his company, leaving the women and children in Civetot, made their way toward the Dracon valley. On October 21 these unfortunate men fell into an ambush laid by the Turks and were horribly massacred. The victors were then easily able to surprise the camp at Civetot, where they killed without pity everyone they found there—men, women, and children.

A man who escaped the slaughter managed to reach Constantinople and inform Peter the Hermit, who hurried to tell the Emperor of the disasters that had befallen his companions. Alexius sent off help immediately. The Turks, however, learned of the coming of the fleet and during the night of October 23 to 24 left Civetot and returned to Nicea with their prisoners. Walter the Penniless and most of the other leaders were among the dead.

The following year Fulcher of Chartres, traveling with the regular soldiers along the road from Nicomedia to Nicea,

saw all along the shores of the Gulf heaps of bones whitened
by the sun. In 1101 it was possible, as Anna Comnena said,
to build

> I would not say a great heap, nor even a mound, nor even a
> hill, but a high mountain of considerable area from this enor-
> mous quantity of bones. Some time later men of the same
> race as these murdered barbarians, while building walls like
> those of a city, used their bones instead of mortar to fill the
> gaps and thus, in a sense, made a tomb for them as they built
> the town. These fortifications are still standing today with
> their encircling walls made equally of rocks and bones.

From a material point of view this was all that was left of the
People's Crusade.

Very soon, however, these people were reborn in folklore
and legend. From the beginning of the twelfth century they
took their places as the heroes of several epic poems such as
La Chanson des Chétifs, La Chanson d'Antioche, and *La Conquête
de Jérusalem.* They are sometimes described as prisoners, forced
to carry stones and haul wagons to build a palace
for "Corbaran" (a deformation of the name of the Sultan
Kerbogha). Sometimes they engage in fantastic combats either against the lions or serpents of the desert or against the
Turks. Some are said to join those wandering bands called
Tafurs mentioned (and then, with due caution) by Guibert
of Nogent alone. These beggars or vagrants were said to be
headed by a Norman knight called King Tafur and were re-
putedly cannibals. In this way, Peter the Hermit and his un-
lucky followers became the heroes of a saga that grew almost
side by side with the events that inspired it, and with which
a wandering singer could stir his audience when he claimed,
truthfully for once, that he was telling a tale of real people.

The song *La Chevalier au Cygne*, for example, begins with this sort of claim:

> Some sing of Arthur and his famous Table,
> But what I tell is neither lie nor fable,
> And though my tale is little fashionable,
> It is from history and veritable.

Thus Peter the Hermit became a hero of minstrelsy and was given a place of honor beside Charlemagne and William of Orange. His biographer, Hagenmayer, ends one of his chapters with this speculation: "What glory and praise might not his contemporaries have lavished on Peter if his expedition had taken another form—if, for example, he had been able to seize Nicea and to hold it until the main army arrived?"

This way of thinking bears the stamp of our own age. In the days of Peter the Hermit a hero was not necessarily successful. In classical times the hero was essentially a conqueror, but it has been said that the *chansons de geste* glorify "not victors, but those who were heroic in defeat". For instance, Roland, who was almost Peter's contemporary, was one of the defeated. It must be remembered that the background is that of Christian civilization, in which an apparent setback of a temporal and material kind often accompanies the state of holiness. Each reverse is thought to be creative, to hold a promise that does not necessarily bear immediate fruit but which will eventually be fulfilled. This indeed is the significance of the Cross and of the death of Christ. It is what distinguishes the pagan hero—the superman—from the Christian hero, who models himself on the One who was crucified for love.

If the Crusaders chose to glorify this little preacher, this tatterdemalion who lost his company in a massacre and was himself a broken reed (he deserted from the siege of Antioch), it was as a form of homage to the lowly yet vital part played in the Crusade by the humble people, the unimportant ones who went on foot. The writers of today are justified in their insistence that the idea of a Crusade is closely linked with the concept of poverty.

The papal legate, Adhémar of Monteil, the spiritual leader of the First Crusade, was called the Friend of the Poor. He is reported to have told the leaders of the crusading forces, "Not one of you can hope for salvation unless you honor and protect the poor. . . . You must pray God each day that your sins may be forgiven." Raymond of Saint Giles, the richest of the leaders, undertook from the outset to pay the expenses of the poor Crusaders, and he had more of them in his army than had any other commander.

Paul Alphandéry has called the First Crusade "the Crusade of Poverty". On several occasions the rank and file forced the leaders to be mindful of the vow, which, distracted by personal ambition, they tended to forget, but which the poor bore always in mind.

This active role showed itself plainly after the siege of Antioch. Adhémar of Monteil was no longer there to rekindle religious enthusiasm among the baronial leaders, who had begun to squabble over the spoils of war. Time was lost, and forces were divided; there was conflict between the good intention that had led to the taking of the vow and the worldly ambition that threatened to damp that early fire. Eventually, the followers took charge. "There are quarrels over Antioch! Quarrels over Maarat! Each town that the Lord gives into our hands causes delay and dispute among our leaders!" So the ordinary folk began to demolish the walls of Maarat an-Numan to force their lords to set off once more. Two days later a barefoot pilgrim marched out of the camp at the head of the army. It was Raymond of Saint Giles. Forced by

the mob to resume his armed pilgrimage, he chose this way
of showing that he had indeed taken up his cross once more.

Throughout the history of the Crusades these popular
movements were to reappear: they were brought to life by
the preaching of Saint Bernard; they exploded into anger
during the Third Crusade when the kings of France and
England wasted time in private quarrels instead of uniting
for the reconquest of the Holy Land; they sometimes took
a pitiful form, as in the strange Children's Crusade of
1212–13—or an eccentric one, as in the shepherd movements of the middle of the thirteenth century, in which it is
hard to distinguish between Crusade and peasant rebellion.
Throughout a long, troubled period of history these movements can be perceived right up to the day when someone
appeared who invested them with their full spiritual significance: the Poor Man of Assisi.

CHAPTER III

THE BARONS

From one end of Christendom to the other during the spring of 1096 volunteers were at work getting ready to set out as an army on the feast of the Assumption in August. This was not in the least like any army of today—there was no state control, no centralization, no system of precedence. Thanks to the unusual nature of the enterprise, a number of descriptions have been left to give us a fair idea of what a feudal army was probably like and the way in which the barons dealt with the problems of its organization.

Every baron was responsible for raising a certain number of men, each of whom provided his own equipment. On this occasion, too, there were a considerable number of "landless" men who came as individuals but were glad to join the company of some lord, usually of one who belonged to their own district. Again, once the march had started, some of the lesser knights found that their resources were not enough for them to manage on their own, and they attached themselves to any baron who was willing to accept their services.

A feudal army had to be self-supporting. Some wheat, forage, and salt meat were carried as a reserve, but the soldiers expected to be able to live off the land as they went along. There had hardly been any chance as yet to find a solution to this problem of long-term supplies, for a feudal army did not usually have to move very far. The King of France was the only ruler who had sometimes to stage a military demonstration at a distance from his domain, either for the purpose of forcing a reluctant vassal to pay homage or to carry out some sort of police operation. Another fact to remember is that the period of military service lasted for only forty days in any one year; once this time was up a vassal went home with his men, whatever stage the campaign might have reached. In order to appreciate fully the limits of time and space that were then set to military service, it is well to remember that the town militias of the communes, most of which originated during the eleventh and twelfth centuries, could not then be taken farther away from their own cities than one day's march.

The leaders of the Crusade were thus faced with problems that were entirely fresh—some military, others concerned with equipment and provisioning. Since they did finally reach their goal, it cannot be denied that they dealt competently with these problems.

A single meeting place was chosen—at Constantinople—a fact that suggests that the general organization was not left to chance. The first link in the chain of ultimate success was the decision to journey to that meeting place in separate groups. Each group had its own itinerary, which simplified both the march and the search for provisions. Godfrey of Bouillon, with a group of Walloons and men from Lorraine and Brabant, went through Hungary, crossing the frontier probably at Tulin, and then at Semlin, and continued through Bulgaria by way of Belgrade, Nish, Sofia, and Philippopolis. He passed through Selymbria and reached Constantinople toward Christmas 1096. In Hungary he had an interview with King Coloman, who, friendly at first, was now very much on his guard, having had trouble with earlier plundering bands. Godfrey saw him in person and left his brother Baldwin, with his wife and children, as hostages; he sent heralds around the army to announce that any act of pillage would be punished by death. Coloman threatened his people with the same fate if they tried any profiteering. After this proclamation there was no more trouble.

Raymond of Saint Giles, who was, at fifty-five, the oldest of the leaders, led the Crusaders from the Midi into Dalmatia and to Skodra in Albania, probably by way of the north of Italy. In Pelagonia they suffered attack by Petcheneg horsemen sent by the Emperor Alexius; after that they followed the old *Via Egnatia* through Salonica, Roussa, and Rodosto to Constantinople, which they reached on April 27, 1097. Raymond himself had preceded the main body and arrived there some days earlier.

The men from the north of France made up a third group, led by Robert of Flanders, Stephen of Blois, and Hugh of Vermandois, brother of the French King. They crossed the Alps and traveled through Italy, where they were received in audience by the Pope at Lucca. They continued by way of Monte Cassino to Bari, where they embarked to cross the Adriatic. They made harbor at Dyrrhachium and then followed the southern French army along the *Via Egnatia*, arriving at Constantinople around May 14, about three weeks later than the others. Hugh of Vermandois had journeyed ahead of the rest of this group. His ship was wrecked, and he arrived almost alone.

Finally, a fourth group provided unexpected reinforcements for the Crusade. This was made up of Normans from Sicily and the south of Italy and was led by the renowned Bohemond of Taranto and his nephew Tancred. They too crossed the Adriatic and landed on the opposite coast somewhere between Dyrrhachium and Avlona. They celebrated

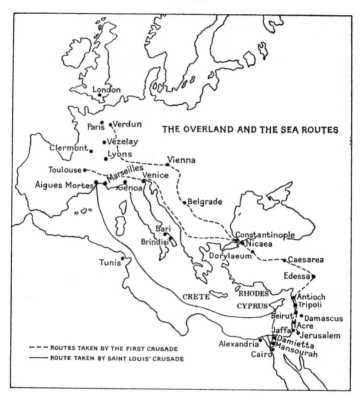

THE OVERLAND AND THE SEA ROUTES

London
Paris • Verdun
• Vézelay
Clermont •
Lyons
Vienna
Toulouse •
Marseilles
Venice
Aigues Mortes •
Genoa
• Belgrade
Bari
Brindisi
Constantinople
Nicaea
Dorylaeum
Caesarea
Tunis •
Edessa
CRETE
RHODES
Antioch
CYPRUS
Tripoli
Beirut • Damascus
Acre
Jaffa • Jerusalem
Alexandria
Damietta
Mansourah
Cairo

- - - ROUTES TAKEN BY THE FIRST CRUSADE
——— ROUTE TAKEN BY SAINT LOUIS' CRUSADE

Christmas at Castoria and then reached Constantinople about
April 16, 1097.

Part of the supplies needed for the journey were carried in the
numerous wagons that always accompanied a large group of
people on the road. A royal army of the time resembled nothing so much as a household removal. A king would take with

him his treasure and even his archives. Philip Augustus lost all his valuables in this way when, after his defeat by Richard Cœur de Lion at Fréteval at the beginning of the thirteenth century, he had to leave everything behind on the battlefield. The soldiers had to carry with them some means of shelter, and also grain, biscuits, dried vegetables, casks of wine and oil, and, a most important matter, oats and hay for their pack animals. It was quite impossible to carry rations sufficient for a journey from the banks of the Loire or the Meuse to the shores of the Bosphorus. Thus the Crusaders chose to leave in August, when the harvests were all gathered in. They bought what they needed in local markets, and from time to time, in places where provisions were plentiful, they would rest a little to allow men and beasts time to recover.

Contrary to what one might have expected, there was little pillaging on the way. Indeed, there was remarkably little, considering the number of people moving along the roads and the difficulty of enforcing discipline among troops—especially those of the People's Crusade—whose recruitment and formation had been left somewhat to chance. Except for the acts of an Emich or a Volkmar, which were pure brigandage and a continuation of the pogroms with which they had celebrated their departure, there was no pillaging except at Belgrade, when Walter the Penniless passed through, and at Bela Pelanka (Semlin) by the followers of Peter the Hermit. The troubles at Castoria were the work of exhausted and starving men. The Normans under Bohemond found that the Greeks—admittedly with good reason—refused to deal with them. Also it was winter, and the journey had been appalling. Bohemond authorized pillage, although with some misgiving, as he did not wish to alienate the local people. Skirmishes with the imperial forces occurred as they went along, but once supplies had become more abundant

Bohemond forbade the raids and even ordered that stolen animals be returned to their owners, who solemnly queued up to thank him.

The troops of Raymond of Saint Giles suffered most on the way, although they had been very well supplied at the start. The count of Toulouse had been able to afford the cost of providing equipment for a great number of poor Crusaders, and as a result the army he led was both the largest and the one which included the greatest number of noncombatants. Raymond himself was accompanied by his wife and his son. In Serbia, probably because of their slow rate of progress, the army began to run short of food. In thick fog they struggled for more than six weeks through a desolate countryside. At Skodra Raymond attempted to negotiate with Bodin, a Serbian prince, but he was forced to realize that there was nothing available for them to buy, and they had to continue as best they could toward the Byzantine frontier. Hunger had made itself felt, and when they reached the *Via Egnatia* the situation scarcely improved. The Normans and the Flemings had preceded them along this route and had taken up all the available supplies. To add to their troubles, the count's men were harassed by the cavalry that the Emperor Alexius had prudently sent to keep watch on them. The Provençals came out of these difficulties with a reputation for robbery and quarrelsomeness, which perhaps they did not entirely deserve.

Finally, there were the raids ordered as reprisals by Godfrey of Bouillon when he learned at Selymbria that Hugh of Vermandois was being held prisoner. Later he did the same at Constantinople to force the Byzantine Emperor to abandon his opposition, but the threat alone was enough to produce the desired result, and the order was immediately rescinded.

The scene at a halt on the way was like an episode from the almost contemporary Bayeux Tapestry, finished ten to fifteen years earlier. Open-air kitchens were organized, where great cooking pots, slung from poles resting on tripods, bubbled over the fires; other dishes simmered gently over the heat of braziers. Oxen, sheep, and pigs were killed to provide joints for the long wooden spits. While the cooks were busy in the background, tables were being laid for the gentry. These would be trestle tables, similar to those used in the houses of the time. The table as a fixture was unknown in the Middle Ages, and before a meal could be served it was necessary first to "set the table". Cloths were spread on which bowls and knives were laid. But most people had to eat as best they could, squatting down or kneeling, and dipping bread or biscuit into their bowls of soup. They had to drink water from the streams and only occasionally for some celebration got a mug or two of wine from the casks carried along with the barrels of oil and salted fish in the baggage wagons.

It has been calculated that an army could travel an average of twenty-five miles a day. A group which included women and children would do very well if they went as fast as this. Messengers were sent ahead of the main body to arrange with the local rulers for what was needed. Before the Crusaders took to the road the pilgrim bands had managed in this way, and a letter exists from the provost of Passau to Günther, bishop of Bamberg, mentioned earlier, telling him of the preparations made for his accommodation in the town.

The chroniclers have left us a vivid impression of the joyful reunions as the various groups met once more. The leaders embraced with mutual congratulations, each telling of his adventures on the way, while the camp fires burned late into the night beneath the ramparts of Constantinople, where the Emperor's sentinels kept silent guard.

At Constantinople the reactions of the East to this movement that had so excited Europe became apparent for the first time. The Crusaders for their part now had to come to terms with the alien world of the Greeks. The Pope had designated Constantine's city as the meeting place for the various forces that, as we have seen, arrived there one after the other between November 1096 and May 1097. Most of them were violently prejudiced against Alexius Comnenus from the moment they came as they had nearly all crossed swords already with his functionaries or his patrols.

The first of the troubles was a tragic episode that had its comic side. Hugh of Vermandois, brother of the French King (Philip I did not take the cross and had been excommunicated), sent a letter on ahead to the Emperor, apparently to ensure a sufficiently impressive reception. Anna Comnena, Alexius' daughter, conveys her feeling of ridicule for this pretension as she writes about it. For the Byzantine Greeks, inheritors of a great empire and its brilliant civilization, these petty princes of the north were mere upstarts, "barbarians" lacking in polished tradition or culture.

The Emperor Alexius had ordered his nephew John, governor of Durazzo, to guide Hugh in his travels. Unfortunately, the Frankish prince had been overwhelmed by a storm in the Adriatic. Several ships had foundered, and he himself lost all his personal possessions. He had nothing left but the clothes he stood up in, and perhaps he felt a little foolish thinking of the grand reception he had hoped for. However, John Comnenus knew how to soothe Hugh's wounded pride, and he led him and his few remaining followers off to Constantinople. Here the Emperor's first concern was to induce

Hugh "to become his vassal by swearing an oath in the usual Latin fashion".

This procedure was repeated as each leader arrived, but while it had been easy to overcome Hugh's reluctance, the other barons turned out to be men of very different caliber. Anna's disdainful words reveal her fundamental contempt for the Franks, those "Celts" whom she calls arrogant, fickle, unreliable. Reading between the lines, we can guess at the atmosphere of bitterness and mutual dislike that strained relations during their stay in Constantinople:

> The Emperor was told about the coming of the great French armies, and he dreaded their arrival. He was aware of their impetuosity and of their inconstant and unreliable nature and all the difficulties that were part of the Celtic temperament. He knew that these men were greedy of treasure and could not be trusted to keep a treaty any longer than it suited them. He had often heard these things said, and he knew they were true, but far from being discouraged, he prepared to meet his troubles and was ready to fight if it became necessary. However, the reality that he had to face proved to be far more serious and terrible than the rumors that had gone before. The whole of the Western world, all the barbarous nations living between the farther shore of the Adriatic and the Pillars of Hercules, was on the move. Whole families had taken to the road and were crossing Europe from one end to the other in their march on Asia.

This well illustrates the lengths to which prejudice can be carried. Anna had only the slightest knowledge of those races that she lumped together as "Celts", but no accusation was too bad for them. She suspected that their real aim was the capture of Constantinople itself; she said that the arrival of each group was preceded by a swarm of locusts, and that these Westerners roasted little children for

food. She was able to recognize that "the simple folk were
genuinely inspired by the wish to worship at the Sepulchre
of our Lord and to visit the holy places", but the actions of
the leaders appalled her. Anna had been born "in the purple", in the Porphyra chamber where by tradition emperors were born. She represented the polished culture of
Byzantium; she had read Aristotle, Plato, Demosthenes, and
Homer; she had studied mathematics and theology, canon
law, and medicine. Such a woman could have nothing but
contempt for "barbarians". She had no wish to imagine
that these men of the north could be anything but brute
beasts whose courage was only an instinctive reaction. "These
Celts are remarkably spirited and mettlesome; once they
have taken the bit between their teeth nothing will stop
them." Even the devout Godfrey of Bouillon earned her
dislike: "The man is wealthy; he takes pride in his noble
birth, his gallantry, and his fine ancestors. Like every Celt
he wants to go one better than the others."

There is another side to the picture. The Crusaders had
their own reaction to the antipathy that they encountered.
These "barbarians" felt strongly that they were the soldiers
of Christ, marching to the relief of a land that Constantinople, its mother city, had been unable to protect. They bitterly resented being treated with suspicion, being watched
by the Petcheneg horsemen whom the Emperor sent to control them, and then being penned up outside the city walls
and faced with a demand to swear an oath of allegiance to
the Emperor.

From more than one point of view this claim must have
seemed completely unreasonable. Oath taking played an essential part in feudal society. All social relations rested on the
oath of allegiance—a pledge linking one man to another,
possessing also a sacred value (*sacramentum*) that made it a

matter of interest to the Church. It was the tie between lord
and vassal. Most of the struggles in France arose because the
King was determined to force some unwilling vassal to swear
allegiance. Once this bond was completed, the vassal became the lord's man and accepted the obligation to give him
every help and advice (*consilium et auxilium*). Each of the
crusading leaders had already made his vow to a suzerain and
could not take a similar oath to another man. They felt
strongly too that their present business was to free Jerusalem,
not to become the vassals of the Emperor. Their unwilling-
ness was quite justified.

The Emperor, however, was able to force the Crusaders
to do what he wished, simply by cutting off their supplies.
Godfrey, the first to reach Constantinople (December 23, 1096),
was soon to discover that he was entirely at the mercy of the
Emperor. His army was confined to one of the suburbs, and
for about three months he refused to take any action, hoping
to be able to hold out until the others arrived. Then famine
began to take control. In April 1097, after various skirmishes, Godfrey was forced by necessity to bow to the Emperor's will. The wording of the oath shows that Alexius had
kept a firm hold on the situation. The Crusaders had to promise to make over their conquests to him; in return, he would
provide them with reinforcements. Thus did the Crusaders
become troops of the Emperor. The rank and file loudly
condemned this action, and the Anonymous Historian of
the First Crusade voices the anger of the ordinary people at
what they took to be cowardice on the part of their leaders.

Very soon after the baron from Lorraine and the Greek
Emperor had come to terms, a man arrived who possessed a
profound knowledge of the character of the Byzantines and
was himself well known to them. The Norman Bohemond
of Taranto personified a type of Crusader described by some

historians and a good number of romantic novelists. He was
an unscrupulous adventurer, savage or astute as it suited him,
quite without any pious motive for joining such an enterprise. He was a son of that Robert Guiscard who had conquered Sicily almost single-handed, and his personality had
been molded by the events of his life. He had inherited the
terrible energy of the Vikings, who, two centuries earlier,
had terrorized Europe as they sailed up the rivers, pillaging,
demanding ransom, devastating as they passed. He was prepared to use every sort of cunning to get what he wanted;
his physical endurance was remarkable, and his cruelty beyond belief. He was like some tremendous natural force. This
savage element appears from time to time in crusading history. It runs from Bohemond to Frederick II and shows up
in Reynald of Châtillon and, in a lesser way, in a man like
Gautier Brisebarre, whose acts of brutality ended the good
relations that had been established with the sultans of Gharb.
Nevertheless there were occasions when Bohemond turned
out to be the right man in the right place and rendered great
service to the other Crusaders simply because he had no scruples and no weaknesses. The capture of Antioch, for instance, was due primarily to his wits and his toughness.

Anna Comnena cannot help letting a hint of liking show
when she comes to talk about Bohemond; it is as though as
a girl she had both admired and hated this handsome adventurer and found these emotions reawakening as she wrote
about him in her old age. She lingers over his description
with some pleasure:

> Everyone admired his appearance and shivered at his repu-
> tation. Nobody in the Byzantine Empire had met a man like
> this before, whether barbarian or Greek. He was more than
> a foot taller than anyone else, slender, with broad shoulders

and chest, and strong arms. His whole person was well proportioned according to the canon of Polycleitus; he was neither too thin nor too fat; he had powerful hands, an erect carriage, burly shoulders.... Remarkably white skin was tinged with red on his cheeks. His hair was fair and was not allowed to hang to his shoulders in the barbarian fashion. He did not like long hair, but had it cut short to his ears. I cannot tell whether his beard was reddish or any other color, for it was shaved and his face was left as smooth as marble. Most likely it was red. His blue eyes expressed both courage and dignity. He breathed easily through a nose and nostrils that were in proportion to his broad chest.

This warrior had a certain charm, somewhat spoiled, however, by the feeling of terror that he inspired. The man's obdurate and savage personality was revealed in his whole person, in the way he stood and in the way he glanced about him. Even his laugh could make his followers shiver. Courage and passion raged in his body and in his soul, and both these qualities were directed toward war. His mind was flexible and cunning, always devious. His words were calculated and his replies always ambiguous. Only my father could better him in the success of his dealings, in persuasive speech and in other such natural gifts.

Bohemond had no objection to taking an oath or to persuading the other leaders to do the same. He was certainly not in the least concerned with the sanctity of a vow. He had fought against the Byzantines some years earlier and knew that they valued the arts of diplomacy at least as highly as military valor. He quickly seized the chance to mend his quarrel with the Emperor, whose help was obviously necessary even if it was limited to the feeding of the armies. Bohemond even asked to be appointed grand domestic of the Orient, one of the many honorary positions in the organization of the Empire. Alexius was evasive in his reply, offering

merely a grant of land somewhere near Antioch, little thinking what the outcome of this suggestion would be.

Bohemond was active now in convincing the others of
the need to bow to the Emperor's demands. Raymond of
Saint Giles alone held out against him. "He had not come
there to recognize or serve any other lord than him for whose
sake he had left his lands and goods", writes Raymond of
Agiles, a member of the Provençal force. It was proposed, by
way of compromise, that Raymond should swear to make
no attack on the life or honor of the Emperor, and, for the
sake of peace, Alexius eventually agreed to this.

A great reception was then held for the crusading leaders
in the Emperor's official residence, the palace of Blachernes.
An incident that happened during the course of this cer-
emonial illuminates the contrast between the elaborate eti-
quette of the court and the rough ways of these soldiers.
They were country louts, in a sense, but they were the men
of the future facing a society that had already passed its peak,
and they were also kin to the men who were beginning,
about this time, to fashion the royal door at Chartres. Anna
Comnena has this to say:

> When all the leaders, including Godfrey, were assembled and
> each one had sworn the oath of homage, a foolhardy noble-
> man took it into his head to seat himself on the Emperor's
> throne. The Basileus himself said nothing, knowing already
> how arrogant the Latins were. Count Baldwin, however,
> intervened. 'He pulled the man to his feet, upbraiding him.
> "You should not behave like this, particularly as you have
> just taken the Emperor as your liege lord. It is not the cus-
> tom of the Roman Emperors [by this is meant the Byzan-
> tines, as they thought of themselves as the heirs of Rome] to
> allow their subjects to be seated in front of them. Men who
> have become His Majesty's vassals must observe the manners

of his court." The man said nothing to Baldwin, but glared at the Basileus and muttered in his own tongue: "What a boor he is! Why should he be the only one to sit when so many brave lords have to stand?" Alexius noticed that the man's lips moved, and he called an interpreter to find out what had been said. When he was told, he appeared to pay no more attention to the matter. . . .

When everyone was leaving the Basileus called this proud and impudent Latin before him and asked him his name, his nationality, and his lineage. "I am a pure-blooded Frank, of noble birth", said the man. "And I'll tell you something. There is in my country an ancient holy place where men go if they want to fight in single combat. They pray for the help of God and then wait there until someone comes along who is brave enough to accept the challenge. I stayed a long time at this place,[1] but no one dared to take me on." The Emperor replied: "If you did not get the chance to fight then, you will get it now."

The reply was humorous, but, having succeeded in transforming the Crusaders into mercenaries—or so he hoped—Alexius wanted to involve himself as little as possible in quarrels with them. Raymond of Agiles, who was well informed on what happened in Constantinople, states quite plainly that the Emperor promised the Latins as much money as they wanted if they would remain in his service. He obviously planned to exploit this crowd of armed men to his own advantage. But, skilled as he was in diplomacy, his schemes were to go awry.

Bad faith soon became apparent. The Emperor sent his fleet to help in the capture of Nicea. However, when on June 26, 1097, the Crusaders entered the town, they were

[1] This probably refers to the burial place near Soissons of the Bishop Saint Drausin, whose fine sarcophagus is now in the Louvre. Men who were to fight in single combat used to go there to pray for his help.

amazed to learn that Alexius had been in touch with the
Turkish garrison and had promised safety to all the inhabitants on condition that the place was surrendered directly to
him. This first success turned to dust and ashes when the
victors discovered that its only result had been to enrich the
Greek Empire. For various reasons, however, it was to be the
last diplomatic achievement of Alexius Comnenus.

A little later, when the army had halted on its way to Antioch, it was joined by a body of men sent by Alexius and
commanded by his general Tatikios—"the man with the
golden nose". According to Guibert of Nogent, his nose had
been cut off, and he wore one made of gold. Anna Comnena says very clearly that her father sent these men "to help
the Crusaders in every way possible and to warn them of
dangers, as well as to take possession of the towns which
they captured". She could hardly be more precise. Later,
though, she seems a little troubled in her conscience when
she has to report the desertion of Tatikios and his band when
the situation of those besieged in that same city of Antioch
had become intolerable.

At the end of the day, Bohemond retained possession of
the city, a prize won by his cunning and his almost unbelievable tenacity of purpose. Then he was able to point out to
the other Crusaders that although possession of the city was
contrary to the oath they had sworn to the Emperor, the
latter had been the first to act like a traitor.

I wish to assure you, my dearest, that the messenger I send to
bring you good news has left me safe and sound outside Antioch, and, by the grace of God, all is well. For twenty-three
weeks we have journeyed steadily in company with Christ's
brave soldiers toward the house of our Lord Jesus. I have
now, beloved, more than twice as much gold, silver, and other

sorts of treasure as you provided when I left, since the other
leaders, backed by the army, but against my will, have made
me, for the moment, the head of the expedition.

You must have heard that after Nicea had been taken we
fought and won by the help of God a great battle against the
treacherous Turks. We then conquered first the whole of Ro-
manie and later Cappadocia for our Lord. Hearing that As-
sam, a Turkish prince, was living in Cappadocia, we attacked
him, captured all his castles, and forced him to flee to a stronghold among the crags. We granted his land to one of our
leaders, whom we left there with some of Christ's soldiers to
hold the enemy in check. After that we pushed on steadily
against the accursed Turks, driving them back toward Armenia and the Euphrates. There they left their baggage and
pack animals on the bank and crossed the river, fleeing to-
wards the land of the Arabs.

Some of the boldest Turks made their way into Syria and
by forced marches day and night hurried to the royal city of
Antioch, hoping to get there ahead of our armies. When the
soldiers heard this, they gave thanks and praise to Almighty
God, then hastened joyfully toward Antioch. We began to
besiege it, encountering many attacks from the Turks. On
seven occasions, led by Christ, we have battled most courageously against the inhabitants of the town and the hosts
who have come to their assistance, and each time with God's
help we have been the victors, killing a great number of the
enemy. Many of our brothers too, have fallen in these battles
and in the many onslaughts on the city, and their souls have
been transported to bliss in paradise.

A description of Antioch follows; then the letter continues:

Throughout the winter in camp outside the city we have
suffered for the sake of Christ bitter cold and torrential rain.
It is not true to say that the heat of the Syrian sun is unbear-
able, for winter here is very like winter in the west. . . . While

my chaplain Alexander was hastily writing this letter on Easter day, some of our men successfully ambushed a party of Turks and returned here bearing the heads of sixty of their knights.

Dearest, I can only tell you a few of the many things that we have done. Since I cannot speak of everything that is in my mind, I can only commend you to good deeds, to the special care of my lands, and to your duty toward your children and your vassals. You will see me as soon as I am able to return to you. Farewell.

The letter is headed "Count Stephen to Adela, his most gentle and gracious wife, to his dear children, and to all the vassals of his blood, greeting and benediction." It was written during the siege of Antioch, in March 1098. We can picture the knight seated on a truss of straw beside his tent, using an interval between skirmishes to dictate the letter to his chaplain while a messenger stood by to carry it to Constantinople and then westward to a castle on the banks of the Loire. The sender was Stephen of Blois, one of the principal leaders of the men from central France; the lady who waited for news was his wife Adela, daughter of William the Conqueror.

In spite of its optimistic tone, the letter reveals the many uncertainties and difficulties which the Crusaders had to meet. It is interesting to compare it with another, which, according to William of Tyre, Sultan Soleiman was meanwhile sending to the citizens of Nicea. Even if its authenticity is a little doubtful, this letter shows how confident the Turks felt as they waited to be attacked in the land where they had firmly established themselves:

There is no need to be afraid of these people in spite of their vast numbers. They have come from that far country where the sun sets, and they are worn out with the exertions and the labors of the way. They do not even have any horses that can bear the shock of battle, nor can their strength or their zeal equal ours, for we have been in this place only a little while. Remember that we have already wiped out a swarm of them without trouble, killing more than fifty thousand in one day. Take heart then, and have no fear. Before the seventh hour tomorrow you will be comforted by liberation from your enemies.

The Crusaders were facing an adversary stronger than themselves, and one who had the advantage of being on his home ground. As if this were not enough, they had to contend with the many hostilities of nature. Everything was against them. The climate took the French barons by surprise— they were poorly equipped to deal with heat, and they were astonished to encounter rain and cold, as Stephen of Blois' letter suggests. It was difficult for them to assess distances. Stephen of Blois hoped that they would be in Jerusalem five weeks after leaving Nicea; in fact it took the Crusaders two years to get there, including more than a year spent besieging Antioch. Finally, time and again, they came up against the most terrible enemy of all in these desert regions, so different from their native France or the Western lands in general, channeled as they are with rivers and streams— thirst. William of Tyre has vividly described the Crusaders' sufferings from thirst, which the natives on occasion pitilessly exploited. The Crusaders suffered from thirst during the journey, but the worst time of all came when they were outside Jerusalem, for the Muslims had blocked up all the wells and cisterns before they retired into the city. The armies were overtaken by famine on two occasions during the siege of Antioch, and the chroniclers spare none of the horrors in their attempts to tell what happened. Finally, the nature of their enemies was quite beyond the Crusaders. They could not understand their method of fighting, and the problem of language was baffling. So many races and so many religions existed side by side in this country that it was almost impossible to differentiate between Armenians, Syrians, or Greeks or to track down spies among the throng.

When Stephen of Blois wrote his letter in March 1098, the Christian army had already been on the move toward the Holy City for almost two years. Fifteen more months were to pass before it reached its goal. Many of the soldiers must have felt discouraged and regretted becoming involved in an adventure whose outcome seemed so uncertain.

This siege of Antioch was one of the most bitter episodes in the whole Crusade. It was to last for two more months and to cost the loss of many lives and to undermine morale before it ended on June 3. There were numerous desertions during these two months, and many more during June itself, when the Crusaders, who had barely taken possession of the city, were besieged by Sultan Kerboga's great army and reduced to utter want.

It is astounding that Peter the Hermit in person and the author of the letter, Count Stephen of Blois, were two of these deserters. The former was seized literally by the scruff of his neck as he was slipping away from Antioch and forced to return by Tancred; the latter simply got fed up and went home. When he reached Blois he was greeted by a scene out of the *chansons de geste*. His wife, Adela, like Guibourc in the *Chanson de Guillaume*, piled such reproaches on his head that Stephen was shamed into going back to the Holy Land. He returned with the second expedition in 1101 and this time completely fulfilled his vow, for he died there.

For the space of fifteen months the history of the march to Jerusalem is the history of the siege of Antioch. Antioch

was a real stumbling block on the Crusaders' route. First there
was the double siege, then the period of rest for the army
ordained by the leaders. This rest was certainly needed after
the sufferings that had been endured, but it was prolonged
beyond all reason and marked by quarrels arising from lust
for the prizes of conquest. These quarrels, and the leaders'
rivalries, proved as demoralizing as the long siege, if not more
so. The Crusade almost collapsed altogether at Antioch, having been undermined first by adversities and then by good
fortune. Throughout the history of the Latin kingdoms we
notice a recurring contrast. The barons frequently triumph
over danger and terrible sufferings only to prove themselves
unequal to the demands of victory and prosperity.

The last stage of their Way of the Cross was also the most
moving. On Tuesday, June 7, 1099, the Crusaders came in
sight of Jerusalem.

> They all wept for joy when they heard the cry "Jerusalem",
> affected by the knowledge that after striving for so long in
> suffering and danger they had at last come near the Holy
> City. . . . In their desire to see the Holy City they pushed on
> hurriedly, sorrow and weariness forgotten, until they reached
> the walls of Jerusalem, and they sang canticles, shouted, and
> wept for gladness as they went.

The siege of Jerusalem began a few days later, for a preliminary attack was made on June 13. The siege has been
described in almost hourly detail by the Anonymous
Historian of the First Crusade,[2] who himself took an active
part in it.

Even the first steps in preparing for the siege were made
in the midst of suffering. The Crusaders had to endure agonies

[2] See Bibliography, p. 353.

of thirst and were forced to fetch water from a place about six miles away, bringing it in stinking bags hastily made from the skins of their oxen. After a careful study of the town, the barons ordered two wooden towers to be made. Three days— the Sunday, Monday, and Tuesday, July 10, 11, and 12—were spent in setting them up before the eastern walls, between the church of Saint Stephen and the valley of the Kedron.

The first assault was launched on the two following days. According to the Anonymous Historian:

> The bishops and priests beforehand led men to believe by their sermons and exhortations that all should walk in procession in honor of God beneath the ramparts of Jerusalem, with prayers, alms-giving, and fasting.

Finally, about midday on Friday, July 15, after twenty-four hours of continuous fighting, the decisive moment came. A knight named Litold of Tournai sprang from the wooden tower where the Duke Godfrey of Bouillon and his brother Eustace of Boulogne were directing the attack and was the first to scale the city wall.

> As soon as he reached the top the defenders all fled from the walls across the city. Our men followed them, killing and butchering, to the temple of Solomon [the Mosque of Omar, built on the site of the former temple in the southeast corner of the city], where such terrible slaughter took place that our soldiers were wading ankle deep in blood.

Meanwhile Raymond of Saint Giles was attacking from the south. The emir in command of the Tower of David on the western side of the defenses surrendered to him with his men during the evening of Friday, July 15, on condition that their lives would be spared, and Raymond sent them in safety to Ascalon.

In the following lines the Anonymous Historian conveys how the feelings of the Crusaders were capable of altering from one moment to another:

> In no time they overran the whole town; they swept up gold and silver, horses and mules, and they stripped the houses of all their treasure. Afterward, exhilarated and crying with delight, they went to worship at the Sepulchre of Our Lord and discharged their debts toward him.

The massacre that marked the taking of Jerusalem is a tale of blood and horror, and it would have been better for the honor of the Crusaders if it had never been told. This wish was being expressed even in the twelfth century by the historian William of Tyre. It must be remembered, though, that these men had journeyed for three years in constant danger of their lives; that they had known hunger, thirst, and terrible suffering; and that many of them did not reach the end of the road. Their feelings had been exasperated beyond all bearing by the insults that the Muslims had flung at the Cross of Christ from the safety of their ramparts. It is not surprising that victory was marked by such an outburst of fury; nevertheless the luster of the achievement has been irreparably dulled.

Two days after the assault, on July 17, 1099, the barons held a meeting in the Holy City to choose a leader, who would keep safe the land they had conquered and guide its policies to the best advantage. The chronicler Albert of Aix specifies that this leader was to be charged particularly with the protection of the Holy Sepulchre. This is a detail that reminds us that the aim of the Crusade from the outset had been the return of the Holy Sepulchre to Christianity; it was for this that men had left their homes and endured such hardships. Whatever may have been the leaders' private ambitions— present from the beginning in the case of Bohemond or arising on the way in the case of the others—the vow that they had taken at the start, and that had been cherished all along by the poor people and the lesser knights, now came back to mind. The business of safeguarding the Tomb of Christ, that common possession of all Christendom, was for the moment of overriding importance.

This council of war, held in the captured city three years after their departure, must have been a solemn occasion for all. Pope Urban's great plan was now a reality, but its survival had to be assured as far as possible. The Crusaders had in fact conquered only a loosely knit strip of enemy territory. Neither Judaea nor Galilee had been completely overrun, and from such powerful neighboring cities as Damascus and Ascalon came the constant threat of an annihilating attack. Furthermore, the coastal towns, except for Jaffa, which was being hastily fortified and restored, remained in Muslim hands, and it was from the sea alone that the barons could expect the arrival of reinforcements, or even of provisions if they were needed.

The clergy emphatically upheld before the council the view that the Holy City should be given to an ecclesiastical leader. They argued that it was the property of the Church, and that since the papal legate had died before arriving there, they must choose from the clergy present a patriarch who would hold the town in trust.

On the other hand, it was only too obvious that the place needed an energetic defender. The council with one accord decided that what was required was a king skilled in warfare, capable of organizing both defense and the conquest of those lands that had not yet been taken, and also capable of uniting the barons who remained in the Holy Land. Once the problem had been stated, the choice that was made—whatever reasons may have been found later to explain it—revealed the barons' desire for fundamental goodness. These men were certainly brutal and had been overcome on several occasions by their own violence and ambitions, but they were not worthless and in fact were no longer dominated by personal interests. They did not choose the most wealthy—Raymond of Saint Giles, to whom many knights owed their equipment and traveling expenses—or the most farsighted—Tancred, of whom it is enough to say that he was related to Bohemond—but the most "pious"— Godfrey of Bouillon. Three years of riding and fighting and ordeals had shown that his courage and wisdom were beyond question.

There is certainly no lack of alternative explanations for the choice. Raymond had been offered the crown by several barons and had declined it. Among the chief barons, others, such as Robert of Flanders and Robert of Normandy, in all likelihood found little to tempt them to remain in the Holy Land. A thousand other reasons, a thousand other intrigues, could be suggested, but the fact is unaltered. Honor was paid to moral worth and confidence given to the man who expressed the ideal of chivalry—physical courage and spiritual goodness.

Some modern historians have imputed various shortcomings to the duke of Basse-Lorraine. They have called him "a mediocre politician, a wretched administrator", and so on. The only things proved by these criticisms is that our standards are not those of the twelfth century. Contemporary chroniclers are unanimous in their judgment of Godfrey as an upright and pious man—so pious that his companions were made impatient by his long sessions in church while the dinner grew cold. No peril could daunt him, and he placed his sword at the service of God.

Proof that the man was worthy of the honor offered to him lies in the fact that he refused it. That is, he accepted the job but refused the honor belonging to it. He accepted responsibility for the defense of the Holy Places, but refused the title of King. According to the phrase popularized later by Guibert of Nogent, he did not wish "to wear a crown of gold in the city where Christ had worn a crown of thorns". Perhaps these actual words were never spoken, but the fact remains that Godfrey's title was merely "the Advocate of the Holy Sepulchre". On August 9, about a fortnight after his election on July 22, he set off to take the offensive against the Egyptian army, which had been sent to the aid of Jerusalem by the caliph in Cairo. No one had imagined that the city would fall so quickly, and help did not reach it in time. If the relieving forces had been a few days later they might perhaps have retaken the city, since a number of Crusaders who were going back to Europe had already traveled some distance on their road home. Godfrey hastily recalled the barons and their scattered troops and defeated the Egyptians beneath the walls of Ascalon.

Most historians have been surprised by this early departure by some of the Crusaders and have deplored their lack of political sense. On the face of it, it would seem to have been essential to send settlers to complete the work of conquest by an effective occupation of the land. However, the facts must be accepted that the Crusaders were not colonists and that their expedition had nothing in common with the sixteenth-century expeditions to the New World or with the nineteenth-century expeditions by which Europeans tried to subjugate other races. Our viewpoint today is quite different from that of the Middle Ages, and if we make so false a judgment of the

Crusaders' reactions it is again because their standards were not the same as ours. It was in the very nature of the kingdom of Jerusalem that its existence should be precarious, maintained somehow or other, as the need arose, by the haphazard arrival of Crusaders, who came later on to continue the work of their predecessors. That a parent state should send out officials and soldiers with specific orders to consolidate the conquest while settlers undertook the exploitation first of the land and then of the inhabitants may be an idea natural to us, but it did not even occur to the Crusaders.

This does not mean that the conquest was left unorganized or that some of the Crusaders did not become settlers. But these things merely happened by chance.

Much the same could be said about the system of kingship that the Franks of Jerusalem and the Holy Land set up—it was definitely not an institution that had been planned or prepared. The barons, as was their way, sized up the facts that faced them and responded according to the spirit of the day. Thus their reactions throw a great deal of light on the main characteristics of the feudal spirit. In fact, the collection of the customs and usage of the Latin kingdoms gathered together later under the title of the *Assises of Jerusalem* is the most perfect memorial of feudal law left to us. It is an expression of the spirit of feudalism caught at its moment of flowering and full maturity.

The personal attachment of a man to his lord is brought out clearly in these decisions made at Jerusalem. As an odd consequence, we find Judea parceled out like a holding in Lorraine, or rather in the Ardennes, for Godfrey, quite naturally, distributed the lands of what was to be the kingdom of Jerusalem to his own followers, those who had belonged to his company. The historian Jean Richard illustrates this point when he lists the names of the vassals: Gerard of Avesnes,

Ralph of Mouzon, Miles of Clermont-en-Argonne, Andrew of Vaudémont, Arnoul le Lorrain, and others. Among them is one sole Provençal, who must have felt somewhat out of place; his name was Gaudemar Carpenel. These vassals were to stand solidly behind their lord when the need arose. Baldwin of Boulogne owed it to them that he was able to succeed his brother when Godfrey died in the following year. The patriarch of Jerusalem had summoned Bohemond, but the barons did not want this and preferred to remain loyal to the family.

The character of feudal kingship is strikingly revealed in the Holy Land, where its nature can be minutely observed as if through a magnifying glass. It has been studied by the American historian La Monte, who sees here "feudal institutions in their purest form" and further notes that it was the French tradition of feudalism that was dominant in the Latin kingdoms.

Kingship in the Middle Ages was the very opposite of absolute monarchy. The king—the title was first taken by Godfrey's brother and successor—was no more than agent for the barons, chief among many other chiefs. The succession was partly hereditary, or, rather, it became so. Godfrey was elected King; Baldwin I, as we have seen, owed his acceptance to the loyalty of the barons from Lorraine. After him, some of the barons wanted to call on his nearest relative, Eustace, count of Boulogne, but others chose a distant cousin, Baldwin of Le Bourg, who had fallen heir to the county of Edessa and who had the advantage of being near at hand, while Eustace had returned to the West. Afterward, the rule passed to the husband of his elder daughter, and the succession was handed on within the family, but the barons continued to intervene, acting sometimes against the wishes of those concerned. When the law of succession, thus established by custom, singled out Isabella, the younger sister of

Baldwin the Leper, to receive his heritage, the barons obliged her to be divorced and then married to the man they thought most capable of maintaining the kingdom.

The jurist Balian of Sidon, in the thirteenth century, solemnly affirmed before the Emperor Frederick II the elective nature of kingship in the Holy Land. The *Assises of Jerusalem* reiterate the same fact. Although, at the beginning, the barons received their fiefs from Godfrey, their council played an essential part in later decisions concerning the kingdom and the kingship. This solidarity between king and council is remarkable. If the king overruled the wishes of the barons, it was at his own risk, and they looked askance at any show of authoritarian power. William of Tyre, seeking to criticize the seneschal Miles of Plancy, who for some time exercised a form of regency, says that he acted quite on his own without taking anyone's advice.

Baldwin I was forced to abandon a plan for an expedition into Sinai because his barons were against it. Tancred's followers forced him to make a reconciliation with Baldwin and to go to his aid at Edessa. The blame for the loss of Jerusalem was laid on the shoulders of Guy of Lusignan, the husband of Queen Sybilla, because he acted on his own and disregarded the barons' advice.

According to medieval thought, personal power was a form of excess punishable by God. Bezzola, the great Romance scholar, has pointed out[3] that in the *chansons de geste* the councils of war held by the barons in the presence of the Emperor were always unruly, with each man voicing his own opinion, often in violent opposition to those of the others, whereas among the "pagans" the emir had only to speak to

---

[3] Especially in his study *De Roland à Raoul de Cambrai* (*Mélanges Hoepffner*, Paris, 1949) and in *Origines de la Tradition courtoise en Occident*, I (Paris, 1944).

see his orders immediately carried out. He was an absolute monarch—and such a person was unthinkable in feudal Christendom until the jurists traced his characteristics from their study of Roman law.

A form of election was still visible in the coronation ceremony as a kind of popular consultation. Certainly it was purely symbolic, but in an age that so valued the symbol in everyday life this was quite sufficient to ensure that no one misunderstood the nature of the power conferred on the king. At the ceremony the king took an oath to defend the church of Jerusalem and to maintain the customs and rights of the kingdom. But first of all, at the moment when the king entered the basilica of the Holy Sepulchre, the patriarch, before receiving him at the door, addressed the people, asking them whether the man whom he was about to consecrate was indeed the rightful heir to the throne. He was answered by a threefold shout, and then, to the chant of the *Te Deum*, the king moved toward the choir, where the ceremonies of anointing and crowning took place.

What power, then, did this king possess? He had the usual privileges expected by a suzerain from his vassals. They were to give him advice and aid, particularly when hostages had to be provided in exchange for his own person after a defeat. No tenant-in-chief could sell his fief or leave the kingdom for more than a year and a day without the king's permission, since a feudal lord was tied to his domain just as a serf was and could not, like a modern landlord, behave as he chose. No lord could sell or alienate his fief—certainly not his principal fief, his *chef-manoir*—since it was more like an aggregation of rights than an estate with an exploitable market value. These rights, moreover, could not even be changed by the lord of the manor, since they were fixed by custom. The king was also the fount of justice. With the help of the

High Court (the council of barons), which frequently sat in his place, he punished offenses and shortcomings. In addition, the tenants-in-chief were required to approve the gifts which the king made and to guarantee the fulfillment of his promises, and as a sign of this they affixed their seals to his writs. In such ways as these was power distributed between king and barons.

Lawmaking was a function carried on jointly by the king and the baronial court. That is, law was made by the way in which they interpreted custom. We must be careful not to think of some legislative body laying down first principles. As cases came up they were judged either by plain common sense or according to the code of the accused's own country. To judge each man by the law of his own land was the method in general use at the time. John of Ibelin, the jurist, writes, "The *assises*, that is to say, legal decisions that have the force of common law, could acquire their value only through long usage or through being seen to be intended as an *assise*." These decisions, eventually collected and sorted out, form the *Assises of Jerusalem*, mentioned above. The oldest part was not written down before the very end of the twelfth century, between 1197 and 1205.

Even within his own circumscribed sphere of activity the king was not able to act entirely on his own initiative. Jean Richard mentions a comparatively insignificant clause concerning the sweeping of streets that in the thirteenth century was not allowed the force of law because the king had promulgated it without consulting either the barons or the townsmen.[4] Warfare, treaties, and taxation were affairs that could be decided only after discussion with the council. They

---

[4] Jean Richard, *Le Royaume latin de Jérusalem* (Paris, 1953), p. 71.

concerned the welfare of the whole state, and in these matters the king only proposed, he could not dispose.

Later on, a burgess court instituted for those who were not members of the nobility met regularly in Jerusalem three times a week, on Monday, Wednesday, and Friday. It was concerned with petty actions and controlled a corps of "policemen", who were responsible for keeping order in the city. The court was made up of twelve jurymen, presided over by a viscount who represented the king and was competent to try cases involving felony, theft, abduction of minors, or treason.

An account of the special tribunals completes the description of the legal system in the kingdom. These were the court of the Fonde, a commercial tribunal having two French and four native jurymen, and the Chain court, with jurisdiction over maritime affairs and the customs. The Arab traveler Ibn Jubayt, although he never let slip a chance to show his hatred of the Franks, had to admit that the customs inspection was not vexatious. The Saracens were dealt with by Arab "scriveners" and the Franks by other Franks. About twenty-two baronial and thirty-three burgess courts were held outside Jerusalem on the estates of the great feudatories and in the chief towns. The people who appeared before these courts always had the advice of counsel, since one of the members of the court acted as advocate. The native population retained its own laws and tribunals.

The king's immediate entourage was made up, as in France, of his chief officials, chosen from among the barons. The seneschal was the master of ceremonies, in special control of the castles and the administration of the royal treasure. The constable took supreme command in battle, was responsible for the disposition of troops, and, here in the East, became the principal officer of the realm. The marshal, who was in a sense the constable's lieutenant, was primarily in charge of the stables, responsible for the buying of horses and the purchase of hay and fodder. The chamberlain was the king's personal assistant and waited on him at table. The chancellor played a lesser role, dealing, with the help of scribes and notaries, with the royal correspondence. This post was usually filled by a cleric in orders.

The kingdom ("I call it a barony as it is so small", says William of Tyre's translator) reveals itself as a little France or England set up in the East—a cluster of fiefs handed over to vassals as the conquest advanced.

These feudal lords lived off the revenue from the lands they had been granted, the income from taxes and from tariffs levied on the commercial interests in the towns. The king did likewise with his domain. He was also allotted such exceptional returns as the special tribute paid by the Bedouins and the tolls collected from caravans passing through the kingdom of Jerusalem on their way between Egypt and Baghdad.

Occasionally, in an emergency, a general tax was imposed: when, for instance, King Amalric attacked Egypt, or when Jerusalem had to be fortified against Saladin, or when the disaster of Hattin had almost wrecked the kingdom.

An interesting example of the method used to apportion lands arose later on, in Greece. After the taking of Constantinople by the Franks and the Venetians in 1204, twenty-four assessors were appointed—twelve Venetians and twelve Crusaders. They devoted themselves to a thorough study of official documents—the register of property and basis of the land taxation in the empire. A little later, in Morea, two knights "took into their employment two knowledgeable Greeks who were well acquainted with the lands, villages, vineyards and serfs, and everything that went on in that part called the Pelloponese" so that the country might be divided among the barons. Here, as in the Holy Land, the peasants were not dispossessed, and the historian Jean Longnon has even found that certain domains belonged jointly to Frankish barons and Greek nobles.

However, these facts belong to a conquest carried out under quite different conditions. In the case of Jerusalem, we have a land acquired at the cost of endless suffering that needed to be preserved and defended from a thousand dangers and whose very survival seemed most unlikely.

CHAPTER IV

THE CHURCHMEN

Among the Crusaders the churchmen must be given a special place. It had been foreseen from the beginning at Clermont that clerics might, in certain conditions, be authorized to take the cross as laymen did. The consent of the superior, bishop, or abbot to whom they were responsible had to be obtained before they were allowed to join in this armed pilgrimage and, in spite of their priestly character, bear a sword. Similarly, the Church herself, during the whole course of the Crusades, played a double role. She took under her protection the Crusaders' property, thus making it as inviolable as her own, and she made an active contribution, in the persons of bishops and of lesser clergy, to the expeditions. Later, one of the conditions imposed on those who preached the Crusade was that they should have vowed to go themselves before they could be allowed to exhort others to do so.

The armed prelate who had appeared first as a character in the *chansons de geste* became, in Adhémar of Monteil and his companions, a real person and continued as such for the rest of the story. The part played was generally one of encouragement, though it could go as far as carrying, as Bishop Aubert of Bethlehem did at Montgisard, the relic of the True Cross in front of the army.

The religious nature of the expedition was emphasized by
the presence, probably in large numbers, of the clergy. Adhémar consecrated some men as priests during the journey. One
of them was Raymond of Agiles, chaplain to the count of
Toulouse and later the historian of the Crusade. It was a
priest, Peter, bishop of Narbonne, who was the spokesman
for the people at Maarat en-Numan when they petitioned
the barons to stop quarreling and continue the journey to
Jerusalem.

The preaching of the Crusade was continued throughout
the journey. It is known, for instance, that William, bishop
of Orange, who was Adhémar's successor for a short while
until he died at Maarat, preached the Crusade at Genoa with
the bishop of Grenoble. Perhaps their sermons bore fruit in
the opportune arrival of the Genoese fleet, which came to
help the Crusaders during the siege of Jerusalem. Some writers have made the point that there is no mention of quarrels
among the churchmen, although there were plenty among
the barons. Indeed, many of the clergy had put aside former
causes of dissension in order to take the cross. For example,
Otto, bishop of Strasburg, a member of the first expedition,
had been a supporter of the antipope Guibert against Urban II. On the contrary, they were active as peacemakers.
The military leaders were accustomed to make their peace
before a bishop, as Bohemond and Raymond of Saint Giles
did after their dispute over the possession of Antioch.

An important psychological function was demonstrated
by some of the clergymen. It was Peter Bartholomew, a
Provençal priest, who discovered the Holy Lance at Antioch. His revelations, although they have been much challenged, had been preceded by those of another priest, Stephen
Valentine, who on June 11, 1098, announced that it had been
revealed to him in a dream that help would reach them within

five days. As time went by, there were several occasions when churchmen were able to raise the Crusaders' morale. At the siege of Acre, for example, in 1189, the soldiers, worn out by famine and disease, were ready to abandon the struggle when the bishops of Salisbury, Verona, and Fano whipped up their morale and organized a collection so that the poorest among them might be provided with food, "each according to his suffering". This action made it possible to await reinforcements from the West and, eventually, to capture Acre.

A good number of these Crusader clerics had been brought out as chaplains to barons rather than as soldiers. Godfrey of Bouillon was the first to set the example, for he took with him monks "noted for the holiness of their lives" to say Divine Office on the journey. Raymond of Saint Giles did the same.

As soon as the Crusaders set foot in Jerusalem they had to decide whether or not the Holy City was to be regarded as a possession of the Church, and as such handed over to the ecclesiastics. Probably if Adhémar of Monteil had been alive this would have seemed the natural thing to do, for he was trusted by everyone, quite apart from his position of authority as papal legate. But things worked out otherwise. Arnulf of Rohes, a Norman priest with an extremely poor reputation, sought by a variety of intrigues to get himself elected patriarch. He achieved his aim, but his election was irregular and was quashed the following year by Pope Pascal II, who sent out Daimbert of Pisa as legate. The latter, after deposing Arnulf, hastened to get himself elected instead and exacted an oath of allegiance from Godfrey of Bouillon and also from Bohemond as prince of Antioch.

It is possible that it was in order to guard the rights of the Holy See that Godfrey refused to be crowned. The coronation ceremony emphasized the position of the patriarch, since it was he who received the king at the door of the Church of the Holy Sepulchre and who accepted his oath to defend both the patriarch and the Church. It was he who was responsible for consecrating the sovereign and for investing him with his dignities.

The residence of the patriarch was in Jerusalem, and according to custom the office was filled by the king from a list of names presented by the canons of the Holy Sepulchre. As well as the patriarch, there were legates who were sent out almost every year as representatives of the Holy See; while they remained in Palestine they had the right to use the white palfrey and the red cope which were otherwise the insignia of the Pope himself.

There had been as many as 102 bishoprics in Syria and Palestine. Most of them were quite insignificant, and in the past the very existence of some of them had been uncertain. Those that did possess some importance—five archbishoprics and nine bishoprics in the patriarchate of Jerusalem— had a precarious state of being. Revenues drawn from the landholders and intended for the support of the churches were sometimes difficult to collect, and although the Church succeeded in obtaining consent to the principle of tithes, it was not without opposition from the barons and from Christians in general, who objected to paying a tax from which the Muslims were exempt.

The part played by those prelates who represented the Church in the Holy Land has been variously assessed. There were men among them like Daimbert, who were out for their own ends and put the satisfaction of their ambitions before everything else. Others were holy men, imbued with the spirit of the Gospels. A few possessed a dual personality, influenced in turn by piety and by their own aspirations. These two types of prelate were opposed in the characters of two churchmen who played equally important roles during the supremely critical period that marked the end of the kingdom of Jerusalem. One of them was the Patriarch Heraclius, who owed his nomination in 1180 to the influence of the Queen Mother, Agnes of Courtenay; she was said by contemporary writers to be "not a wise woman, but overfond of power and too concerned with her money bags". Heraclius, like the lady, was covetous and contemptible. He led a scandalous life, and in the streets of Jerusalem his mistress was pointed out as "the patriarchess". He was to head the plot that, contrary to the King's own last wishes, forced Count Raymond III of Tripoli out of the regency after the death of Baldwin the Leper. In spite of opposition from the barons, he engineered the coronation of the King's sister Sibylla and Guy of Lusignan, the incompetent husband she had chosen for herself. Furthermore, popular opinion accused Heraclius of having arranged the poisoning of William of Tyre, his antithesis in character and the man whom he had elbowed out of the See of Jerusalem in order to get it for himself.

William of Tyre, the historian of Frankish Syria, stands out in marked contrast to Heraclius as one of the country's most attractive figures. Born in Palestine, probably of French parents, he was completely representative of that generation which had formed a twofold culture from its own double origins. Although he had finished his education by going to study the liberal arts and canon law in the West and was thoroughly at home in French and Latin, he could speak Greek and Arabic like a native and even knew a little Hebrew—quite a normal thing, probably, for a cultivated man living in the land of the Bible. He was a canon at Tyre when in 1167 King Amalric, attracted by his brilliant qualities, appointed him archdeacon of Tyre and asked him to write the history of his reign.

He acted on many occasions as ambassador or negotiator for the King, who, a few years afterward, made him tutor to his son Baldwin. This responsibility continued for four years, from 1170 to 1174, and during this time he wrote his *History of Overseas Affairs* (*Historia Rerum transmarinarum*), one of our most important sources for the story of the Latin kingdoms from the time of their creation until the fall of Jerusalem. He also demonstrated his own mental activity and breadth of interest by writing a *History of the Eastern Princes*, the story, unfortunately now lost, of the Arabs since the days of Muhammad.

A single quotation is enough to show the way in which William of Tyre interpreted the historian's role. He describes the finding of the Holy Lance at Antioch and how it restored the Crusaders' morale, but he also gives the other side of the story, telling of the doubts which were cast on the veracity of Peter Bartholomew, the Provençal priest who had started off the affair. He had submitted to ordeal by fire as proof of his good faith.

> Peter Bartholomew died a few days later, and there were some who argued that since he had seemed in good health beforehand, so sudden a death must have been the result of the ordeal that he had insisted on undergoing and that he had sought to die in the pyre rather than stand as an upholder of deception. There were others again who claimed that he had passed unharmed through the flames and that his death was entirely due to the pressure of the crowd, which had rushed upon him in an ecstasy of devotion after his escape from the fire. It was thus impossible to decide the truth of the matter, and the controversy darkened the issue still further.

That is all William says. He states the facts and refrains from judgment between two opposing opinions so long as neither seems more convincing to him than the other. He had, too, a strain of deep compassion in his nature, and the passage in which he describes his discovery that his nine-year-old royal pupil was a leper is most moving in its restraint:

> We took as much care over training his character as we did over his academic education. He was always playing with the young nobles who were his companions, and they often pinched each other on the arms or hands as children of that age do when they are together. The others cried out when this hurt them, but the young Baldwin displayed a remarkable fortitude as if the pain meant nothing to him.... I thought at first that this showed courage on his part and not lack of sensation. Then I called him to me ... and I found that he could feel nothing in his right arm or hand.... This was the first onslaught of a much more serious and quite incurable disease. By the time he had reached the age of puberty we realized, and we weep as we speak of it, that the young man was a victim of leprosy.

We can do no better than repeat the judgment of A. C. Krey, his most recent historian, on William of Tyre: "His work surpasses all other Latin and Arabic histories of his time in vitality, power, and knowledge", and, it could be added, in fairness of interpretation.

William of Tyre was appointed chancellor of the kingdom when his pupil came to the throne at the age of fourteen. In the next year, 1175, he became archbishop of Tyre. He accompanied the King on all his military campaigns and sustained him in all the acts of a heroic life. This young man, consumed by the disease from which he was to die at twenty-four, had to withstand not only the Muslims, regrouped and unified under Saladin, but also the plots that were being hatched by the Queen Mother, together with his uncle Joscelin of Courtenay, the Patriarch Heraclius and Gerard of

Ridfort, the treacherous grand master of the Temple, and that were to end in the destruction of the kingdom. It is comforting to know that death, from whatever cause, had come to both the King and the archbishop who was his teacher before the disastrous battle at Hattin, which was to lead to the loss of the Holy City and wipe out the victories— sometimes against unbelievable odds, as when five hundred knights beat Saladin's army of thirty thousand at Montgisard— that had distinguished the reign of the Leper King.

At the time of the departure of the crusading expedition, Urban II was hoping, among other things, for the restoration of the links between the Eastern and Western churches that had been broken since the schism in 1054 when the Eastern Church had severed all ties with the See of Rome. This hope came to nothing. Several attempts were made to improve relations, but although certain groups such as the Maronites were reunited with the Roman Church, the many conferences that met to put an end to the discord between East and West achieved no practical results.

Between 1204 and 1206, after the Crusaders had captured Constantinople, Benedict of Sainte Suzanne, the papal legate, and Nicholas of Otranto, a Greek priest from southern Italy, tried hard to reconcile the outstanding differences. However, their attempts came at an unpropitious time. The Westerners had by force made themselves masters of the Byzantine capital, the seat of the Greek patriarchate, and now dissensions of a religious nature were accompanied by the hatred felt by the conquered for the conquerors who occupied their city.

A few years later, in 1213, negotiations began again, but conditions then were even worse. The leader this time was the famous Legate Pelagius, a dictatorial and hotheaded man, who in later years was to blame for the failure of the campaign against Damietta in Egypt. He began badly by taking harsh action against the schismatics. Most of the Greek clergy then fled to Nicea to join the "resistance movement" under Theodorus Lascaris, which was carrying on the struggle against the Latin emperors. Presently Thomas Morosini, a Venetian, was elected patriarch by the western canons of Saint Sophia in place of the Greek incumbent, who then turned all his energies to the task of combatting the Pope's attempts to reestablish unity. Meanwhile the Eastern and Western rites were performed side by side in the Church of Saint Sophia, which had become the Cathedral of Constantinople, and on the whole, the lesser Greek clergy were left to work unmolested. A special dispensation allowed the monks of Mount Athos to continue their life of prayer and penance. The union of the churches was proclaimed at the Council of Lyons in 1274, but this had no practical result, and negotiations for the return of the Greek church achieved nothing until two centuries later, when at the Council of Florence in 1439 Pope Eugenius IV was successful. The time coincided with a threatening advance of Islam, which made the Byzantine Emperor feel, somewhat late in the day, the need to unite himself with the rest of Christianity—a sentiment that was not shared by his subjects.

On the other hand, the Crusades made possible an exchange of religious ideas between the West and the reconquered East. Ties such as those that today link one city to another were created in the twelfth century between the churches. A letter written between 1132 and 1146 by Anselm, bishop of Bethlehem, to the bishopric of Rheims gives some idea of this:

We have learned from your letters that you wish to be united in spirit with the glorious Church of the Nativity of Our

Lord, and we are glad to know that we are linked like brothers in the prayers of the holy Church of Rheims. Since we
asked for your charity, we have decided that your godly company should join in joyful devotion in the Church at Bethlehem. The fine psalter that you have sent to us as an offering
will bear witness to this holy spirit.

Another aspect of the relationship that was built up between
Christians in Europe and those in the East is shown by the
growth of religious foundations here as well as in Syria or
Palestine. In France, for instance, a number of churches were
dedicated to the Holy Sepulchre, from fine buildings like
Neuvy-Saint-Sepulchre to such tiny chapels as the one at
Peyrolles in Provence. When Peter the Hermit returned to
the West he entered the monastery of Neufmoutiers near
Huy, which had been built about 1099–1100 as a depen-
dancy of the Holy Sepulchre at Jerusalem.

As soon as the Crusaders reached the Holy Land, they
began to establish monasteries there. Godfrey of Bouillon
founded the monastery of Saint Mary in the valley of Je-
hoshophat and installed there the monks, probably Cluniacs,
whom he had brought with him. Other abbeys were almost
immediately set up on Mount Zion, on the Mount of Olives, at the temple, and, at a greater distance, on Mount Tabor and Mount Carmel. The Cistercians, expanding rapidly
in the middle of the twelfth century, founded in 1157 the
Abbey of Belmont to the south of Tripoli as a daughter-
house of Morimond in Burgundy. In the following century
they built the cloister of Daphni in Athens, an offshoot of
the Burgundian monastery of Bellevaux. It became "the Saint
Denis of the dukes of Athens", for it was there that they
were buried. Some of these abbeys, particularly those belonging to the Cistercian order, quick to branch out in Syria

and Palestine, obtained permission to have armed guards. This gives a clear indication of what their situation was in threatened districts.

A few things still survive today to remind us that our Church once moved in the Eastern world. A breviary from the Church of the Holy Sepulchre is in the Conde Museum at Chantilly, and a fine book of ritual from the same place is to be found at Barlotta in Italy. The Church of the Holy Sepulchre had a place in its liturgical use for an annual celebration on July 15 of the entry of the Christian army into Jerusalem. A procession was made to the place where the first of the soldiers had forced their way over the walls, and a sermon recalling the event was preached there. One result of the capture of Jerusalem had been the recovery of the relic of the True Cross. The liturgical calendar was now to be enriched with feastdays celebrating the solemn translation of some of its fragments to churches in the West. Some interesting letters were written between the chapter of Notre-Dame in Paris and Anseau, the precentor of the Church of the Holy Sepulchre in Jerusalem. The French canons were anxious to know in detail the history of the piece of the Holy Cross that Anseau had sent to them about 1108 or 1109. He explained how the original relic kept in Jerusalem had been cut up after the Turkish conquest for greater safety and how the pieces had been divided among different cities. Some had gone to the patriarchal sees of Antioch, Edessa, Alexandria, and Damascus, others to Constantinople, Cyprus, and Crete. The fragment that went to Paris had belonged to a King of Georgia. His widow, who had retired to a convent, had, during a time of distress, sold it to the patriarch of Jerusalem to provide for the needs of her community.

The Church, by her creation of the military orders, provided the answer to the ever-present problem of the defense of the Holy Land. Their creation was not, however, either organized or intentional; as so often happens, it was the completely spontaneous response of some Christians to the problems facing them in the Holy Land. The pilgrims had to be protected and the sick and needy among them cared for, and, above all else, the safety of the captured holy places had to be assured. One of the most astonishing of Christian institutions arose in answer to these problems and flourished until, like all the others, it declined, fossilized by formality and acquired wealth and by the avoidance of necessary change.

Those who started the movement had no idea how successful the outcome of their work would be. Gerard Tenque, a humble knight from Martigues, founded the Hospital of Saint John of Jerusalem, probably about 1080 and certainly before the First Crusade. His only thought then was to care for poor pilgrims who had fallen ill on their journey and for those who had been reduced to poverty by theft or exactions. In 1118 Hugh of Payens and his eight companions—a mere handful of knights from Champagne and Flanders— troubled by the dangers that beset travelers, particularly those on the way between Jaffa and Jerusalem, had sworn to devote themselves to the escort and defense of pious folk on their journey. Barely ten years later, at the Council of Troyes in 1128, the Templars emerged in the character of warrior-monks. A rule was drawn up for them by Saint Bernard himself. It made a break with what was already familiar to the Christian world by giving the knight a place in monastic life, where the characteristics that made him a knight also made him an alien. The warrior, a strong man, taking pride in his strength, was asked to use this strength and his sword in the service of the weak, to step out of his own world and become a monk, yet keep his sword by his side and his lance in his hand, "to serve in the chivalry of our Supreme King".

The Templars and, following their example, the Hospitallers, took part in the normal conventual offices. They said
daily the prayers laid down by their rule and took the three
canonical vows of poverty, chastity, and obedience, following the teaching of the Gospels. They consecrated themselves to the defense of the Church in the Holy Land, and
their rule encompassed both physical training and the care
of their horses. But the military character of their lives was
not allowed to drive out austerity, and they were obliged to
observe all fast days, including not only Friday and the eve
of a feast as laid down for all Christians of that time but the
whole of Advent from Martinmas (November 11) to Christmas, and, of course, the whole of Lent from Ash Wednesday
to Easter. They were forbidden to flee in battle, to leave the
ranks, or to disperse their forces by, for instance, going hunting. They were permitted to hunt only the lion.

The daily life of these soldier-monks has often been described, for example, by Marion Melville, and their role in
the Holy Land has been treated in a number of books with
the justice it deserves. The Templars, wearing over their ar-
mour a white surcoat with a red cross, and the Hospitallers,
in black or red with a white cross, were to be found practically everywhere in the Holy Land, and from there they spread
to the West, attracting both gifts and new members. Other
military orders such as the Teutonic Knights or the Knights
of Saint James of the Sword, who protected the road to Compostella, were founded on similar lines.

From the year 1131 onward the diocese of Rheims made an
annual collection for the benefit of the Templars. A few years
earlier the Hospitallers had founded their first priory in Europe, at Saint-Gilles-du-Garde, in Provence, not far from the
home of Gerard the Blessed. From such modest beginnings
came the enormous wealth that the two orders were to amass

both in Europe and in the East. It must be admitted that the construction and upkeep of their fortresses alone justified the accumulation of these vast funds. The Templars built Castle Pilgrim, Chastel-Blanc, Tortosa, Beaufort, and many others of lesser importance; the Hospitallers were responsible for Krak des Chevaliers and Margat and for a whole network of fortifications, mostly in the districts around Antioch and Tripoli.

It is well known that the orders, because of their dual establishments in Europe and in the Holy Land, were entrusted with the money that pilgrims intended to use overseas. On presentation of an order for payment at one of the commanderies in the Holy Land the amount was returned, and thus the risk involved in carrying large sums was avoided. This most useful role of banker held its own dangers, for knights could not easily turn themselves into administrators. In the end the wealth of the Templars caused their downfall in Europe, as their independence and its resulting disunity had ended their days of power in the Holy Land.

A grand master of the second half of the twelfth century, Odo of Saint-Amand, was said to be "an evil man, proud and insolent, breathing fury, and without fear of God or respect for any man". The reputation of his immediate successor, Gerard of Ridfort, was no better. Gerard was one of the men responsible for the terrible defeat at Hattin. For some inexplicable reason, Saladin granted him his life afterward, although the other surviving Templars were massacred. There were, however, other grand masters, both before and after these two, whose lives were exemplary, and, as René Grousset has said, "these knights knew how to die nobly". Probably the day of their defeat at Acre on May 28, 1291, when the last of the Crusaders' cities fell, was one of their finest, when the decadence of the twelfth century was lost and they regained the spirit of their earlier, heroic years.

The Hospitallers remained more faithful to the ideals of their founders and never allowed their charitable functions to lapse. A great deal of evidence remains to show what this charity was like. The Hospital at Jerusalem not only cared for the sick but also looked after the elderly and fed nearly two thousand poor people every day. At that time a sick man was received "like the master of the house" at all the Hospitaller establishments, and infirmarians were ordered to treat a patient as if he were Christ himself. A story has been handed down that bears witness to the faithfulness with which this rule was kept. Apparently, Saladin wished to test for himself the Hospitallers' fine reputation and got himself admitted to the Hospital at Jerusalem disguised as a poor pilgrim. Once inside, he was given every attention, but he absolutely refused to eat. When he was asked if there was anything at all that he would like, he said that he would take only some soup made from the foot of Morel, the grand master's own horse. When the latter heard the request, he was heartbroken, but he led out his charger, prepared to offer this sacrifice to the whim of a sick man. Saladin then revealed his identity and departed, full of admiration for the monks.

A hospital was the first building to be set up in Rhodes by Fulk of Villaret, the grand master who conquered the island in the thirteenth century. The words of the fine "prayer for the sick" which was spoken every evening in the great hall, now a museum, are still known today:

Our lords, the sick, pray for peace, that God may send it from Heaven to us on earth.

Our lords, the sick, pray for the fruits of the earth, that God may increase them to his service and to the use of Christianity. . . .

And pray for all Christians who journey by land or sea on pilgrimage, that God may guide them and lead them home again in safety of body and soul. . . .

Our lords, the sick, pray for yourselves and for all Christians who are sick throughout the world, that God may grant them health sufficient for the needs of their bodies and their souls. . . .

Our lords, the sick, pray for the souls of your fathers and mothers and for all Christians who have passed from this world into the next, that God may grant them everlasting rest. Amen.

CHAPTER V

THE WOMEN

The hackneyed situation of the knight who departs for the Crusades, leaving his wife alone in the castle to pass her time spinning wool—and in fact allowing herself to be consoled by some young page—has been fully exploited by the pseudo-romantic writers and their followers. It has attracted to itself various racy details, most typically the famous "chastity belt", which, according to a persistent legend, may still be seen in the Musée de Cluny.

The real state of affairs was quite different. Not all barons took their wives with them on the Crusade, but most of them did, and in these cases the wives shared closely in the life led by their husbands. They played a most important role in the Holy Land, all the more so since according to feudal custom, the wife could succeed her husband and might thus find herself at the head of a fief, perhaps even of the kingdom of Jerusalem. The celebrated "Salic law" was not at that time invoked and actually had no real force in France until fourteenth-century legists made it important.

From the time of the First Crusade, it is apparent that the principal leaders did not all behave in the same way. Godfrey of Bouillon traveled alone, whereas his brother Baldwin took with him his wife, an Englishwoman, Godvere of Tosny. Together with their children, they were held as hostages by

King Coloman to prevent further disorders as the Crusaders moved through Hungary.

Raymond of Saint Giles was also accompanied by his wife, Elvira of Aragon, who was related to the royal family of Spain and who shared with him the dangers of travel and battle. Their son, Alfonso, went with them but died during the expedition. Another son was later born to them at the castle of Mount Pilgrim and was named Alfonso-Jordan, half for his birthplace and half in remembrance of his brother.

The chroniclers have made a point of mentioning how the women in times of danger such as the siege of Antioch, rose to the occasion and took an active part, carrying water to the fighting men. The Anonymous Historian of the First Crusade says, "That day the women were a great help to us, taking water to the soldiers and never ceasing to encourage them to fight well." Much later, at the siege of Acre, another decisive moment in the history of Frankish Syria, the women slaved to fill in the moats, and Ambroise describes how courageously one of them met her death there.

Those barons such as Robert of Flanders and Stephen of Blois who left their wives in the West looked to them to continue the administration of their fiefs while they were away. Stephen's letter gives some idea of how thoughts of his wife helped him during the setbacks suffered by the army before Antioch. Certainly, the energetic Adela of Blois, left in charge of her husband's vast estates, could not have found time hang on her hands during his absence.

Women's faces look out from every page of the story of the Crusades and the overseas kingdoms, but they have not attracted the attention of modern historians. It would be worth making a study of those peasants and townswomen who worked with the ordinary soldiers in the Holy Land and who sometimes stayed on in Syria. There they played beside their husbands the humble yet vital role played a great deal later by the wives of the pioneers in the United States, to whom the Americans have erected a memorial in Maryland. Their presence can be felt, or guessed at, throughout the chronicles, but so little has been written about them that the eye must be content with the portraits of the great ladies, painted in more detail by the scribes.

These ladies, naturally, were of many different types. There is the Amazon: the Margravine Ida of Austria, a celebrated beauty and apparently an incorrigible tomboy. She took the cross on her own behalf with the barons who went on the second expedition of 1011 and set off in company with the Duke Welf of Bavaria. She disappeared after the terrible battle of Heraclea when the Frankish forces were annihilated, and a legend grew up telling how she had ended her days in some distant harem, where she became the mother of the future Muslim hero, Zengi, the conqueror of Edessa.

There is the child-wife such as the little Princess Isabella, daughter of John of Brienne. An unkind fate made her the wife of Frederick II, of all men the least likely to understand a child. The German Emperors had long dreamed of uniting their crown with that of the Latin kingdom, and this marriage brought the reality within reach. Immediately it had taken place, Frederick seized this kingdom from his father-in-law, ignoring the agreement they had made to leave him as regent during his lifetime. Three years later, Isabella's life of tears ended—she was not yet seventeen when she died. Her husband had provoked such violent feelings that for some time hatred of the imperialists took precedence in the East over the struggle against the Muslims—a situation from which the latter drew great profit.

There were ladies who caused trouble through their flirtations. One of these was the lovely, frivolous, and ill-omened Eleanor of Aquitaine. Her husband, Louis VII of France, had many reasons for regretting that he had not left her behind when he responded to Saint Bernard's call and became the first King of France to take the cross. At Antioch Eleanor met again her young uncle, Raymond of Poitiers, who had become prince of Antioch through his marriage with the heiress Princess Constance. The passionate friendship that soon developed between them was to cause the failure of the Crusade, for the King soon became jealous and refused to listen to the advice of Raymond, well versed in local affairs, who wanted to use the newly arrived troops to attack Aleppo and its fierce ruler Nur ed-Din. This would have been a wise decision, but Louis VII, wishing to thwart Raymond, insisted on a siege of Damascus. Politically, this was ill advised and made this defeat the most costly of all in the history of the Crusades, since the Sultan had been an ally of the Franks some years before and could have been so again. After this Louis VII took himself back to France, where the first thing he did was to divorce Eleanor.

From a husband's point of view, Louis was perhaps right, for a few weeks later Eleanor married Henry Plantagenet, the young count of Anjou. From the point of view of a ruler, however, his action involved the loss of the fine southern duchies that Eleanor now brought as a dowry to her new husband. She also brought him many troubles, for in the end she turned his own children against him, and he died of grief. As for Raymond of Poitiers, less than a year after the Crusaders left, he was killed in battle by the Atabeg of Aleppo who seized at the same time half the principality of Antioch. He was another to whom Eleanor had brought little good.

A hundred years later there was the even more dramatic love story of Robert of Courtenay, the Latin Emperor of Constantinople. The barons had chosen him as leader at a time when their Greek conquests were closely threatened by the advance of the resistance leaders John Vatatses and Theodorus Angelus. The young Emperor, however, was completely blind to his duties and preoccupied by his love for the daughter of Baldwin of Neuville, a knight of Artois who had died at Andrinopolis. The infuriated vassals were goaded into taking a terrible revenge. They killed the girl's mother for favoring the meetings and disfigured the girl herself by cutting off her nose. Robert did not live long after this dramatic episode.

Alongside the femme fatale is the woman of strong character. There are many stories of occasions when a desperate situation was saved by a woman's courage. The best known concerns Margaret of Provence, the wife of Saint Louis, who accompanied him on his first Crusade. In Damietta, three days before giving birth to a child, she heard that their army had been beaten, that the King had been taken prisoner, and that the town itself was in danger. The line she took has been described by Joinville with his usual vigor and sobriety:

> Before she was brought to bed, she sent everyone out of her room except an eighty-year-old knight, a trusted old man who slept in her chamber. She knelt before him and begged him for a favor. He swore to grant it, and she said, "I ask you, by the oath you have just taken, to cut off my head rather than let me be captured if the Saracens enter the town." The knight replied, "You may rest assured that I will do that. I had already decided that I would kill you rather than let you be captured."

Even this is not the whole of the story. Margaret had hardly given birth to her child when she heard that the Italian merchants who had followed in the wake of the Crusaders wanted to leave Damietta and to abandon the women, the sick, and

the elderly who had remained there. The day after little John
Tristan's birth she called their leaders into her room and
begged them to be compassionate. "At least take pity on this
poor little soul in his cradle and wait until I can get up."

But she was talking to merchants, men not much affected
by sentiment. "How can we do that? We shall starve to death
in this town." The Queen then suggested that she would
requisition, and herself pay for, all foodstuffs in the city and
that these should be distributed, on condition that the Italians agreed to stay. Margaret of Provence set aside 360,000
livres for this purchase. The system of rationing that was then
organized saved Damietta, and the town was later exchanged
in ransom for the King and his men. The Queen did not
leave the town until it was handed over, when she departed
for Acre to meet her husband. Each of these two people,
faced with a dramatic situation, had shown themselves equal
to the demands made on them and had brought to reality
the medieval ideal of the Knight and the Lady.

The women of the overseas kingdoms were not all "Crusaders". Right from the beginning of their long adventure
the Frankish knights showed themselves completely indiffer-
ent to any sort of racial prejudice and willingly chose for
themselves native wives, so long as they were Christian or
would accept conversion. About 1180 there were some five
thousand men-at-arms living in Palestine, many of them married to natives, either Armenian or Saracen. Consequently,
there were many people in Jerusalem who were of mixed
blood and who spoke Arabic.

The barons themselves set the example. Baldwin of Le
Bourg, the cousin and successor of Baldwin of Boulogne,
became count of Edessa and married an Armenian princess,
Morphia, daughter of Gabriel, the lord of Melitene. He proved
an excellent husband, although his early relations with his

wife's family had been marked with more than a touch of farce. In order to induce Gabriel to pay his soldiers' wages, he pretended that he had sworn to shave off his beard if he ever failed to do so. Gabriel was horrified at the thought of a beardless son-in-law and gave him without hesitation the amount he needed, begging him to be more careful in future about the possible outcome of his oaths.

Baldwin of Le Bourg was only following the example of Baldwin of Boulogne, who, after the death of his wife, Godvere, had married an Armenian princess named Arda. He repudiated her some time later, accusing her of adultery. He was probably right about this, for when she was sent to the Convent of Saint Anne in Jerusalem, she lost no time in making her escape and getting away to the big city, Constantinople, where she proceeded to enjoy herself for the rest of her days. Baldwin then looked around for some rich heiress and decided that Adelaide, the countess-regent of Sicily, would suit. Her son, Roger II, had just come of age, and she was no doubt weary of her long widowhood, so she agreed willingly when he asked for her hand in marriage. In August 1113 she arrived at the port of Acre, staging the most impressive entry yet known in the history of the kingdom. The prow of her galley was plated with gold and silver, and her chair stood on a carpet of spun gold; two escorting triremes carried her Arab guard, robed all in white, and seven other ships followed behind, laden with her treasures. Not to be outdone, Baldwin and his suite, waiting for her at the landing place, were arrayed in gold and purple, while their horses were caparisoned magnificently in the same colors.

In spite of this promising start, the marriage did not last long. When the Pope heard about it he made vigorous protests, accusing Baldwin of bigamy as his former wife was still alive, and ordered the pair to separate. They were obliged to obey, and four years after her triumphant arrival, Adelaide set sail again for Sicily.

During the history of the Latin empire at Constantinople in the following century, many matches were made with local ladies. Henry of Hainault, when he became Emperor, married the daughter of Boril, King of the Bulgars. According to Greek folk stories she was later accused of poisoning him when he met a painful death at Salonica at the early age of thirty-nine. The Emperor Baldwin II used such marriages to further his political aims. He made an alliance with the half-savage Coumans, and to consecrate this alliance took part in a solemn ceremony at which, following their custom, drops of his blood were mingled in a goblet with that of their principal chiefs and each then drank a little. Two of his knights, Narjot of Toucy and William of Morez, married daughters of two chiefs called Jonas and Saronius. The Coumans were still pagan, but these ladies accepted the Christian faith and thereafter lived in high style as members of the imperial suite. Conversely, a Bulgarian prince named Slav married the natural daughter of Henry of Hainault, and this also led to an agreement between the princes.

Many years earlier, during the assaults that were to win them possession of the Byzantine capital, the Franks had entered the palace of Boucoleon and found there "a great number of ladies of the very highest rank who had sought refuge in the castle". Among them was Agnes of France, Philip Augustus' sister, who at the age of eleven had been married to the Emperor Andronicus. Robert of Clari has described the meeting, which was a great disappointment for his fellow-countrymen: "The barons called upon her to greet her and to offer their services, but she made a poor impression . . . and did not wish to speak to them. She called an interpreter, who explained that she understood no French."

After the death of Andronicus, this Frenchwoman who was too much at home in her adopted country had married a Greek knight, Theodorus Vranas. Usama tells of the more surprising wedding of a young Frankish girl to the Muslim lord of Tabar. However, although her son was ruling as prince, she later returned to her own people and found a second husband among them.

Family alliances and possessions had the same great importance in the kingdom of Jerusalem as in the rest of medieval society. Ties of blood counted for as much, or almost as much, as the normal feudal links between vassal and lord in the various exchanges carried on between these disparate baronies. When Pons of Tripoli was besieged in Montferrand, it was the entreaties of his wife—who was Pons' sister—which decided King Fulk to go to his aid. On several occasions a woman was appointed regent, but the rules of succession varied from place to place. At Tripoli it was not possible for women to succeed, but their patrimonial goods, their dowries, were secured to them, and they could dispose of them as they wished. Thus the Countess Cecilia, married first to Tancred and then to Pons of Tripoli, could make a gift in her own name to Mount Pilgrim. For almost ten years in the thirteenth century (1253–61), Plaisance of Antioch was regent of Cyprus, where she won the reputation, as Martin de Canale tells us, of being "the bravest lady in the world".

The regency that produced the most remarkable crop of stories was probably that of Queen Melisende in the early years of the kingdom of Jerusalem. She was the cause of the first really serious quarrel to break out among the Franks of the Latin kingdom. The Arab chroniclers noted the fact with surprise. "This is not a thing that often happens among them", wrote Ibn al-Qalanisi.

Melisende was the daughter of King Baldwin. As a young girl she had enjoyed the companionship of Hugh of Le Puiset, whose Crusader father and his mother, Mabilla, had both died in the Holy Land. Hugh had been brought up in Apulia and at the age of sixteen arrived in the Holy Land to claim the fief of Jaffa as his father's heir. He was received at the court of Jerusalem and struck up with Melisende a close friendship that was not interrupted by her marriage with Fulk of Anjou.

Hugh, meanwhile, married the Countess Emma, a lady older than himself and the widow of a baron, Eustace Garnier, by whom she had had two sons. It was not long before disagreements arose between these two and their youthful stepfather. One of them, Walter, accused him in public of some misconduct and challenged him to a duel with swords. Whether because of cowardice or guilt, Hugh failed to appear on the day appointed. Everyone then turned away from him, and, unable to bear the weight of this silent criticism, the knight did something that he certainly should not have done. He fled to Ascalon, which in 1132 was still in Arab hands, and sought the help of the town's Egyptian garrison. The Muslims were only too happy to seize the chance thus offered to them and immediately set out to raid the countryside around Jaffa and Sharon. This brought Hugh back to his senses, and he hastened remorsefully to Jerusalem to throw himself at the feet of the King and beg for pardon.

Fulk had never shown much desire to listen to accusations against his vassal. As a wise man, he was concerned at the proportions the affair had assumed and had no wish to see the Saracens profiting from the discords which fermented as the barons took sides for or against Hugh. He pardoned the wayward young man and, on the Queen's intervention, sentenced him only to three years' exile. However, as he was leaving the town, Hugh was attacked and stabbed. Although he did recover, it was thought at the time that he was dying. This was a serious matter for the King, who might well have been suspected of wishing to rid himself of him. He lost no time in arresting the assailant and having him tortured in public. The man swore that he had acted entirely on his own account.

The strong feelings stirred up by this affair subsided gradually. Some years later, in 1143, Fulk died suddenly after a fall from his horse, and Melisende ruled in the name of her thirteen-year-old son, the future Baldwin III. It was she who received the Crusaders who came out to the help of the kingdom and she who presided over the famous assembly at Acre on June 24, 1148. Nearly all the crowned heads of Europe had by then taken the cross, and their presence made this a most brilliant occasion. Louis VII of France was there, and also the Emperor Conrad and his brothers, among them Frederick of Swabia, father of the future Frederick Barbarossa; in addition, of course, all the prelates and princes of the Holy Land were present.

Another guest was Alfonso-Jordan, the son of Raymond of Saint Giles, a living link with the First Crusade since he had been born at Mount Pilgrim at the height of the siege of Tripoli. He died quite soon after his arrival, and the story got about that Count Raymond of Tripoli, fearing that he had come to claim his inheritance, had taken the chance to get rid of him.

Melisende's taste for power grew with the years, and she had no wish to let it pass out of her hands. Her son Baldwin III had reached the age of twenty-two and was impatient to rule on his own, but Melisende was always able to find some excuse to defer his coronation. On the Tuesday after Easter 1152 Baldwin went to the Church of the Holy Sepulchre

and ordered Fulcher, the Patriarch of Jerusalem, to crown
him there and then. The prelate had no choice, and Baldwin, alone in the Church, was anointed and received the
crown. Then he went to tell his mother, the Queen, what
had been done. A period of squabbling followed before Melisende recognized defeat and retired from politics. A little
later, Baldwin gratified the wishes of his subjects and the
hopes of the realm when he married Theodora, niece of the
Emperor Manuel Comnenus, in the midst of celebrations
that lasted for several days.

Time and again the figure of a woman moves through
decisive episodes in the history of the Latin kingdoms. There
is Constance of Antioch, who delivered her principality into
the calamitous grasp of Reynald of Châtillon as the result of
a romantic love affair. At the age of twenty she was the widow
of Raymond of Poitiers, but refused one after the other various eligible gentlemen who wished to marry her. A chronicler wrote, "The princess knew only too well how trying
life could be under the domination of a husband and how
little freedom was left to ladies when they had a lord." She
refused Roger of Sorrento, the Emperor's brother-in-law, who
turned monk out of vexation, and another Byzantine "Cae-
sar", Andronicus John Comnenus. Then suddenly, and most
unfortunately for the Holy Land, she fell in love with Reynald, a penniless younger son in the King's service who came
from Châtillon-sur-Loing in France. All the same, she behaved with scrupulous regularity. "She did not wish", writes
William of Tyre, "to make her decision known until the King,
her cousin and the protector of the principality of Antioch,
had confirmed her wish by his authority and consent." Baldwin III was at that time besieging Ascalon, and Reynald hurried down from Antioch to see him.

He carried the princess' request to the King, received the royal permission, and went back to Antioch and married her immediately. But many people were surprised. They could not understand how so distinguished, powerful, and renowned a lady, the widow of such a great prince, could stoop to ally herself with a man who was no more than a knight.

A fancy of the same kind led Sybilla, sister of Baldwin the Leper, to marry Guy of Lusignan. He was a young nobleman from Poitou and, like Reynald, a younger son without fortune. Sybilla had earlier been married to William of Montferrat, nicknamed Longsword, who died a few months after the wedding. He left a posthumous son, little Baldwin, but the child lived only until he was nine. The King's illness made it urgently necessary to find another defender for Palestine, and everyone was busy weighing up the merits of various suitors for Sybilla when she announced that she had fallen in love and chosen a husband for herself. Unfortunately, Guy of Lusignan, charming though he might be, had none of the qualities essential in a ruler, particularly in one faced with the task of guiding the Holy Land through critical times and against the opposition of such an adversary as Saladin. Baldwin the Leper was by now too ill to hold out for long against his sister's wishes. In 1180 he consented to the marriage and at the same time made Guy regent of the kingdom. However, his brother-in-law gave such evidence of incapacity when Saladin invaded Galilee in 1183 that the King revoked his decision; made his nephew, little Baldwin, co-ruler; and appointed Raymond III of Tripoli as his regent. Baldwin IV died two years later, and these final arrangements were not honored. Guy of Lusignan, together with Reynald of Châtillon and the Patriarch Heraclius, was in fact the person chiefly

responsible for the utter defeat at Hattin and thus for the loss
of Jerusalem and the larger part of the Latin kingdoms.

Isabella, the youngest sister of Baldwin and Sybilla, makes
her appearance after this disaster. For a while, the barons had
hoped to put forward her claim to the throne, but she too,
although betrothed at the age of eight and married at eleven,
was in love with her husband, the young and handsome Humphrey of Toron. He was the son of a family distinguished for
its services to the Holy Land, but he had inherited from his
ancestors the gift of scholarship rather than standfast courage. He spoke Arabic like his mother tongue, acting as interpreter in discussions with Saladin, and he was a delightful,
good-looking person. An Arab writer said of him, "I have
seen this young man. He is indeed extremely handsome."
The barons, gathered at Nablus, suggested that he should
have the crown, which, against their wishes, had been assumed by Queen Sybilla's husband at Jerusalem. But, either
out of loyalty or in a panic at what was being expected of
him, Humphrey slipped quietly away from Nablus by night
and sought an audience of Guy and Sybilla, "like a naughty
child caught red handed", as the chronicler put it.

The barons never forgave him this defection. After Hattin, when Sybilla had died without leaving children and when
the kingdom needed a strong protector more than ever before, they offered the crown to Isabella, but urged her to
divorce her husband. The situation demanded "a mighty man
of war", and such a man was at hand. He was the Marquis
Conrad of Montferrat, from Piedmont. He had arrived in
Tyre at a moment when the besieged town was ready to capitulate and by his cool bravery had rallied the defenders. In
return he demanded the lordship of the town, and, furthermore, he told the King and Queen, Guy and Sybilla, that "it
was as much as their lives would be worth to set foot in the

place". There were those who said that the marquis of Montferrat already had a wife living in the West—some chroniclers
said he had two. Isabella put up a determined resistance to the
plan. She was devoted to her handsome husband and did not
intend to be parted from him. Even Humphrey was prepared
to make his protest in front of the barons. However, one of
Montferrat's supporters, Guy of Senlis, challenged him to single combat by flinging his glove down before him, and Humphrey lacked the courage to pick up the challenge.

Isabella was obliged to submit to the demands of the state.
The Pope, when he heard of it, made a strong protest against
such a violation of religious law, but by then Isabella had
become the bride of Conrad. But the forced marriage was
not to last long. Conrad was preparing for his coronation
when on the evening of April 28, 1192 he dined with the
bishop of Beauvais. Going home afterward through the streets
of Tyre, he was met by two Muslims who had been converted to Christianity a short while before. One of them
handed him a letter. Suspecting nothing, the marquis stopped
to read it and was stabbed to death by the other. These men
were "Assassins", members of that terrible Islamic sect that
was fanaticized and dedicated to political murder by their
grand master, who was called by the chroniclers "the Old
Man of the Mountain".

The problem of succession to the throne of Jerusalem had
to be met once more, but it was speedily solved this time by
calling upon Henry, count of Champagne, who had only
recently arrived in the East. He was not at all desirous of
becoming the ruler of such a precarious kingdom, and he
had had no intention, when he took the cross, of remaining
in the Holy Land, but the interests of Christianity were used
as an argument to persuade him. On May 5, 1192, he, in his
turn, became the husband of Isabella, who was expecting a

child by Conrad. The chronicler Ambroise comments that even if Henry II had been hesitant at the beginning, he was well pleased afterward, "for she possessed a remarkable beauty and charm". When Isabella gave birth to a daughter, Henry retained his rights to the crown. He was worthy of his position, showing himself as wise in peace as he was valiant in battle. Several times he took effective action to reestablish order. A remarkable example of his methods was shown at Acre when a newly arrived band of German Crusaders came ashore and immediately, as if they were invaders in a conquered land, began to drive off the inhabitants and molest the women. As a result of the endless lawsuits coming up since its capture between former owners who wanted to recover their premises and successful besiegers who wished to install themselves there, order was already hard to keep in the town. Henry of Champagne threatened to put the women and children under the protection of the Hospital and then to take up arms against the inhabitants. As part of the plan the leaders of the newly arrived Crusaders hastened to quarter their men in the suburbs.

Henry wisely restored his contacts with the Assassins, a discordant element in the body of Islam, who were valuable allies but most formidable foes, and he made friends with the Armenians in Cilicia. Saladin had died in 1193, and it seemed that Frankish Syria could look forward to some years of tranquility. Then a strange accident intervened. On September 10, 1197, Henry of Champagne fell from the balcony of his palace at Acre to the street below and fractured his skull. He brought down with him his dwarf Scarlet, who had seen him tumble over backward and had grabbed at his clothing to try to save him.

Isabella, now aged twenty-five, had lost a husband for the third time. Knowing that she was bound to the will of the state, she raised no opposition to a fourth marriage, and, by a strange chance, Amalric, the brother of Guy of Lusignan, was chosen for her. In 1194 he had succeeded Guy as ruler of Cyprus. No two brothers could have been more unlike. Amalric was both a prudent diplomat and a hardened warrior. He recaptured Beirut from the Muslims in October 1197 and then concluded a profitable peace with the Sultan Saif ad-Din. He was the last in Isabella's series of husbands.

The most affecting portrait of a woman that emerges from crusading history is on a tombstone and not in the pages of a chronicle. There is a portrayal in the Church of the Greyfriars in Nancy that is surely the most touching of all twelfth-century sculptures that have survived. It depicts Hugh and Anne of Vaudémont and has been for centuries a symbol of "the Crusader's return". It shows a ragged Crusader being welcomed by his wife with a close embrace. The monument commemorates a lifetime of waiting. According to tradition Hugh of Vaudémont was held prisoner in the Holy Land for sixteen years. When his death was reported, his wife, Anne of Lorraine, was urged to remarry but always firmly refused. Then at last the man who was no longer expected came home. The sculptor has recalled this moment on the tomb where, some years later, the knight and the lady who had been faithful to each other all their lives were laid to rest side by side.

CHAPTER VI

THE GRAIN AND THE CHAFF

While the People's Crusade was making its way through central Europe, certain things happened in Germany that popular opinion has confused with events marking the passage of Peter the Hermit's followers. These events showed the dark reverse of the crusading movement. They revealed leaders who were either priests of dubious character like a certain Gottschalk or another named Volkmar or else brigands like Emich of Leiningen, who for years had been known as an outlaw. Men like these gathered their followers for a Crusade, but before setting out they were responsible for a number of atrocities against the Jews.

The savage attacks began at Speyer early in May 1096, when Emich killed twelve Jews and a Jewess. The bishop of the town took the Jews under his protection and punished the murderers by cutting off the hands of any of them he was able to catch. Emich reached Worms on May 18. Here he launched a full-scale attack on the Jewish quarter and killed over five hundred people, after breaking down the gates of the palace of the bishop, who had protested and given shelter to the persecuted. A week later the scene was repeated at Mainz, where Bishop Rothard gathered the Jews into his palace behind barred doors and where once more the mob of thugs overpowered them. At Cologne, on June 1, Jews were killed in a massacre lasting for two days as they fled in terror before the approaching bands. There was news of a similar massacre at Treves, while at Metz twenty-two Jews were killed. On May 30 Volkmar's gang slaughtered Jews in Prague in spite of Bishop Cosmas' intervention; Gottschalk's men did the same at Ratisbon.

This perversion of crusading fervor into ferocity was condemned by contemporaries exactly as we ourselves condemn it now. Chroniclers of the time, describing the leaders of these bands, used the phrase "the tares among the wheat". Ekkehard of Aura always makes a point of standing up for his countrymen, the Crusaders from Germany, but even he calls Gottschalk "not a true but a false servant of God" and says that Emich was "a man of violence, a noted oppressor". Ecclesiastical authorities everywhere protested strongly, as Saint Bernard did later, whenever the news of fresh massacres, coming invariably from the cities of Germany, reached them.

These lawless gangs came to a violent end, and their complete annihilation was regarded as a punishment for the scenes of horror that had marked their departure. Some, like Volkmar's followers, were massacred in Hungary. Others died in the Balkans. Still others met their deaths in ways that seemed beyond explanation. Emich's men, for instance, were crossing a bridge they had just made when a sudden panic arose, and they were all lost in the confusion that followed. Oddly enough, men from Germany bore a poor reputation all through the time of the Crusades. Their first departure had been marked by a pogrom, and, in spite of all their efforts, they attained only a limited degree of importance in the East. One German traveler mentioned rather tartly that he had barely heard a word of his own language spoken in the Latin cities.

To confuse these bloodthirsty mobs with the People's Crusade would be, to parody a celebrated phrase, "more than wrong; it would be wrongheaded". Peter the Hermit's following left Cologne in the middle of April 1096. Consequently, they would have traveled as far as Hungary or the Balkans before these riots broke out in May. None of the contemporary writers is guilty of such confusion. All of them distinguish between those who got themselves massacred within Christendom—evidently as a punishment for the crimes and excesses to which they had abandoned themselves—and the followers of Peter who died "in pagan lands" at the hands of the infidels.

Slaughter on such a scale recurred on several other occasions. The history of the Crusades demonstrates most vividly the mixture of fineness and brutality characterizing the men of that age. Their impulses, whether of courage or of ferocity, went to extremes, and they brought as much enthusiasm to killing as they did to their religious acts, and even to the expiation of their sins. Raymond of Saint Giles set out from Maarat an-Numan shoeless and dressed as a penitent, although he was one of the men responsible for the delays to the expedition that resulted from quarrels over completely materialistic ambitions.

It is possible to hold totally opposing views on every aspect of the Crusades and to produce facts to justify them all. Some historians eagerly present the Muslims as patterns of moderation and the Crusaders as savage brutes, while others see things differently, showing the former as ferocious beasts and the latter as stained-glass saints. Both sides can find plenty of massacres in Crusader and Saracen annals alike to ornament their theses; they can even set off one slaughter against another, canceling out the massacre of Peter the Hermit's followers by that of the people of Jerusalem. The study of history has nothing to gain from this.

It is obvious that the Muslims, who used the holy war as an acknowledged part of their religious propaganda, had more excuse for their massacres than had those who fought under the sign of the Cross. There is no room for doubt, however, that the Crusaders included among their number, in the biblical phrases favored by the preachers of the time, "tares as well as wheat" and "chaff among the good grain". These could crop up in the most unexpected places, since, as we have seen, feelings of ambition or nobility could in turn unleash conflicting reactions in the same individual.

Probably the most amazing example of this emotional type of character is Richard Cœur de Lion. He demonstrated his incredible bravery at the siege of Acre, when Arab chroniclers describe him as returning from combat bristling with arrows "like a pincushion stuck full of pins". But he was also capable of acts of savagery as violent as they were unexpected. After the town had surrendered, he suddenly, on August 20, 1191, ordered the slaughter of three thousand prisoners because his adversary was too slow for his liking in carrying out the terms of the capitulation. Saladin reacted by putting to death all the Frankish prisoners who were taken in the ensuing campaign, thus bringing the bitterness of unappeasable warfare into a Crusade that until then had been marked by an astonishing degree of fraternization between Franks and Muslims. An Arab writer says, "During the siege of Acre, from 1189 to 1191, a kind of friendliness grew up between the opposing camps. Talking would begin when the battle was over, and out of long association the men would dance and sing together. Then, an hour later, they would start fighting each other again."

These outbursts of useless brutality were nearly always the work of newly arrived Crusaders who had not yet learned to weigh up their opponents or to behave with the caution necessitated by the numerical inferiority of the Crusaders in Syria. The most typical example of all is undoubtedly that which marked the last act of the Crusade and the end of the Latin kingdoms.

In 1291 Frankish power in the East was being upheld only by a miracle, and Acre was the only town that was still resisting the Mameluke attacks. Two years earlier, the magnificent town of Tripoli, one of the most prosperous of the Latin lordships, had been besieged by the armies of the Sultan Qalawun and taken by assault (April 26, 1289). Its capture was followed by scenes of appalling slaughter. The chronicler Abu'l Feda gives us this description:

> The inhabitants fled toward the harbor, but very few got away by sea. Nearly all the men were put to the sword, while the women and children were taken into slavery. When an end was made of killing, the town was razed to the ground. A church dedicated to Saint Thomas had been built on a small island near the town, and here an enormous crowd of refugees gathered. The Muslims plunged into the sea on horseback or else reached the island by swimming. All the men captured there were slain. I visited the place myself a little later and found it full of rotting corpses. The stench made it impossible to remain there long.

Christians everywhere were horrified to hear of the loss of Tripoli in such circumstances. Two years later some Crusaders, nearly all from Italy, landed at Acre, and the first thing they did was to destroy their own usefulness as reinforcements by a most senseless act of savagery, which, as things were, was also highly impolitic. These Crusaders, anxious to get into battle, attacked the Muslims who habitually thronged the market at Acre and killed them without provocation. Gerard of Montreal writes:

> These men arrived in Acre at a time when the truce made between the King and the Sultan was working well. The poor

villeins [the Saracen peasants] came into Acre bringing goods
to sell as they had always done. Then one day, the old enemy
of mankind, eagerly fanning the flame of evil among people
of goodwill, so arranged things that these Crusaders, who had
come to bring help to the city as a good deed and for their own
souls' sake, ended by causing its destruction. They ran through
the city and killed all the poor villeins who had brought in their
produce, wheat and suchlike, for sale. These men were Saracens from the villages around Acre. Several bearded Syrians,
members of the Greek Church, were mistaken for Saracens and
killed also. This most disastrous affair was the reason why Acre
was taken by the Saracens, as you will hear.

In fact, we shall see how this massacre, both stupid in itself
and in disloyal contravention of the existing treaties, caused
the fall of the last Christian city in the East.

A moralist would have plenty of opportunity for observ-
ing that in the history of the Latin kingdoms it was almost
always barbaric acts of this type which sparked off the worst
catastrophes. The situation is summed up in the deeds and
exploits of one man, who symbolizes the brutality and cruelty of the age. That man was Reynald of Châtillon.

Reynald represents among the Crusaders the type of dare-
devil adventurer found down through the years in every army
in the world, apparently born only to fight and able to turn
his energies only toward murder or robbery. With his soldierly bearing and his undeniable courage he was extremely
attractive to women, possessing a power that his brutality
merely enhanced. It brought him unbelievable success. This
petty knight from Châtillon-sur-Loing, apparently a landless
younger son, literally dazzled the Princess Constance of Antioch, widow of Raymond of Poitiers.

This infatuation of a temperamental princess was to prove
a real catastrophe for the Holy Land. If he had kept his place,

Reynald of Châtillon might well have performed wonders. He was a man whose intrepidity was useful only when it was firmly restricted and held by an iron discipline to the right course. This unexpected elevation made him lose his head completely and opened the way to all kinds of excesses.

Reynald had as much of the brigand as of the soldier in his makeup, and from now on brigandage on a large scale was made easy for him. The first thing he did showed how far he was prepared to go. On the subject of the marriage the patriarch of Antioch had allowed himself some little jests that had touched the humorless parvenu on the raw. Reynald ordered his immediate arrest, had him beaten until he bled, and then left him lying for a whole day, with his head smeared with honey, to endure the blazing Syrian sun and the attentions of the insects. It is easy to imagine the anger that this barbarous performance aroused, and Baldwin III intervened at once to ensure the release of the patriarch, who spent the rest of his days in Jerusalem, though retaining his patriarchal seat. However, the end of the tale was to match its savage opening and to lead at last to the downfall of the kingdom of Jerusalem.

Scarcely had Reynald of Châtillon come to power in Antioch than he started off on a series of raids and forays undertaken without the least concern for any political or moral obligations. He struck first against the Armenians of Cilicia, although it should have been the business of a Christian state to befriend them; then he sent a force against Cyprus, another Christian possession, belonging to the Byzantine Empire, and here he behaved exactly like a pirate, robbing, killing, ravaging as he went.

Reynald returned to Antioch with immense spoils, but also, as William of Tyre writes, "cursed by the Greeks as well as the Latins". The Byzantine Emperor Manuel Comnenus was at that time detained far away by affairs in Europe, and this barbaric behavior might well have ruined all Baldwin Ill's efforts to improve relations with him. Luckily both rulers were sagacious men who realized that their mutual interest demanded a united stand against their dangerous enemy, Nur ed-Din, the atabeg of Aleppo.

Baldwin III asked for the hand of Manuel's niece, the Princess Theodora. His request was granted, and the marriage was celebrated at Tyre in 1158. At that time the Byzantine army, under the command of Manuel, was stationed at Missis in Cilicia, not far from Antioch. Reynald considered it wise to take advantage of the Emperor's friendly mood to sue for pardon. He presented himself before him bareheaded and barefoot, with a rope round his neck, and groveled. A chronicler relates, "He cried out for mercy and cried so long that everyone was sickened, and many Franks thought him contemptible and looked down on him."

After this unexampled humiliation, Reynald returned to his own state with the Emperor's pardon, having recognized his suzerainty over Antioch. Afterward he joined his forces to those of Manuel and Baldwin III in an alliance against Nur ed-Din. For a while it almost seemed as if the future of Frankish Syria had been assured against this dangerous emir, who was gradually rallying the whole of the Turkish and Arab forces around himself to make Aleppo the center of a movement increasingly united against the kingdom of Jerusalem. As it turned out, however, Byzantine diplomacy disregarded the interests of Christendom. Manuel refused to besiege Aleppo, contenting himself with obtaining the release of Christian prisoners, and returned to Constantinople without involving himself in warfare.

This left Reynald of Châtillon free to apply himself once more to brigandage. But his adventures came to an abrupt end and Frankish Syria gained a short respite when he was captured raiding, in violation of a truce, the country near Edessa. He was taken to Aleppo and remained a prisoner there for sixteen years.

Reynald was freed in 1176, and by that time many changes had taken place in the kingdom of Jerusalem. His wife, Constance of Antioch, had died twelve years earlier, and since he had held Antioch only through her, he could no longer lay claim to his former principality. He lost no time in marrying Stephanie (or Etiennette) of Milly, "the lady of Kerak". She brought him as her dowry the distant seigneury of Oultre-Jourdain (Transjordan), with its castles of Kerak of Moab and Montreal (Chaubak) lying beyond the Dead Sea on the caravan route from Damascus to Cairo. From one point of view, to entrust the remote frontier marches, whose safekeeping demanded a warrior of proved courage, to this lawless baron, was to make an intelligent use of his qualities. But getting him out of the way also had its dangers. He was now beyond the reach of royal authority, and his independence was to have awkward consequences.

At this time Baldwin IV, the young leper, was King of Jerusalem, and it was only his sublime courage that kept the unstable kingdom going. It was menaced both by internal dissensions—we have already noted the weakness shown by his own entourage, particularly by his brothers-in-law Guy of Lusignan and Humphrey of Toron—and by the development of a new Muslim alliance linking Egypt and Syria under the leadership of the heroic Saladin.

Events now demonstrated emphatically the sort of thing that could be expected from a soldier like Reynald of Châtillon. First he fought extremely well at the battle of Montgisard, one of the most extraordinary exploits of the Crusades, when five hundred knights, led by the seventeen-year-old leper King, put to flight the Kurdish and Sudanese hordes under Saladin's command. Then, three years later, in time of peace, without regard for the treaties guaranteeing the safe conduct of pilgrim caravans to Mecca, he attacked one of them and carried both loot and prisoners back to Kerak.

Baldwin was horrified when he learned of this act of aggression. He ordered his vassal to release his captives at once and to go and make his apologies to Saladin. Reynald refused, and neither threats nor prayers could move him. However, he had no qualms about appealing for help to the King when in retaliation the Egyptian army invaded Transjordan. The series of attacks that followed would have put the Frankish possessions in grave danger if it had not been for the young King's courage and the remarkable speed of his strategic moves.

It might have been thought that the terrible lord of Transjordan would this time have learned his lesson. But all the evidence suggests that he was incapable of resisting the attraction of pillage, and now he began to scheme on a grand scale. His imagination had been fired by tales of the fabulous riches amassed in Mecca and Medina, the holy cities of the Prophet Muhammad, and he plotted to extend his operations to these points. For this end he formed a plan that must be recognized as a considerable achievement from the technical as well as from the military point of view. He had a fleet of ships built in Transjordan and then had them carried in sections on camelback to the Gulf of Akaba on the Red Sea. There the galleys were rebuilt one by one and launched near Suez, and then they set sail for Ailat, which Reynald had besieged. After a voyage of more than five months, lasting from the end of 1182 until early in 1183, these five galleys began their career of piracy along the coasts of Egypt and the Hejaz as far as Aden. A vessel carrying pilgrims back from Mecca and two merchant ships from the Yemen fell to them. "The inhabitants of these lands were greatly terrified", note the Arab historians. The piles of plunder heaped on the pack animals mounted until, when Reynald was no more than a day's march from Medina, a strong Egyptian squadron sent against him by Saladin defeated his flotilla and brought him to a halt. His irreverent action had aroused more than terror. It had stirred up the anger of the Muslims and succeeded in uniting them against Frankish Syria. Reynald returned to Kerak of Moab, like "a wolf taking cover in the valley", as the Eastern historians put it, and Saladin followed to besiege him there.

Now there occurred a chivalrous incident, reported by chroniclers of the time. Stephanie, the lady of Transjordan, sent to tell Saladin that Humphrey of Toron, her son by her first marriage, was celebrating his wedding to Isabella, the half-sister of the leper King, in one of the castle towers. In her message she reminded him that as a child he had carried her in his arms—an odd evocation of the intimacy that could exist between the Franks and their Muslim prisoners. Saladin asked for the tower where the wedding was taking place to be pointed out to him and forbade any attack on it. By way of thanks, those in the castle sent out to his army some of the dishes from the feast. This exchange of courtesies, however, did not prevent the Mamelukes massacring the unfortunate inhabitants of the Kerak township in November 1183. The blame for this also could be laid at Reynald's door, for he had persisted in trying to defend the township instead of giving the people shelter inside the castle walls. Once again Kerak was saved by the intervention of Baldwin IV. The leprosy had by now advanced so far that the King was blind and little more than a breathing corpse carried about in a litter, but he remained

in charge of the army. The following summer Saladin re-
sumed the siege, again without success.

Reynald of Châtillon committed one last act of banditry,
and in so doing set a match to the train of events leading to
the disaster of Hattin, the dramatic finale to the history of
the Holy Land. In 1184, while Saladin was discussing a three-
year truce, a caravan with which his own sister was traveling
passed on its way from Egypt to Damascus. Reynald was
quite unable to keep his grasp off its treasures, and he way-
laid it. This time the Sultan swore to kill him with his own
hands. He was to keep his word.

It has been said that the entourage of the admirable leper
King included all the worst possible types, as a foil for his
own wisdom and unbelievable courage. At this same time,
Baldwin's brother-in-law, Guy, who, by his marriage with
Sybilla, was the next in succession to the kingdom, also committed an unpardonable act of savagery. He massacred a party
of Bedouins, dependents of the King, who, relying on the
latter's protection and on arrangements made in the earliest
days of the kingdom of Jerusalem, were pasturing their flocks
near Ascalon.

This attack was actually a base act of revenge on Baldwin
himself, against whom the count was now in open revolt.
The King was aware of Guy's incompetence and had been
trying to withdraw from him the "baylie", the power of regency. The reign of the leper King was to end with the news
of this lamentable affair. Baldwin called his vassals to Jerusalem and in their presence gave the power to Count Raymond III of Tripoli before he died on March 16, 1185. He
was twenty-four years old. With the last breath he drew and
with his last words he tried to ensure that control of his kingdom would pass to the most worthy person. Raymond of
Tripoli appeared to be the only man capable of exerting any

authority over the barons or of preserving a kingdom apparently doomed to anarchy. Unfortunately the forces of anarchy were to prove the more powerful, and to rise in opposition to the leper King's last wishes.

At this point Gerard of Ridfort, another unprincipled adventurer, makes his appearance. He too had risen from the ranks and come to Palestine in search of the fortune denied him in his own land. He was Flemish and had landed in Palestine some years earlier. He had quickly attracted the attention of Raymond of Tripoli, who appointed him marshal of Jerusalem. From that time on Gerard's great ambition was to follow Reynald's example and marry some wealthy heiress and thus become a powerful lord.

Gerard had designs on Lucia, the only daughter of the lord of Botrun. But when her father died, Raymond had other ideas and gave Lucia's hand to another suitor, an enormously wealthy Pisan. The tale is told that he offered to give for his bride her own weight in gold. The chronicler who reports this glittering bargain adds, "The Franks do not look on the Italians as gentlemen. They are so rich and so gallant." Gerard of Ridfort, thus rejected, fell ill with vexation. He was cared for in the Templars' infirmary at Jerusalem and on his recovery expressed a desire to join the order. The story is told that he added a fourth vow to the usual three, swearing to have his revenge on Count Raymond of Tripoli.[1]

One may wonder what intrigues he used to get himself named first seneschal of the Temple and afterward grand master of the order. All we know is that when a chapter was held in 1184 to choose a successor to Arnold of Toroga (Red Tower), there was difficulty in deciding between him and

[1] Marion Melville, *Vie des Templiers*, pp. 105–6.

the commander, Gilbert Erail. In the end, and to their misfortune, the Templars chose Gerard of Ridfort.

Gilbert Erail was immediately sent away from the Holy Land and did not return until after the disaster. Gerard and Reynald were two of a kind, and they easily struck up an alliance, which was then completed by a third person who was in every way a perfect match for the other two. This was Heraclius, the patriarch of Jerusalem, who had been elected, in preference to William of Tyre, through the interest of the Queen Mother.

Joint action by these three men secured the surprise coronation of Guy of Lusignan, the circumstances of whose marriage to the heiress of Jerusalem have already been described. The young Baldwin V, the son of Sybilla's first marriage, died when he was nine years old, and his funeral had just taken place. Raymond of Tripoli, detained in his fief, had not been present. The patriarch and Reynald were his personal enemies and were not anxious to have to deal with a man of his quality, for Raymond could exert an authority they would have found displeasing, and, moreover, he could count on the support of the other barons. As for Gerard, his only thought was of vengeance. The three confederates took the chance that was offered and decided to have Guy and Sybilla crowned at once. The regalia were kept in a chest with three keys. One was in the keeping of the patriarch, and the others were held by the grand masters of the orders of the Temple and of Saint John of Jerusalem—an interesting indication of the way in which power was divided within the mother Church of the kingdom. Gerard and Heraclius went together to the Hospital. At first Roger of Les Moulins, the grand master, refused to hand over the key in his possession, but in face of their insistence and the threatening behavior of the crowd that they had stirred up in Guy's favor, he ended by flinging his key on the floor of the room and walking out. The others made their way immediately to the Church of the Holy Sepulchre, where Heraclius placed the crown on Sybilla's head. She then crowned her husband. Gerard of Ridfort was heard to exclaim, "This crown is well worth the Botrun marriage."

It did not take long for the new King's personality, or rather lack of personality, to become apparent. He was easily influenced, impulsive, and at the mercy of his courtiers, and these courtiers being the men they were, the worst could be feared. And the worst happened. Saladin was then preparing an expedition in reprisal for Reynald's robbery of the caravan, and on May 1, 1187, Gerard of Ridfort rashly—and against the advice of the grand master of the Hospital and the marshal of the Temple—threw 140 knights into an attack against seven thousand Mamelukes. The knights were immediately cut to pieces. Then, under pretext of avenging the dead, the fatal march toward Hattin began. The army was drawn up unwisely in the arid hillsides, without water and without shade. The last assault was made on the orders of Guy to a plan influenced by Gerard of Ridfort but against the advice of the other lords. The men, thus engaged in the worst possible conditions, offered an easy target to the Saracens. The unfortunate soldiers were literally stifled when smoke from burning brushwood was blown toward them. Raymond III and his followers succeeded in a desperate dash through the Turkish ranks, but all the others fell into Saladin's power.

Saladin showed his generosity in pardoning Guy of Lusignan. He received him in his tent and reassured the frightened man, "A King does not kill another King." But he behaved quite differently to Reynald of Châtillon, and the story goes that he killed the adventurer with his own hands, as he had sworn to do. Then, on the Sultan's orders, the 230

Templars who had been captured were tied one by one to the execution post, where each was offered his life in return for "calling the law", or accepting the Muslim religion. None of them agreed to this, and each in turn had his head cut off. Curiously enough, the grand master, Gerard of Ridfort, alone escaped this treatment and was spared. He then did something that had never been done before and that was never done again in Templar history. He exchanged for his own freedom the castle of Ghaza, the property of the Templars, thus breaking one of the vows on which the life of the Holy Land depended. But Gerard of Ridfort was not only a perjurer. Members of his order accused him of having "called the law".

After the total loss of the Frankish army, it might have been expected that the Holy Land would now be quite lost to the Christians. Yet they clung to their hold there for another hundred years. At Jerusalem, where the capitulation was negotiated by Balian of Ibelin, the citizens were armed as knights so that at least a semblance of resistance might be offered. It was only because reinforcements came from Europe that a genuine resistance, concentrated first on Tyre and then on Acre, could be made to Saladin's armies.

PART TWO

TECHNICAL METHODS

CHAPTER VII

THE ORGANIZATION OF THE CONQUEST

Historians have been particularly interested in finding out how many people went on Crusade. Like all medieval problems involving numbers, the answer to this one is utterly obscure. Nowadays we find it difficult to ignore numbers, since only assessments based on figures seem to us exact and reassuring. But in dealing with the world of the Middle Ages we have to accept that no one then knew precisely how old he was or told the time by any other clock than the sun or the bell of the nearest monastery, which came to the same thing. We also have to accept that estimates provided by contemporary witnesses are in general based on pure convention. In those days either 60,000 or 600,000 might serve equally well as a number to suggest that a crowd was really enormous. Modern writers have thus had to make use of a more or less personal scale in assessing the size of the crusading armies. Ferdinand Lot has strictly reduced their numbers by counting only the effective troops. Others have been more generous, allotting between 60,000 and 100,000 combatants to the Christian army. Runciman, for instance, thinks that each expeditionary force must have been made up of at least 10,000 men. Peter the Hermit would have had more, perhaps as many as 20,000. Bohemond certainly had fewer than 10,000, for the chroniclers have noted that he lacked the means to raise an army of any great importance.

Of those who set out, how many actually reached Jerusalem? We have seen how Peter the Hermit's followers were wiped out and how the battles, the hunger, particularly during the siege of Antioch, the killing marches across desert country, and the assaults on Nicea and Jerusalem took their toll of the others. But, more than anything, a custom of feudal warfare was responsible for the extremely vulnerable and unprotected state of the Holy Land, for, once Jerusalem had been taken, the majority of the Crusaders considered that they had accomplished their vow and went back home. As a result, by the spring of 1100, Godfrey of Bouillon was left with a contemptible fighting force of 300 knights, a figure which, for once, is well substantiated by the chroniclers. Raymond of Saint Giles, according to his contemporaries, had sworn on leaving never to return to his own lands. His example evidently did not appeal to many others.

Similarly modest numbers are mentioned on various other occasions. Tancred was accompanied by 80 knights when he seized Tiberias and won the title of prince of Galilee. Later, King Amalric could muster only 374 knights to meet Sultan Shirkuh's army of at least 2,000 Kurds. Such forces were weak indeed in comparison with a modern army. It should be remembered that mobilization of priests or peasants was quite inconceivable in the Middle Ages, hence the enormous difference between medieval and modern warfare. It was this departure of a peasant population who would have done better to stay on their own lands, and which Urban II himself had tried to restrict, that gave its unique character to the First Crusade. Even the Children's Crusade a hundred years later made no greater impression on contemporaries than this mobilization of land workers, a measure that nowadays we regard as a necessity.

When the news that Jerusalem had fallen reached the West, other Crusaders set out from Lombardy, from Burgundy, and from Germany and western France to reinforce the armies of the Advocate of the Holy Sepulchre. In succession the three armies were defeated by the Turks, and it has been estimated that at most only 3,000 combatants escaped.

A little later, in 1102, Raymond of Saint Giles had 300 knights under his command at the battle of Tortosa. In 1115 Pons of Tripoli led 200 knights and 2,000 foot soldiers to the relief of Antioch, while William Jordan, cousin of the count of Toulouse, had 300 knights with him when he raised the siege of Al Akma in 1108.

In 1146, when Louis VII of France and the Emperor Conrad took the cross in response to Saint Bernard's appeal, the number of people who set out with them may have totaled about 140,000, but about three-quarters of these were to die in Asia Minor. The Provençal contingent, under Alfonso Jordan, the count of Toulouse, traveled by sea and was the only one that arrived almost without loss.

More precise information is available for some of the expeditions of the twelfth and thirteenth centuries. The Emperor Henry VI wrote to Pope Celestine III in 1195 that he would lead on Crusade a force of 1,500 knights and as many foot soldiers. At about the same time the Crusaders from the Rhineland and Franconia under the Archbishop Conrad of Mainz needed thirty ships for their embarkation at Messina. Those who accompanied the count of Brunswick and the archbishop of Bremen needed forty-four.

Ferdinand Lot has set the number of Frederick Barbarossa's cavalry in 1190 at 3,000, but the Greek historian Nicetas stated that there were 5,000. The transport vessels used were

70 *huissiers*[1] and 150 other ships lent by the Emperor Isaac Angelus. These were apparently sufficient to carry—in two sailings, as the chronicles tell us—the 15,000 horses required for 5,000 knights. Since each knight took two squires with him, one knight implied three men and as many horses. Barbarossa brought only cavalry on his expedition. He was anxious to avoid the disaster suffered by one of his predecessors, the Emperor Conrad III, who had lost nearly the whole of his infantry during the march across Turkish Anatolia, either through starvation or through disease in the hot climate. Misled by the Byzantines, he had provided food for a journey of only eight days between Nicea and Konya, when supplies for twenty days at least were required. Barbarossa's expedition was organized with infinite care, and for the first time supply depots were prepared in advance. The capture of Konya made a brilliant beginning, for it deprived the Seljuk Turks of their capital. The Emperor suffered only the loss of many of his horses. A witness says that two years after his departure he had only 600 left. But after the senseless accident when the Emperor was drowned in the waters of the Selef, his army was disbanded.

To make the same journey, Philip Augustus set off at the head of 650 knights, with the customary number of squires, and three or four times as many on foot, making a total of at least 10,000 men. One hundred vessels were needed for their conveyance. The fleet gathered by King Richard in the same year of 1191 for the transport of his followers was greatly admired at the time. According to Richard of Devizes it comprised 156 *nefs*; 24 *busses*, which had double the burden of

[1] These were vessels used to transport cavalry; they were the Liberty Ships of the Middle Ages. In the stern of the ship, below the water line, there was a door that opened for the horses to be taken on board.

the *nefs*; and 39 galleys. These numbers make it doubtful whether Ferdinand Lot was right when he reduced the total of this army to 10,000 men. One *nef* had space enough as a rule for 500 persons, together with their horses and all necessary equipment.

Villehardouin, a member of the next expedition, at the beginning of the thirteenth century, gives us very exact details of the expenses charged to the Crusaders by the Venetian contractors who undertook to arrange their passage:

> The doge of Venice personally told them, "We will provide a sufficient number of *huissiers* to carry 4,500 horses and 9,000 squires, and also *nefs* to convey 4,500 knights and 20,000 foot soldiers. Further, we agree to take nine months' rations for all these horses and men. This is the minimum that we will do for a charge of four marks for a horse and two for a man. All the agreements we shall enter into with you will be binding upon us for one year from the day on which we leave the port of Venice to take up the service of God and Christianity wherever that may be. The total charges stated above amount to 94,000 marks."

Unfortunately, these plans came to nothing, for some of the more important Crusaders—Geoffrey of Le Perche, for example—died, and others decided to embark from different ports. Thus the Crusade was broken up, and those who did arrive at Venice, although they were expected to pay the agreed sum, were fewer than Villehardouin and his committee had foreseen. Thirty-four thousand marks were still needed to complete the amount, a figure that suggests that in the year 1204 the number of Crusaders must have been about 14,000. In the end the expedition turned aside to attack the Byzantine Empire and balanced its accounts by the capture of Constantinople. An equally precise valuation followed in

1206, when the Latin Emperor, Henry of Hainault, demanded 600 knights and 10,000 infantrymen so that he could consolidate his conquest and safeguard the empire, now in Latin hands.

The next expedition, which took Damietta for the first time, consisted of 2,000 knights, 1,000 horsemen, and 20,000 foot soldiers. Saint Louis' Crusade consisted of 1,500 knights and 6,000 infantry in 1248, while in 1270 there were about 10,000 men and 4,000 horses, one-third of them intended for the knights, the rest for their squires.

The letter of 1195 from the Emperor Henry VI, quoted earlier, contains details that give some idea of the method of assessing the cost of feeding the troops. He had allotted to each knight thirty ounces of gold in ready money and as much again for the purchase of corn, while each foot soldier received ten ounces of gold and ten to buy corn. This gave an equal share to everyone, since each knight provided for two squires.

The help brought by the later Crusaders, however, was occasional, intermittent, and irregular. Obviously a standing army was essential for the defense of a state that was no more than a strip of territory roughly 370 miles long and 40 wide and surrounded by peoples who could never be other than hostile, since, as far as they were concerned, a Christian was an unbeliever. Thus, when Godfrey of Bouillon allotted fiefs to his followers, he followed the normal feudal custom of exacting military service in return for a grant of land.

Eventually these services were standardized and acquired the force of custom. By the thirteenth century it was possible to draw up a tariff of the number of soldiers to be provided—even at a time when many of the fortresses on the list had already been retaken by the Saracens and could be included only in a figurative sense. Thus a barony might owe "the service of 100 knights"; the castle and lordship of Krak, for instance, owed 60 knights.

This list was the work of John of Ibelin, who accounts for 675 knights in Latin Syria in the year 1265; in the principality of Antioch the numbers were probably much the same. The period of service was not, as in the West, restricted to forty days in the year; a man could be required to serve at any time and in any place in the kingdom. A knight called upon by the King was obliged to report with his "harness" complete within fifteen days. During this period he was not paid. For the rest of the time he received an allowance to cover his daily needs. Some knights were not, properly speaking, possessed of a fief in the Holy Land. These were the "pilgrims", wandering knights who arrived without any intention of settling and who were hired and retained in the King's pay for a certain period. They became his mercenaries. A few were granted land as payment. The notorious Reynald of Châtillon, who played so disastrous a role, began his career as a mere mercenary.

As well as the fiefs of the nobility, ecclesiastical possessions and towns could be called upon to provide soldiers. Thus the King of Jerusalem could demand 500 men at arms from the patriarch and 150 each from the archbishops of Tyre, Nazareth, and Caesarea. Some of the abbeys were similarly called upon. Josaphat owed the service of 150 men, and Mount Zion the same number; Mount Tabor owed 100 men, and so on. The townsfolk supplied their own contingents—500 men at arms from Jerusalem and from Acre, 100 each from Tyre and Jaffa, 50 from Caesarea, and so on—as well as performing their duty of watch and ward upon the battlements. According to John of Ibelin, the normal levy could raise 5,025 soldiers.

The army in the Holy Land was also kept up to strength by the employment of mercenaries.

We have, among others, the receipts given during the Crusade of 1270 by one Enguerrand of Bailleul, who "in the host before Carthage" received a sum of 300 *livres tournois* for the expenses of his force.

But for the most part the mercenaries were drawn from the local people, Syrians or Armenians. Among them there is repeated mention of the Turcoples (or Turcopoles), who were perhaps half-breeds, sons of Turkish fathers and Christian mothers, or perhaps converted Muslims, or perhaps merely native soldiers who could be recruited to serve either side. Thus at the time of the campaign against Egypt, the grand master of the Hospital promised King Amalric "500 knights and as many well-equipped Turcoples". It has been estimated that in normal times the kingdom of Jerusalem could call upon a force of some 20,000 to 25,000 men, of whom 1,000 to 2,000 were knights.

It should be added that in times of danger a universal levy was enforced. This was the case when the attack on Damascus was planned in 1126 and when Ascalon was taken in 1153. On these occasions the pilgrims passing through the country enrolled for service with the Crusaders and the settlers.

The armor worn by these knights was not in the least like the weighty shells with which history textbooks traditionally equip them. These date only from the end of the Middle Ages, when the advent of firearms compelled warriors to encase themselves in steel as an effective protection. Hence the armor of the fifteenth century. Most of the suits of armor in our museums belong to the sixteenth and seventeenth centuries. It would be hard to find in all the museums throughout the world more than two or three complete suits of armor that genuinely date from the fifteenth century.

During the feudal period a knight was protected only by a flexible coat of mail known as a hauberk, by a casque or helmet, and by a shield. A surcoat, a light garment made of cloth, or of silk for the wealthy, was worn over the mail to avoid the blinding reflection of sunlight on metal. Sometimes the legs too were protected by a kind of breeches made of chain mail.

In the crypt of the church at Tavant there is a picture of a knight painted about the end of the eleventh century and thus contemporary with Godfrey and his companions. He is transfixing an enemy with his lance, is wearing a coat of mail and a helmet, and is carrying a long shield. A fresco at Cressac shows Templars of the twelfth and thirteenth centuries in similar light armor. Frequently, as we see in the miniatures in the Psalter of Saint Louis, the coat of mail was carried right over the head like a balaclava helmet, leaving only the face uncovered. The coat was slit at the side to allow the sword to pass through. The shield was pointed and elongated, like the one depicted on the lovely enamel plaque from Geoffrey of Plantagenet's tomb now in the museum at Le Mans. The devices with which it was emblazoned were an exact language of lines and colors, used to identify the owner. The horse, also, was given protective armor—a caparison of leather, or of metal plates, or of chain mail, covering chiefly its breast and shoulders.

Armor became slightly more intricate during the twelfth century. The wrists, hands, and feet were protected by articulated steel plates, and the former conical helmet with nasal was replaced by a flat-topped casque, entirely enclosing the head except for an eye slit and some holes at the level of the nose and mouth to allow for breathing. It was not until the end of the thirteenth century that the pointed basinet with hinged visor was developed.

Eventually a loose cloak, as protection against the cold, came to be fastened to the right shoulder in such a way as to leave the right arm free. In the East, as protection against the sun, knights adopted the custom of covering their casques with a kind of veil, and they are represented on seals with it floating behind them on the breeze. Altogether they made a fine sight, and one that can still be admired by anyone who goes to see the carved figure of a knight inside Bamberg Cathedral. The foot soldier was protected by a "tin hat", and by a fitted suit of armor, normally made of leather. He usually carried a shield, a sword, and a bow.

Of course this equipment was intended for battle, and the Crusaders were not called upon to wear it until they reached Constantinople. Until then, even if their swords hardly ever left their sides, their coats of mail and their helmets were carried in wagons, like their lances, the principal weapons of attack. The Bayeux Tapestry illustrates how the coats of mail were loaded on the wagons or the ships. Each was borne between two servants on a pole slipped through the sleeves and shoulders so that front and back fell straight down as from a modern coat hanger; the servants carried the helmets and swords in their hands. Probably hauberks also traveled hanging in the same way from poles, on the carts on which the helmets were stacked.

The crossbow completes the list of offensive weapons. Anna Comnena, who was much impressed by it, called it the *tzangra*—the canker—"a truly diabolical weapon". She describes how the archer stood with his two feet on the semi-circle of the bow and pulled on the cord with his two hands, releasing a short thick bolt with enormous force. The use of the crossbow was in fact forbidden by the Pope in 1139 as too murderous in its effect. From then on it was employed only for hunting. (However, Philip Augustus and Richard

Cœur de Lion brought it back into use.) Although the Saracens' corps of archers gave them a definite superiority over the Frankish cavalry, the barons continued to regard the bow and the crossbow as cowards' weapons, and Joinville echoes the feelings of the knights of his day when he writes of one of the battles in which he fought: "You must understand that this was a great feat of arms, for no one drew a bow or a crossbow. It was a hand-to-hand combat with maces and swords between the Turks and ourselves."

It was necessary to provide equipment for the horses too. Richard Coeur de Lion, preparing in England for his Crusade, ordered fifty thousand horseshoes to be made in the forest of Dean. Arrows, maces, and "quarrels" for the crossbows had to be provided; the sappers and miners needed axes, picks, and mattocks. The siege engines had to be considered, from ballistas and mangonels to straightforward ladders, and there were those curious "flamethrowers" shown on the Bayeaux Tapestry, pikes with blazing tow on the point that at the right moment were flung against wooden fortifications.

It has been possible to study the military tactics of these armies in which knights were complemented by foot soldiers. They alone took their places in the line of battle, for the squires, even when mounted, were unarmed and were simply servants. One of them bore the lance, while the other, in the rear, guarded the horses.

The soldiers were under the command of their respective lords. Beforehand, by common agreement at a council of war, a plan of action was decided and a supreme commander chosen. During the battle this man would be responsible for directing the reserve troops and for sending them to the help of whichever wing happened to be in need of reinforcement. The less important lords, those who had the fewest followers, were grouped together.

Generally speaking, the battle front did not extend for much more than half a mile or a mile. The foot soldiers were in the front rank and made the first move, discharging their bolts and arrows. Then they returned to the wings or the rear when the time came for the charge. This was the moment for the cavalry to go into action. They were usually ranged in two ranks, but closed up so that they formed a compact body whose solidity gave it strength. The chronicler Ambroise tells of a battle in which the ranks were drawn up so closely that an apple tossed among them could not have failed to touch either a man or a horse.

Such great importance was attached to the maintenance of order and close contact on the field of battle that the statutes of the Templars included a strict ordinance that no knight should ever leave the ranks, except to look to his horse or its harness or to go to the help of a Christian in immediate peril. A knight who broke formation for any reason except these two would be expelled from the order.

It had not been forgotten that in 1147, during the march across Asia Minor of Louis VII's armies, a Turkish attack against the flank of the column was successful because of the insubordination of Geoffrey of Rancogne, one of the leaders of the advance guard, who had broken away from the main body. Some time later, at Mansourah, Robert of Artois rashly broke formation and, refusing to wait until all the troops were in position, charged the enemy ranks in defiance of his orders. In so doing he put the whole of Saint Louis' Crusade in jeopardy.

Apart from stupid recklessness of this sort, which became much more frequent toward the end of the Crusades than at the beginning, the barons maintained excellent discipline among themselves during a battle. Even their enemies commented on it. According to Usama, they were "in combat the most prudent of men". Their cavalry charges were especially feared, because their ranks, bristling with lances, gave such an impression of a close-packed, invincible mass. The whole point of their charge was to ensure victory, and so from the first moment action had to be swift and decisive. It follows that the timing of the charge needed careful calculation, and the fate of all the principal battles was decided by the tactical ability of the man who gave the order. Bohemond possessed this ability to a high degree and was renowned for it.

The choice of the exact moment when the cavalry were brought into action was particularly important because the tactics of the Turks were based principally on their extreme mobility. Their speedy horses gave them a flexibility in maneuver that the Franks could not imitate. The Turks made similar use of their bowmen. They moved in detached bodies, withdrawing and trying to destroy the unity of the mass of knights by striking at them on the flanks or even from the rear; then, fleeing at the first hint of attack, they would return to torment their enemies "like flies". The maneuver is well described by William of Tyre:

> When our forces met, the Turks shot so many arrows at us that the sky could hardly have been darker in rain or hail, and many of our people had great cause for grief from them. When the first group had emptied their quivers and shot off all their arrows, the second followed them, and going to a place where there were still many knights, they began to shoot arrows more thickly than we could believe possible.

By killing the horses the archers achieved the double effect of weakening the dreaded charge and of spreading disorder through the ranks.

The Franks, in compensation, were superior in hand-to-hand fighting as well as in the charge. Thus they preferred to take the initiative, and on the few occasions, as at Dorylaeum, when they were attacked on the march and forced to defend themselves, victory was more dearly bought. Their aim was always to achieve a breakthrough, while the Muslims, even when they were on the offensive, sought to surround their opponents.

The Turks made frequent use of the tactical maneuver of feigned withdrawal. The Franks, however, were also aware of its possibilities; the classic example of this strategy is the Battle of Hastings, which ensured William the Conqueror's victory on English soil in 1066. Little by little the two armies reorganized their forces so that they achieved a better balance of strength. The Franks made up for their lack of mobility by adding battalions of lightly armed Turcoples, while the Muslims recruited mercenaries—particularly Sudanese archers—and formed them into a permanent body to offset the irregular composition of their own armies.

Some of the most famous battles fought in the East have been studied from a tactical point of view. René Grousset thought that Montgisard (November 25, 1177) was "the Crusaders' most perfect victory". It was gained by the leper King Baldwin IV with 500 cavalry and the help of 80 Templars—3,000 men altogether—over a force of at least 30,000 Mamelukes under Saladin.

A little later on, Richard Cœur de Lion was attacked at Jaffa, on August 5, 1192, by the Turks, again led by Saladin. He set a party of foot soldiers out in front, knee to the ground and lance at the ready. Behind them the Genoese and Pisan crossbowmen stood to shoot over their heads, each one of them with a soldier beside him ready to hand over a newly bent bow every time an arrow was discharged, so that the rate of firing continued without interruption. After this came the charge of the knights. Another way to fight a battle was demonstrated by Henry of Hainault, Emperor of Constantinople, near the Lake of Apollonia on October 15, 1211. He had only 260 knights against 90 divisions, perhaps 1,700 men, under the Greek Theodorus Lascaris, so he made the knights charge in squadrons of 12. He achieved a complete victory without losing a single man.

Clearly no action was undertaken without preparation. Apart from spies, the knights dispatched ahead lightly armed horsemen to act as scouts and reconnoiter the terrain. Before a siege, the Franks quickly learned how to gain an advantage by taking possession of the water springs. When Louis VII's Crusade was attacking Damascus, his soldiers cut down all the brushwood around the town and took control of the canals that watered it. Relays of scouts continually patrolled every encampment, and as a result surprise attacks were comparatively rare. In the same way columns of men on the march were protected by archers on foot.

Little is known about the arrangement of the camps. The miniatures show tents which are either conical or have a roof with a double slope—the *tref*. The army made camp on grassland, if possible, in order to provide pasture for the horses. The responsibility for choosing the camp site then fell on the marshal. But when marching through occupied territories the quartermaster's assistants would be sent on ahead to arrange billets in a town. It has been estimated that armies in the field could cover as much as thirty miles in a day.

The use of scouts and dispatch riders ensured communication between the various bodies of troops. Besides this, and surprisingly enough, a fairly regular, though slow, correspondence between East and West was maintained. From the very beginning of the expedition, the Crusaders had sent letters to the Pope, or simply to their own families, and had received answers. This implies a continual movement of messengers. They were not slow to use carrier pigeons when on campaign or to communicate between one place in the East and another. According to the chronicler Raymond of Agiles, the Crusaders were beyond Caesarea, where they had celebrated Pentecost, when they killed for the first time a pigeon carrying a letter from the emir of Acre to the emir of Caesarea in Palestine. Afterward they are mentioned frequently. William of Tyre says:

> When they wanted to report to their master, it was not possible to go to him in person, since the enemy had surrounded the castle on all sides, and there was no way of going in or out. So they took two pigeons that had been trained for this work and fastened beneath their tails two letters telling the governor the result of their negotiations and the promises they had obtained. Then they released the two birds. The pigeons flew at once to the place where they had been reared and were caught by the men who had fed and cared for them. The letters they had carried were then taken to the governor.

The care of their horses always posed a problem of crucial importance for the Crusaders. Lack of food, the heat, and the desert marches took their toll of beasts as well as men, and to carry them by sea often presented other difficulties. The chroniclers make satisfied comment on the number of animals captured in battle, for if the horses could be seized, so could the victory. The Anonymous Historian of the First Crusade tells how in January 1099 five thousand horses were lifted in a raid on the countryside around Caesarea, but the capture of six animals a few weeks later by a patrol of fourteen knights was not too trivial to mention. Clearly

distinguished from the *destrier*, the warhorse, which was controlled with the right hand, were the palfrey, or saddlehorse,
and the common *ronçin*, the ordinary draft animal.
There was one occasion when King Baldwin ordered the
squires to be armed as knights to make up the number of his
pitifully reduced forces, but the plan came to nothing because there were not enough horses. Some time later, Bishop
Gottfried of Würzburg, an eyewitness of Barbarossa's Crusade, reported that losses had been so heavy that in 1190 the
Emperor had mounts for only six hundred knights.
The man who held the position of marshal to the kingdom
of Jerusalem was always hard put to it to keep the army supplied with horses. The chronicle written by Villehardouin, who
had once filled this office in Champagne, is full of remarks about
"good warhorses". He was observant on this point.

It was on June 19, 1097, shortly after the siege of Nicea, that
the Crusaders came face to face for the first time in open
country with the Muslims whom they had come to fight.
The first impact was shattering. William of Tyre bases his
description on the various accounts he was able to collect
and emphasizes the terror of the Franks, who were thrown
into confusion by the tactics of this new enemy. They were
ignorant of the use of the bow by mounted horsemen, and
they charged the Turkish cavalry, not knowing that they were
armed in this way.

> The Turkish squadrons immediately attacked our army, shoot-
> ing off a great cloud of arrows that fell from the sky like hail.
> The first shower, flying in a half-circle, had barely fallen when
> a second, just as heavy, followed it. Those who were not hit
> in the first minute had little chance of avoiding being struck
> in the next. Our soldiers had had no previous experience of

this sort of warfare, and they were the less able to stand up to it as they were so unaccustomed to it. Also they had to watch their horses fall all the time without being able to do anything to protect them. Taken by surprise, unable to escape wounds that in many cases were mortal, they tried to repulse their adversaries by charging them with glaives and lances. The enemy, in their turn, could not stand up to this kind of attack and withdrew immediately to avoid it. So our men found no one to oppose them and, failing in what they had tried to do, were obliged to fall back into the main body of our army. While they were thus retreating, having failed in their attempt, the Turks were quickly rallying their forces and beginning to send another shower of arrows raining down on our men, few of whom escaped a mortal wound. Our soldiers resisted as long as they could, protected by their helmets.

Probably the soldiers who survived this first encounter owed their lives to their defensive armor. However, from then on, they had some idea of the adversary with whom they had to deal. The Muslim world they were attacking had behind it a battle roll of victories that left no doubt of its military prowess. For several hundred years the West had lived in fear of the Arabs, who had caused each power in turn to totter and who had only just failed to take the city of Constantinople itself. When the *Reconquista* began in the eleventh century, the known world was divided in two. By far the greater part was Muslim territory; the smaller was Christian. Such was the geography of the Middle Ages. The Saracens had conquered their larger portion by force of arms—by the jihad, the terrible Muslim "Holy War".[2] The barons must certainly

---

[2] Gaudefroy Demombynes, a historian of Arab affairs, writes, "Only the Caliph Omar ben Abd al-Aziz (717–720) entertained for an instant the strange notion of substituting for belligerent apostleship the peaceful conversion of the infidels."

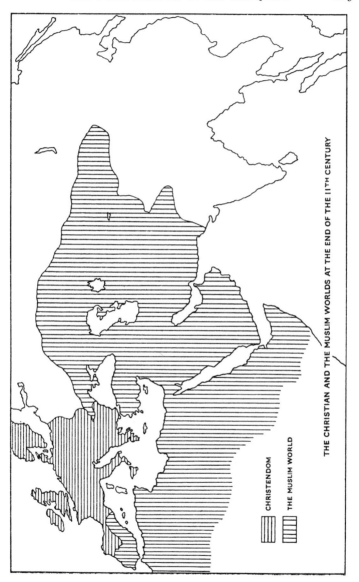

THE CHRISTIAN AND THE MUSLIM WORLDS AT THE END OF THE 11ᵀᴴ CENTURY

CHRISTENDOM

THE MUSLIM WORLD

have known all this. A period of decadence had given the Byzantines the chance to retake various strips of land in Syria and Armenia, but now the Seljuk Turks, converted to Islam, had come on the scene to strengthen the enormous military might of the Muslim world.

After their entry into Ispahan in 1051 and Baghdad in 1055, the Seljuks had taken up the holy war on their own account under the authority of the Arab caliphs. Armenia, Georgia, and the neighboring regions were the first to feel the consequences. The Turks had seized the Armenian capital, Ani, and the Sultan Alp Arslan had had the great silver cross pulled away from the dome of the cathedral and melted down. It was sent to Nakhitchevan, where it was used to mark the doorsill of the mosque. The disaster of Manzikert in 1071, some twenty years before the Crusade, had allowed the Turks to establish themselves firmly in Asia Minor. This tremendous defeat of the Byzantine armies, made even worse by domestic troubles in Constantinople, was still fresh in people's minds when Urban II launched his appeal. It had happened only a short while before Alexius Comnenus established himself on the imperial throne.

Thus the Franks could not have had any illusions about the military power they were being asked to attack. Only the Normans had ever made a successful stand against the Muslims. Their operations, however, had been little more than lucky forays against isolated points such as Sicily and the south of Italy, while in Spain, the enemy was at that time in a fairly weak position.

The men of the West were about to attempt the impossible venture of hewing by main force a way through the Muslim world to their "promised land". It is interesting to inquire how much, apart from its military reputation, they knew about this world. They certainly knew that they were up against an enemy whose resources were almost unlimited, whose caravans were loaded at the central markets of the widely coveted spice trade. They had heard of the legendary Baghdad, where the mosques, it was said, could be counted in their thousands, and the spoils that the Crusaders later took from Sultan Kerbogha's camp were to confirm the tales of the luxury of the Muslim palaces:

> Among the wonderful things that were seized was a very remarkable tent. It was an admirable piece of work and had belonged to Prince Kerbogha. It was made to look like a town, decorated with towers, walls, and ramparts and covered with rich hangings of many-colored silk. The principal quarters were in the center of the tent. From there partitions radiated in all directions, forming passages like streets, in which were many other sleeping places, resembling inns. It was said that two thousand men could find plenty of room in that huge structure.

Any other ideas that people had about Muslim civilization were probably rather vague. In the poem *Le Couronnement Louis*, which is very nearly contemporary with the First Crusade, the sultan is made to say, in a challenge addressed to the Pope in Rome itself:

> Mine is the heritage I rightly claim.
> Of old my fathers built it, and their name
> From Romulus and Julius Caesar came.

This idea that the Arab world was a continuation of the classical world of the Caesars is found more than once in the *chansons de geste*. In other words, the Arabs are regarded as the inheritors of paganism. There was no hesitation in ascribing to the Muslims all the attributes of paganism in general and idolatry in particular. "Unless you deny Apollo and

Sorapus", threatens Raynouard the Giant when he challenges an adversary to single combat. In *Le Jeu de Saint Nicholas* the sultan is described as praying to a "horned Muhammad", an idol that he calls Tergavant. This, of course, was a complete misapprehension of the essential nature of the Muslim religion. Nevertheless this misapprehension indicates a recognition of the regressive nature of Islam in comparison with Christianity. The teaching of Muhammad does in fact turn back from the conception of the God of Love, God in Three Persons, as revealed by Christ, toward the God of All Power and Might of the Old Testament. The Arabs had used the Old Testament texts to declare themselves the sons of Abraham. For them, a Christian was primarily a "polytheist", one who believed in the Trinity. In other words, it is chiefly the refusal of the essential message of the New Testament that characterizes Islam, and there is great significance in the fact that for a Muslim his religion is the "law". The Gospel teaching, on the other hand, ushered in the rule of grace instead of that of law. Hence Christians of the time associated this backward-looking characteristic of Islam with all other anti-Christian forces. The general feeling was that they were setting off to fight "the pagans".

The churchmen certainly knew more about the Muslim religion, or at least they quickly took steps to become better informed. In 1143, at the time of the Second Crusade, Peter the Venerable, the abbot of Cluny, had a translation of the Qur'an made by Robert of Chester and sent a copy to Saint Bernard so that he could refute it. The desire to fight at the doctrinal level is already apparent.

This desire had been awakened much earlier in the East. Among the works of Saint John Damascene, who lived from 700 to 754, there is a *Dialogue between a Christian and a Saracen*. It was also known by scholars that through the Arabs access could be obtained to the learning of the ancient world, for in the tenth century Gerbert had gratified his insatiable curiosity by going to Spain to copy various treatises that interested him.

Although the Arab invaders of Syria and Egypt sometimes behaved like destructive savages—the loss to the world of the famous library at Alexandria, which they burned in 645, has been irreparable—they were not slow to take an interest in the treasures preserved by the Christians of these two countries, who had kept safe the great philosophical and literary works of antiquity. Toward the end of the eighth century and the beginning of the ninth, that is, about 150 to two hundred years after the conquest, they began, under the Abbasids, to translate into their own tongue the Greek manuscripts found in the conquered countries. Syria and Egypt had been deeply influenced by Hellenism, and philosophical studies were pursued with great interest in the schools and monasteries that existed at the time of the Muslim invasion. In these schools classical writings had been translated from Greek into Syriac. Several of the principal translators are known to us by name, such as Paulus Persa, or Sergius of Rassain, who died at Constantinople in 536.

About the year 800 the great Arab schools were beginning to become important; Cairo, Baghdad, and Cordova later acquired immense prestige. Classical philosophy was included in the syllabus. Recent research has established that the list of subjects studied was the same as in the Syrian schools that had preceded them; they included the *Timaeus*, the *Republic* and the *Laws* of Plato and the *Treatises*, but not the *Politics*, of Aristotle.

The Christians of Syria and Egypt came to use Arabic as their everyday language, and so the impulse toward translation from Greek into Arabic came also from the conquered peoples. A letter, dated in the year 917, written by Severus, bishop of Ashmounein in Africa, says, "I have asked the Christian brothers to help me in translating the documents that we have found from Coptic and Greek into Arabic, the tongue of the Egyptians, since few of them understand either Coptic or Greek."

A Jew called Ibn Shabru had the help of a Greek monk when he translated the famous manuscript of the Dioscorides which the Emperor of Constantinople, Constantine Porphyrogenetes, addressed to Abd ar-Rahman, the caliph of Spain.

On this basis the Arab studies of science and philosophy were established. About the year 835 Ibn Luqa, the first of their philosophers, wrote a short treatise on the distinction between mind and soul. By the tenth century the learned men of Islam were dividing knowledge into two groups. Grammar, ethics, history, and literature were called the Arabic sciences; philosophy, natural science, and medicine were the ancient, or non-Arabic, sciences. Their philosophy was a synthesis of Eastern Christian teaching and of Gnostic and Mazdean authorities, together with certain elements drawn from the Neoplatonists. Jewish thought was also to play a large part, and the influence of Maimonides (1135–1204), who was doctor at Saladin's court at Alexandria, is well known.

Meanwhile the study of Greek had died out in the West, except in the monasteries of Ireland or in those, like Saint Gall, that were filled with Irish monks, and the philosophers of antiquity were no longer read except for those works that had been translated into Latin. Such translations had been made since the time of Saint Augustine.

After the standstill caused by the conquest, the Eastern world saw the development, under Arab domination, of the hoard of classical works held in trust by the Syrian

Christians. The rediscovery of this hoard by the West was to be made through Arabic translations or through the medium of the works of the Arab philosophers themselves. Saint Thomas used the proof of the uniquity of God which Avicenna (Ibn Sina, 980–1037) formulated, while the commentaries on the work of Aristotle by Averroes (Ibn Rashid, 1126–1198) formed the basis of a whole school of thought in Paris.

The action of Peter the Venerable, mentioned above, which dates from less than fifty years after the first expedition, suggests that the churchmen who went out with the soldiers were not slow to appreciate the importance of Islamic thought, philosophy, and religion. At a very early stage, and even while Crusades and battles were succeeding one another, men were busy discussing Arab ideas. From the twelfth century, Toledo was a center of Islamic studies, and later the newly founded Franciscan and Dominican orders took a lively interest in the learning of the Arab world.

Most writers have noted the changes in customs that very soon overtook the Crusaders and transformed them from conquerors into feudal landowners who had brought with them into the Holy Land their Western way of life. This change is first noticeable about 1110, the date of the fall of Sidon. From that time on, there is no longer any question of banishing the people they had been fighting, but rather of organizing them and of working out modes of coexistence. The population was remarkably mixed and was not made up of Muslims alone. It has been mentioned earlier that, right from the start of the conquest, the Syrian Christians had formed a kind of "fifth column" for the Crusaders, and their contribution was far from negligible.

The Armenians were the most important of these Christians. They had suffered terribly over the centuries at the hands both of the Byzantines and of the Turks, who had perpetrated horrible massacres, notably after seizing Ani, the Armenian capital, in 1064. Their chronicler, Matthew of Edessa, says, "Who could tell all the misfortunes of the Armenian people, all their sorrows and their tears? Who could tell all they have had to suffer from the Greeks since our kingdom lost its legal rulers, who were removed by its false defenders, the ineffectual, effeminate, ignoble nation of Greeks?"

It goes without saying that the Armenians, crushed between two oppressors, found some comfort in the approach of the Frankish armies. They gave help to Tancred's forces, and at the taking of Jerusalem Armenian contingents fought beside the Franks. A genuine liking seems to have grown up among the Armenian population of the principality of Edessa for the counts who governed them. When Joscelin of Courtenay was taken prisoner in 1123, the help of the Armenians of Kharpurt enabled a small group of resolute men—fifty in all—to take possession of the town, attack the garrison, and allow Joscelin to escape. The Armenians themselves paid with their lives for this audacity, for the Turks returned in strength and killed them all to the last man. Joscelin, who had fled, succeeded in getting back to Edessa, thanks to the devotion of an Armenian peasant whom he met on the way. This man dressed him in his own wife's clothes and, so that he would look as much as possible like a countrywoman, even gave him his little daughter to carry. Count Joscelin bore the child gently in his arms until they reached the town.

Apart from the Armenians, most of the Christians in the Holy Land were Syrians or Greeks. Their religion varied. They either were members of the Orthodox church or belonged to different heretical sects; usually they were Monophysites. In spite of the schism, recognized fifty years earlier, between the Greek church and the See of Rome, relations were friendly and only gradually became embittered, after acts of treachery by the Byzantines (the Emperor Isaac Angelus congratulated Saladin after the fall of the Holy City) and, particularly, after the capture of Constantinople by the Crusaders. Adhémar of Monteil, the papal legate, showed his willingness to cooperate with the Greeks, and the patriarch of Antioch was reestablished there immediately after the siege. Some time later his successor, Michael, the Jacobite patriarch of Antioch from 1166 to 1199, wrote an account of his reception by the Latin patriarch of Jerusalem and King Baldwin IV himself at Acre in 1179. About the same time, in 1181, the Maronites of the Lebanon were restored to communion with Rome. This afterward cost them dearly at the hands of the Muslim conquerors, who, on the whole, tried to win over the Syrian Christians but showed no pity toward those belonging to the Latin rite.

The bulk of the population, however, was made up of Muslims. They were consequently under the subjection of their conquerors and in circumstances comparable to those of the Christians in Spain, and they bore their yoke with no more patience than did the latter. Jean Richard, one of the most recent writers on the Crusades, says, "It would be wrong to regard the native peoples as a mass of tenant farmers and artisans oppressed by the dominant race of Franks." The Muslims, like other groups, benefited from a principle peculiar to the mental attitude of the time—that each individual should be judged according to the laws of the social group to which he belonged. This did not encourage unification. The Muslims kept their own customs and continued to control their own administration.

The most striking testimony on this subject is the frequently quoted description by the Arab traveler Ibn Jubayr. He was resolutely hostile to the Franks, and yet in 1184, in an account of a journey which he made from Damascus to Acre, he could write:

> We left Tibnin (Toron) by a road running past farms where Muslims live who do very well for themselves under the Franks—may Allah preserve us from such a temptation! The regulations imposed on them are the handing over of half of the grain crop at the time of harvest and the payment of a poll tax of one *dinar* and seven *qîrâts*, together with a light duty on their fruit trees. The Muslims own their houses and rule themselves in their own way. This is the way in which the farms and big villages are organized in Frankish territory. Many Muslims are sorely tempted to settle here when they see the far from comfortable conditions in which their brethren live in districts under Muslim rule. Unfortunately for the Muslims, they have always reason for complaint about the injustices of their chiefs in the lands governed by their coreligionists, whereas they can have nothing but praise for the conduct of the Franks, whose justice they can always rely on.

It is good to remember this tribute paid to Frankish justice by an Arab. His remarks show clearly that there had been no robbing of the indigenous population for the benefit of the conquerors. They were in the position of any farmers who paid rent in kind, and the personal tax owed to their seigneurs was far from excessive. One *dinar* and seven *qîrâts* was worth one besant or twelve gold francs.

The same traveler remarks farther on, "We stopped at a small town on the outskirts of Acre. The mayor in charge was a Muslim put in office by the Franks and appointed to superintend the local farmers."

So the Muslims were even entrusted with administration. A certain Arab khadi has also been mentioned, Mansur Ibn Nabil, whom Bernard III, prince of Antioch, put in charge of all Muslim affairs in the Lattakieh region.

It comes, finally, as no slight surprise to find in the same account, which was written, as already mentioned, by a man particularly hostile to the Crusaders, a description of two mosques in Acre. These had been converted into churches, but the Muslims were granted the right to use them as meeting places and to pray there facing toward Mecca according to their established custom. This example of simultaneous worship was paralleled, though only very occasionally, in the southern villages of France, where the Protestant minister and the curé used the same church for the gathering of their flocks. The situation in Acre was not exceptional, for the same fact is reported by Usama, another Arab writer, who states that in Jerusalem he was able to say his prayers in a former mosque, now a chapel, where the Muslims were nonetheless allowed to come to pray according to their own rites. In short, there are many examples, given by Western writers such as Fulcher of Chartres and by Muslims like Ibn Al-Qalanisi, of the friendly relations established almost everywhere in Palestine between the different peoples, particularly between the country population and the conquerors.

An exact comment on this state of affairs has been provided by the historian Claude Cahen, who writes:

The establishment of Frankish domination did not necessarily cause a great upheaval in the native population. A new ruling class took the place of the old and superimposed itself on the existing rural society. Since it knew nothing of soil conditions there, it naturally relied on this society to continue its exploitation of the land for the benefit of the new masters but according to the traditions of the old.

An odd point that has been brought to light is that from a fiscal point of view the Muslims were treated better than the Christians, for the latter were required to pay a tithe to the churches, whereas the Muslims were not. The Armenians who wanted to establish themselves in Jerusalem were loud in complaint about this inequality of circumstances. All this suggests a much more tolerant regime than one has come to imagine.

The Turcoples must not be forgotten, those auxiliaries who very soon took their place beside the Frankish troops in the battles fought in the Holy Land. They were horsemen who wore a light armor resembling that of the Turks, but, while it is true that the role they played in the campaigns has been recognized, their origin is still a matter for argument. Were they simply "men armed in the Turkish fashion", or were they actually Muslims? It does seem as though some of them at least were Muslims, perhaps converted to Christianity. This may explain Saladin's fury when in 1169 he ordered the massacre of all those of his captives who had been in the service of the Temple—as though he was dealing with apostates.

Natives were quite frequently found among the close personal attendants of the barons. King Baldwin I had as valet a Saracen who, according to the chronicler, became his intimate and whom the king trusted more than anyone else. "He had been a Saracen but had asked to be baptized, greatly wishing to do right, as it seemed. The King therefore took pity on him, stood as his godfather, and gave him his name. Then he received him into his household."

It turned out badly for him in the end that he did so, for the man later tried to poison him. Similarly, the knight Reynald of Sidon was accompanied by a Muslim—though this one was not baptized—who acted as his "scrivener". In the administration of their new domain interpreters ("dragomen") were indispensable, so the Franks did not hesitate to recruit them. Often, it seems that they willingly gave their confidence to these men, as though a rather surprising familiarity had grown between Franks and Saracens. William of Tyre denounces the favor that the Syrian doctors enjoyed among the *poulains*, the Franks born in Syria. It had become fashionable to be cared for by them. Some Arab treatises, on the other hand, mention the medical practices of the Franks.

> We who were Westerners find ourselves transformed into inhabitants of the East. The Italian or Frenchman of yesterday, transplanted here, has become a Galilean or a Palestinian. A man from Rheims or Chartres has turned into a Syrian or a citizen of Antioch. We have already forgotten our native land. Now we hold our houses and domestic life with as great a sense of security as if they came by right of age-long inheritance in this land. Some men have already taken as wives Syrian or Armenian women, or even Saracens if they have been baptized. Through them we are involved in a whole network of family relations with the native people. We make use in turn of all the various languages of the country.

Fulcher of Chartres wrote this account about 1120. He had gone on the First Crusade as chaplain to Baldwin I. He had then remained in the Holy Land and so knew from personal experience a great deal about the settlement of the Franks in Syria. All the writers on the Crusades have quoted him to a greater or less extent. He deserves quotation, for his history emphasizes one of the most astonishing facts about the Crusades—the speed with which the Franks made themselves at home in a land conquered under conditions that were themselves surprising. Everything there—climate, race, language, and, above all, religion—was strange to them. But although religion made the Saracens their enemies, race in itself presented no obstacle to friendship. Provided that a Saracen woman had accepted baptism, no Christian would refuse to make her his wife. The idea of racial discrimination, which was used by sixteenth-century slave traders as an excuse for their traffic, had no meaning for a man of the twelfth century. He fought the Muslims, but at least he considered them his equals. In comparison with colonial practice of the nineteenth century, and indeed with certain prejudices of our own, which involve, for instance, segregation, this attitude seems remarkably "advanced". No Crusader would have hesitated to choose a wife from the native population.

Language presented no more difficulty in the Latin kingdoms than did race. In the Holy Land each different group spoke its own tongue. The barons and their men naturally used among themselves the dialects of their own countries. That is to say, the *langue d'oil* predominated, for the most part, in Jerusalem and Antioch, whereas in the Saint Gilles fief of Tripoli, the *langue d'oc*, the French of Provence, was chiefly used. Many of these barons learned Arabic. The *poulains*, those who had been born in the Holy Land, found it quite natural to speak the native languages. Many of the personalities who are known to us did so, and this includes not only a man of letters like William of Tyre, but also barons like Reynald of Sidon, who has been mentioned earlier, or Humphrey of Toron, the man who might have been King of Jerusalem. In the coastal towns Italian was most frequently heard. It was the mother tongue of most of the merchants—men from Genoa, Pisa, or Venice—who traded there.

The history of the Latin kingdoms shows, in short, that the Crusaders were quick to understand the peculiarities of the Muslim world and to turn them to their own profit. They learned how to exploit the many divisions which existed within Islam. Early on, in 1115, they made treaties with the sultans of Damascus. This alliance was often broken, notably at the time of the imprudent expedition sent off against the advice of the Eastern barons during the Second Crusade, but it was afterward renewed. They also formed an alliance with Egypt—a fact which provides the material for one of the principal chapters in crusading history.

Above all, they were quick to appreciate the power of the Ismailians, who were at that time a dissident sect at the heart of the Muslim world. Baldwin II, in 1129, was the first to accord them his protection. This alliance with the terrible and fabulous "Assassins" was renewed from time to time during the history of the Crusades.

The Assassins were in fact representatives of the Shi'ites, the most important dissenting sect in Islam. A little while before the arrival of the Crusade, Al Hassan, one of their chiefs, had seized the castle of Alamut, an eagle's nest in the country to the south of the Caspian. From here he could defy the rest of the world, and here was to be established the residence of the grand master, the "Old Man of the Mountain" of medieval legend. It was said that the castle walls enclosed marvelous gardens where the followers of the Old Man of the Mountain passed their days encompassed about with subtle perfumes and every sensation of pleasure. Drunk with delights, they became robots, prepared to carry out any sort of mission on the orders of their chief. The word *assassin* comes from *hashishin*, a taker of hashish, a drug that was probably the cause of the voluptuous dreams alluded to in the histories.

The term *grand master*, used by the Old Man of the Mountain, was the title of the *imams* who succeeded each other as head of the Ismailians. Each was the symbolical descendant of Ali, Muhammad's son-in-law. Ali's followers preferred him to Abu Bakr, who had had him assassinated in 661. Their doctrine was founded on an esoteric interpretation of the

Qur'an and exercised a great intellectual influence. It reappeared in Cairo in the founding of the famous mosque Al Ahzar, which has now become the principal university of the Arab world.

The Assassins committed murder as a religious duty, using always a dagger, never poison. They had a good number of followers in Syria, and they held castles as far off as Iraq and Persia. They lived an almost secret life, making proof of their absolute submission to the will of the grand master. Those men who were marked out for the daggers of his devotees hardly ever escaped. Among the Franks the first victim was Raymond II of Tripoli, who was assassinated beside the city gate in 1129–1130. Later Conrad of Montferrat and, in 1213, Raymond, son of Bohemond IV of Antioch, were overtaken by the same fate. The Assassins tried twice to kill Saladin. But the kings of Jerusalem, particularly Henry of Champagne, were not afraid to visit them in their lair. The story goes that the Old Man of the Mountain arranged for him to watch, by way of entertainment, the suicide of one or two of his bodyguard. Saint Louis, a little later, reinforced the bond with the Assassins and exchanged gifts, which Joinville describes in detail, with the grand master. The power of the sect was finally crushed by the Mongols, who captured Alamut in 1256. Much later on, their *imams* moved from Persia to India. The Aga Khan is their lineal descendant.

The relations between the Franks and the Assassins undoubtedly form the most curious of all the chapters in the history of the Crusades. It is one that shows the Franks influenced, in the most extraordinary fashion, by a way of thought completely opposed to their own. However, apart from these dangerous allies, the relations that they established with Islam, even in the midst of battle, show a mutual regard, in which are combined admiration for the gallantry of good soldiers and appreciation of the qualities of an enemy. The Anonymous Historian could write during the First Crusade, "What man is there wise enough and knowledgeable enough to attempt a description of the sagacity, the soldierly gifts, and the valor of the Turks? It would be nothing but the truth to say . . . that if only they had held firmly to the faith of Christ and Holy Christianity . . . no one would be found to equal them in power, in courage, and in warlike skill."

Furthermore, it was commonly said in the East that the Franks and the Turks had sprung from the same race. The Anonymous Historian has this to say: "In fact they [the Turks] claim to be of the same race as the Franks and assert that none, except the Franks and themselves, have the right to say they are knights."

Paradoxically enough, this admiration attained its peak in relation to Saladin. He was the great conqueror, the man who had torn Jerusalem and the Holy Sepulchre from the Christians, yet his bravery and generosity won for him not only the regard of his opponents, but also a hero's place in their folklore. The Franks liked to think of him as a knight among the Saracens. A romance, the *Ordene de Chevalerie*, actually shows him seeking knighthood from one of his Frankish prisoners. The man explains to him the duties that this implies and then begins to go through the process of making him a knight. He continues until he comes to the symbolic *colée*, and there he is obliged to stop. It is impossible to make a knight of a man who does not believe in Christ. The feeling behind this is the same as that which was already being expressed in the *chansons de geste*—the only fault in Saladin was that he was an infidel.

"What a knight he would have made for Christianity."

CHAPTER VIII

THE ENGINEERS AND THE BUILDERS

At nightfall a fire blazed into life on the mountainside. Presently another flame began to sparkle in response, and then, leaping from hilltop to hilltop, a message sped from the tiny fortress of Kirch across the fifty miles that separated it from Jerusalem. Kirch, besieged by the enemy, was seeking help. A few hours later it received in reply a promise of reinforcements. Meanwhile a small troop of knights equipped themselves hastily in the capital to go to the assistance of the isolated outpost. Some years later, in 1187, this method of sending a message from one signal station to another carried the fearful news of the defeat at Hattin from the Holy City over the Jordan to distant Kerak of Moab—Petra Desertae. But, on that occasion the relief troops dispatched by the garrison of Kerak were of no avail.

No one would have anticipated that the Frankish kingdoms could survive for more than a hundred years after the catastrophe that wiped out their army and delivered Jerusalem into the hands of Saladin. That they did survive was due largely to the fortresses with which the Crusaders had marked the boundaries of their conquests.

These strongholds were not planned merely as a system of defense. They also allowed for the establishment of a chain of communications, a vital need in a country where bands of

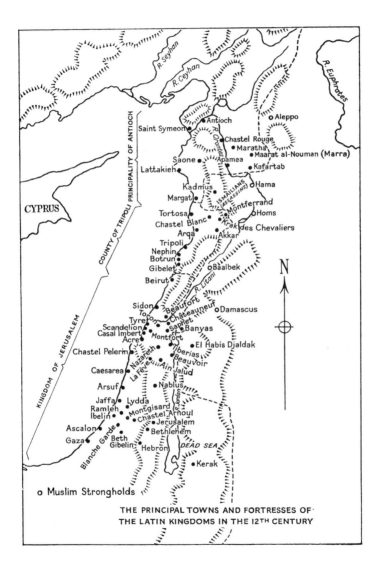

THE PRINCIPAL TOWNS AND FORTRESSES OF
THE LATIN KINGDOMS IN THE 12TH CENTURY

soldiers, scattered among hostile or uncommitted peoples, had to be able to keep in touch. It has been contended that they did not form a true defensive system, and it is undeniable that the first of them were sited more or less by chance. But it is also undeniable that, once the Crusaders had gained possession of a large part of the region, they set themselves to organize the fortresses into a real network. They could send messages between the castles and the principal fortified towns more swiftly than by courier by using a rudimentary system of optical telegraphy; semaphore was the latest example of such telegraphy in the days before radio. A similar system was in use at the same time in the West for, among other things, the defense of ports and places on the coast. At Marseilles, for example, the *farots*[1] marking the shoreline reefs for the benefit of pilots could also make signals between themselves from one hill to another by means of lights during the night and columns of smoke during the day.

On the coast of Palestine the port of Jaffa was in communication with Ibelin, and the fortress of Ibelin with Montgisard and Blanche Garde, while Blanche Garde relayed messages between Ascalon and the castle of Beth Gibelin.

A few of the castles had been erected at the time of the conquest in order to facilitate, for instance, the capture of a town. The castle of Mount Pilgrim was built during the siege of Tripoli; that of Toron was constructed to help in the taking of Tyre, and Beth Gibelin to overcome Ascalon, the "Virgin of the East", the impregnable city that the Crusaders captured in 1153. But the builders devoted their most systematic efforts to the defense of the open eastern frontier of the new state and to guarding themselves against the perpetual

---

[1] One of the hills overlooking the *Vieux-Port* has taken its name from this and is known as *le Pharo*.

menace of the two towns of Aleppo and Damascus, which remained in Muslim hands.

Palestine was actually a long fringe of territories edged on the one side by the sea and on the other by the desert. Castles were raised above every defile and every road, always on guard and ready at need to bar the way. The number that still remain standing today give an amazing impression of the Crusaders' activity as builders. This was of course the great period of building throughout the whole world of the West. It was the period in which from Saint Sernin in Toulouse to Cologne, or to Lund in Sweden, buildings rose in a profusion unknown at any other time. Side by side with this went the phenomenon of the growth of towns at a speed not seen again until the nineteenth century in America. This fever to build was nowhere so sensational as in the East, where its development took place both in an adverse climate and in the midst of a hostile people. The Crusaders had barely set foot on Eastern soil than they began to build, and their activity ended only with the fall of the Latin kingdom. The story of these two centuries is the story of stone, as much as or even more than it is the story of the sword. In that story the buildings played a less illustrious part than the battles, but a more effective one.

The Crusaders raised their first building in 1097, before they had even taken possession of the Holy Land. It was a church, the Cathedral of Saint Paul at Tarsus in Cilicia. Five years later, Hugh of Vermandois, brother of Philip I of France, was buried there. It is amazing to realize that in five troubled years—those of the advance into the Holy Land and the sieges of Antioch and Jerusalem—such a great monument of Romanesque architecture could have been brought so near to completion that a solemn service was held in it. The implication is that it had been consecrated. The nave and its two aisles, which are separated by piers and columns ruled by the principle of alternation dear to Romanesque designers, form the oldest religious building in the Holy Land. It was followed by scores of others. The Church of the Holy Sepulchre is still the most important of them. In it are joined in splendid material form the ancient rotunda raised above the Tomb of Christ, the Chapel of Golgotha, and four chapels built separately and dedicated to the Virgin at the north of the rotunda; to Saint John, to the Holy Trinity, and to Saint James at the south. It also includes the Chapel of Saint Helena and the Grotto of the Invention of the Cross. This church was begun immediately after the capture of the Holy City. It was consecrated on July 15, 1149, the fiftieth anniversary of the assault. The work was crowned with a spire some time about the year 1175.

The city of Antioch, which cost the Crusaders so dearly in suffering, was defended by a whole string of castles: Roche de Roissel, Trapesac, Gastin, and Cursat, which were themselves covered by a line advanced beyond the Orontes and held by the fortresses of Hazart, Corsehel, and Bathemolin. Most of the latter were mere watchtowers, accessible only by a ladder reaching to a door seven to ten feet above ground level—eagles' nests, like Akkar, close to Krak. Similar towers guarded the roads used by pilgrims and offered shelter to them in time of need; one of these was Chastel Arnoul, between Jaffa and Jerusalem, on the busiest of all the routes.

Sometimes these fortresses were set up as sentinels in desolate places. Le Moinestre, six thousand feet up near the source of the Adonis, in a region deep in snow for part of the year, guarded the pass of the B'kaa valley where it opened out toward the coast. In the south, the garrisons of Li Val Moise and Sela "lived among leopards and deserted Nabatean temples".[2] Sometimes, like El Habis Djaldak, the fortresses commanded a river; sometimes, like Saphet, a ford; or sometimes they were used to cut communications between two towns or two regions held by the Muslims. Thus Toron guarded the road from Damascus to Tyre; Montreal, south of the Dead Sea, watched the routes between Damascus and Egypt; Banyas or Subeibe kept the ways between Damascus and the upper Jordan.

These castles were often given into the charge of a baron and his men; for several generations the Embriaco family, who came originally from Genoa, defended Gibelet. But when the military orders were fully developed the castles were more frequently entrusted to these knights—Templars, Hospitallers, or, later, Teutonic Knights—who were both their builders and their defenders. Toward the end of the twelfth century the Templars held eighteen fortresses, which provided a living for the *casaux*, the agricultural communities beneath their walls.

Between Antioch and Tripoli, to the north of Tortosa, lay the Assassins' country. There the Crusaders built the castle of Margat (*Marqab*—the lookout), one of their finest structures, at the entrance to a mountain-dominated gorge. The surrounding walls, fragments of which are still standing, enclosed about ten acres of ground. Huge storerooms, cellars dug out of the rock itself, could hold sufficient provisions to last a thousand defenders for five years. It belonged to the Hospitallers, and four knights and twenty-eight sergeants stood guard every evening upon the ramparts. In 1285 it was besieged and taken when Sultan Qalawun brought up an enormous number of men, including a whole army of sappers.

[2] Robin Fedden, *Crusaders' Castles* (London, 1950).

After eight days of siege he invited the masters of the fortress to come out and inspect the extent of the mines that his men had dug underneath the round towers. The knights understood the situation and surrendered their arms.

The fortress of Sayoun, called Saone by the Franks, is remarkable even now. It guarded the region around Lattakieh, the great port at the mouth of the Orontes, whose position both on the sea and on the river gave it a double importance. The castle ruins are among the most impressive of all the Crusaders' buildings, covering an area of roughly eleven acres. It was cut off from the mountain by a trench hewn from the rock. The stones that were taken with picks and hammers from this quarry were then used for the construction of the fortress. A column of stone still rises out of this trench, a witness to the nature of the toil exacted by the solid rock. It served as support for the bridge that crossed the great ditch to provide a means of communication with the outside world. The column is about ninety feet high. A similar method was used at Edessa, which was a small Byzantine castle when the Crusaders reached the Djebel Alawi. Out of this they made a stronghold, extracting in the process a mass of stone that the historian Robin Fedden has calculated at 150,000 tons.

But Krak des Chevaliers is of course the finest and the best known of these castles. Its position was particularly important strategically, since, from its lonely summit to the north of the plain of La Bocquée, it commanded the whole of the district between the two strong towns of Homs and Hama. This plain was the channel of communication between Tortosa to the north, Tripoli to the south, and the Orontes valley to the east. The Homs gap leading into it was the scene of some of the most desperate fighting between Franks and Muslims. Of the surrounding fortresses Montferrand stood highest up the pass, and it was taken and retaken several times during the course of the Crusades. In the end it remained in the hands of the Arabs, who destroyed it in 1238 or 1239. Opposite Krak stood Akkar, a castle of more modest size, used as a relay station, which had its place in a defensive system further strengthened toward the east by strongpoints such as Archas; Arima, held by the Templars; and the two castles of Chastel Rouge and Chastel Blanc—the latter also in the possession of the Templars.

This was a region where the power of the Franks was firmly assured only by these huge piles of stone. The men in charge of the Latin kingdoms were trying with their walls and their towers to compensate for their appalling numerical inferiority. The fortresses at least created a strategical advantage for the Crusaders and allowed them to withstand attacks by superior forces.

This was the reason for the importance of the fortresses. For a long time the development of the art of fortification was attributed to Muslim influence. It was one of the commonplaces of the history of this art that as an immediate result of the Crusades military architecture in the West had an Arab or Byzantine origin. T. E. Lawrence was the first archeologist to hold the opposite view, and he was received with raised eyebrows. The accuracy of his observations has now been recognized, and the Crusaders are credited with introducing to the Middle East a system of defense that they were continually driven by circumstances to perfect.

Within its two encircling walls Krak enclosed a rough oblong space of about five acres. The outer wall had five round towers toward the western side, and the inner one had four. The eastern side, less easy of access, was defended by ordinary salients. A crenellated parapet walk, upheld by well-laid courses of stone, surrounded the whole. There was room for two thousand soldiers, and the garrison of Krak did actually reach this number in 1212, without including the people from the country round about who sought refuge there in time of need. The ruins, which have been admirably studied by Paul Deschamps, are impressive even today. The ramparts are still standing, while the chapel, the great hall, and parts of the undercroft are complete. Excavation has provided a good deal of information on the layout of the whole.

As well as quarters for the men and stables for the horses, there were at Krak wells and cisterns like those in all similar constructions in East and West. Water supplies were, of course, guarded much more carefully in the East. The wells were eighty-four feet deep and still bear on their curbstones the channeled marks of the ropes that drew up the water. In addition, nine enormous cisterns collected the rainwater that ran off the roofs and fed it into an immense *berquil*, or stone-built horse trough, used also as a swimming bath by the men. It was 234 feet long by 26 to 52 feet wide.

The windmills of Krak crushed not only corn but also sugar cane, for sugar was used in food in the Middle East in the twelfth century. An oven[3] and a winepress provided for bread and drink. Twelve latrines that have been found were connected to a sewage system carrying the refuse beyond the walls. At Saone also the stores of water were guarded with particular care—in this case in huge chambers vaulted like a Romanesque church and measuring 117 feet long by 52 feet wide.

The great hall of Krak looked like a Cistercian chapter house, and was 390 feet long. Its doors and windows opened

---

[3] The oven alone had a surface area of twenty-two square yards. Presumably it was always kept hot, or at least warm, for nowadays it takes a month of continuous stoking to prepare an oven about twelve yards square.

onto a covered gallery where the breadth of the walls would make a pleasant coolness in the heat of summer. The chapel, with three bays of broken barrel vaulting, and the grand master's chamber in the southwest tower of the inner wall display in the ruins of their delicately ribbed columns some of the beauty of our finest Gothic art. The total effect reminds us a little of the work of the master builders of Champagne.

It was in the great hall of Krak that Paul Deschamps discovered an inscription, and a cast of this, with a model of the castle, are in the *Musée des Monuments Français:*

> Yours may all wisdom, wealth, and beauty be,
> But pride, the only arch-corrupter, flee.

On several occasions Muslim forces tried to reduce Krak, which seemed in itself alone to stand as a symbol of the might of the Franks. Nur ed-Din, the lord of Aleppo and Edessa, encouraged by the repulse of the Second Crusade, had already tried to seize it. He had wiped out the armies of Raymond, prince of Antioch, and of Joscelin of Edessa and was passing from one triumph to another when he made camp beneath the walls of Krak. The garrison was reduced to a token force, and its surrender seemed inevitable. Then one blazing midday, when only a handful of men were on watch in the overpowering heat, the knights charged out, fully armed from head to foot, and scattered the Sultan's troops before they had even got over their surprise, chasing them as far as the shores of the Lake of Homs.

This battle of La Bocquée, which freed Krak in 1163, was one of the outstanding feats of arms of the Crusades. Later, Saladin himself failed to take Krak. After the fateful day at Hattin that destroyed the Frankish army, the great fortresses fell one by one into his power. Krak was besieged for more than a year before it gave in. Montreal held out for even longer. Saphet surrendered after a month of relentless assault, and among the others Saône, Beauvoir in the Jordan valley, and Châteaueuf at Hunin also fell. But the Hospitallers kept their hold on Krak as they kept Margat, and the Templars gathered their strength within Tortosa.

Construction on a scale like this makes us consider the problem of manpower. Among the barons' followers were evidently architect-engineers capable of using the strategical resources of the places they passed through in order to plan their strongholds. There is the case of the Lombard engineer at the siege of Nicea who came to the barons with an invention to help them in sapping the defenses. To protect the sappers he built a shelter that was fixed to the walls. It had a sloping roof, so that stones and burning material slid off instead of landing on the workers beneath.

Progress in metallurgy, in the forging of iron tools, made possible in the twelfth century, in the East as well as in the West, the immense labor called for in hewing stone. The use of various hoisting devices facilitated the setting of the blocks in position: winches, pulleys, elevating wheels such as those still to be seen in place at the Mont Saint-Michel—all the devices in fact that were being used at the time in the construction of the cathedrals.[4] The huge size of the buildings presupposes an abundant labor force. The scene described in the chronicle of Ambroise was probably repeated many times over:

> The foundations for a gate were being prepared, and everyone came to help in the work. They all labored away so hard that they were surprised themselves by the amount they accomplished. The fine knights, the squires, and the sergeants

[4] See Jean Gimpel, *Les Bâtisseurs de Cathédrales* (Paris, 1958).

passed the stones from hand to hand. Everyone toiled without slackening, and so many clerics and laymen came that in a short time the work was well advanced. Later, they sent for masons to carry on. It took a long time to finish.

William of Saint-Pathus in a famous passage describes Saint Louis, hod on shoulder, helping to carry the stones for the fortifications of Caesarea, and he alludes to the voluntary work done by the fighting men. Ambroise depicts King Richard bearing on his own back the timber needed for siege engines. The sentences from his chronicle quoted above are sufficient to show that when necessary the knights and men at arms took over the job of laborers, while specialized craftsmen were called in to complete the real work of construction.

According to Villehardouin, this is how the castle of Pamphilon in Thrace, later destroyed by the Bulgars, was rebuilt. Masons were brought in, and everybody helped in the work by carrying stones, lime, and mortar. Probably the assistance given by Crusaders and pilgrims was augmented by that of native workmen, fatigue parties of peasants, and prisoners of war.

These buildings were completed with astonishing speed. Work on the castle of Pamphilon was begun in August. Villehardouin returned to Constantinople before the end of the year. In that time he had finished the reconstruction and manned the fortress with troops. The castle of La Mahomerie holds a better record still. The Crusaders besieging Antioch built it in twelve days, between March 8 and 19, 1098. It had two towers and two inner works and could shelter five hundred soldiers.

Much later, the *château de mer* at Sayette (Sidon) was built in less than four months, between November 12, 1227, and March 2, 1228. Its two towers rose out of the sea and were linked to the shore by a bridge built at the same time as the fortress. A castle like Saphet took two and a half years to build. It sheltered seventeen hundred men in peacetime and could provide a refuge for a large number, perhaps ten thousand, of the peasants whose lands surrounded it.

It is not difficult to imagine what it must have been like to besiege the great walls of these fortresses and fortified towns— for the towns themselves, with their wide ramparts, had all the appearance of vast strongholds. Ludolph of Sudheim, a German traveler of the fourteenth century, said that on the walls of Acre two wagons could pass each other comfortably.

In the coastal towns the fortifications were often planned so that the sea could be used as a natural defense. The tower at Maraclaeum, not far from Tortosa, where only the footings of the walls now remain, was built right in the water. Boats loaded with stone were scuttled to make its foundations. At Tyre and at Sidon, the *châteaux de mer*, like regular keeps, could be isolated by opening a sluice gate and releasing the waters. After the middle of the twelfth century, it was the sea, not the land, that seemed to the Crusaders of prime importance. Therefore, especially after the defeat at Hattin, they concentrated all their genius on the construction of fortresses in the coastal towns. The fortifications at Jaffa date from 1193, those of Tyre from 1210, Chastel Pelerin from 1218, and Sidon from 1228, while it is well known that Saint Louis paid a great deal of personal attention to the walls of Caesarea.

The siege of a place of this sort demanded, as one can imagine, some deployment of forces. An attempt might be made to get inside the curtain wall by bringing up ladders against the ramparts. Ladders, like hurdles and the wooden bridges thrown across moats, played an important part in medieval wars. It is not surprising to find the barons recruiting carpenters as well as stonecutters for their expeditions. In the fifteenth century, when the duke of Bedford was fortifying Paris in preparation for an attack led by Jeanne d'Arc, the first men he called upon were the carpenters and the stonecutters.

Assailants found that a more certain approach lay in constructing a wooden tower, higher than the walls and sometimes mounted on wheels for mobility. It had to be covered with raw hides as protection from Greek fire. At the right moment a drawbridge could be dropped onto the ramparts to allow the attackers to gain a foothold. At the same time, to help the scaling parties, others strove to breach the walls, using ways known throughout history—the ram, the sap, or the mine. The method known, before the invention of gunpowder, by this name consisted in digging holes in the base of the walls and putting fires into them. The stone would break up under the action of the heat and cause the wall to collapse. Mines of this sort, dug by the Sultan Qalawun's sappers beneath the towers of Margat, forced the Hospitallers to surrender their fortress without making a fight of it. The slow advance of a mine, the succession of blows that could be heard even in the heart of the beleaguered castle, sometimes induced a state of tension that, quite as much as the famine to which they were reduced, led to panic among the besieged. In 1182, this sort of panic fear led to the surrender of the Saracens besieged in El Habis Djaldak.

William of Tyre tells us:

> The men hidden behind the mobile rampart, sheltered from all their enemy's attacks, toiled ceaselessly and with the greatest eagerness to demolish the wall so that they could overthrow the tower. As they brought out the stones, they replaced them with balks of timber and small pieces of wood. They

were afraid that if the lower part crumbled, the wall above might come down too soon and crush their machine, which could not possibly sustain such an impact and the immense amount of debris falling upon it. When they had demolished as much as they thought necessary to accomplish the fall of the tower, they set fire to the props, which would support the wall for only a little while longer. To keep the fire blazing, they threw in anything that would burn, and then they rushed away toward the camp, abandoning the machine. Toward midnight, when all the underpinning was burned through and reduced to cinders by the raging fire, the tower fell in with a tremendous crash.

The whole history of the Crusades is built up of stories of this kind, and they all help to reveal what man in feudal times was really like. He was certainly a warrior, but a warrior who did not confine himself to the use of his sword. He was capable of doubling as a technician and of making the best use he could of the materials to hand. Above all, he displayed imagination. For example, the chroniclers describe the barons themselves making a search among the various kinds of trees growing in the country for those which would best serve them for a bridge or for a tower:

> The princes then searched with great care for places where they might find the timber they needed, for there was no way of obtaining suitable materials in the surrounding countryside. A loyalist, a local inhabitant of Syrian origin, by good fortune led some of the princes into deep valleys about six or seven miles from the town. There they found trees that were not entirely suitable for the purpose they had in mind, but among them were several that were tall and well grown. They sent at once for workmen and woodcutters, as many as were thought necessary for the work to be done. The trees were cut down, loaded onto wagons, and drawn back to the

camp by camels. The leaders called together their craftsmen and others who had some knowledge of this skill, and they all set to with tireless zeal. They used axes, hatchets, and many other tools suitable for shaping wood, and one after the other they constructed mobile towers, ballistas, petraries, rams, and other engines that would serve for mining beneath the walls. . . .

While those of highest rank among the leaders were thus occupied with the matters of greatest importance, some of the other nobles and distinguished men left the camp, banners flying, and led their followers to the secret places, to the coppices pointed out to them by the country people. There they ordered the collection of brushwood and osiers. These were then dragged to the camp by horses, donkeys, and other beasts of burden and were used to make hurdles and to help in greater works.

The Anonymous Historian of the First Crusade shows us also how the barons scouted ahead and marked out the routes as they advanced:

The duke [Godfrey] realized that there was no road by which he could lead his troops to Nicea, as the way followed by the first Crusaders was not adequate for so large a number of people. He therefore sent off an advance party of three thousand men armed with axes and swords and ordered them to hack out and widen the path sufficiently for our pilgrims to march along it to Nicea. They made a road across the defiles of a high mountain,[5] and as they went they fashioned crosses of iron and wood and set them up on cairns to show the way to our pilgrims.

[5] The Ouzoun Tchair Dagh, between Nicomedia and Nicea—five thousand feet high.

At the very beginning of hostilities the Crusaders thought up a stratagem that thoroughly confounded their adversaries. The Turks had shut themselves up in Nicea and were able to bring in supplies at will, as the waters of the lake came up to the walls of the town. The Crusaders had no ships, but they completed their blockade by bringing across dry land the fleet that the Emperor Alexius had put at their disposal. Albert of Aix writes:

> It was decided at a general council to send large bodies of knights and foot soldiers to the port of Civitot. They were to transport across the dry land between the sea and the Lake of Nicea the ships that had been requested from the Lord Emperor and granted by him. These ships were big enough to carry a hundred men. They were dragged in silence through the night across seven miles of roads, and by sunrise they were in the water of the lake, anchored against the banks.

William of Tyre relates the same episode with rather more detail. He is emphatic that the transport was made in one night, but this would seem to be unlikely. In a similar manner, after the capture of Nicea, the Crusaders built a bridge of boats across the Orontes to ensure their food supplies:

> The princes judged that it would be possible to build a bridge with the materials they could find. This would allow the soldiers to resist more easily the ambuscades of the enemy and to cover the return of those who had gone out, at the same time providing them with a much shorter road. It would also offer a safer and more convenient way to people on foot who wanted to go in search of provisions or down to the shores of the sea. Several boats were found on the river and on the lake, which was higher up. These were lined up close beside each other and then tied strongly together. Beams and a sufficient quantity of wood were fixed upon them and the

whole linked together with a stout trellis of osier. This made a boardwalk wide enough and firm enough for several persons to pass along it together and side by side. The people found many advantages in this new construction. The stone bridge was close to the town gate, and this wooden bridge was nearly a mile away from it. It was near to the duke's camp and thus went across in the region of the gate he had been ordered to guard.

Later on, at the siege of Acre, to augment the stores of flour, the Crusaders built the first windmill seen in Syria. The rhymed chronicle of Ambroise reflects the astonishment of the Saracens at this invention as yet unknown to them:

> They were the first who fashioned there
> The earliest windmill, such as ne'er
> Had stood before on Syrian sod,
> On which the race accursed by God
> Did look askance with startled gaze
> And shrank away in sore amaze.

Exploits such as these, like the sieges of castles and towns, displayed the ability of the Frankish technicians. Their enemies were astonished by the ingenuity of their machines. Apparently, however, the Crusaders did not often make use of Greek fire, that device that gave the Arabs an incontestable superiority. Incendiary materials had been used in the West as well as in the East, and it was current practice to set fire to the enemy's machines with blazing tow. The Bayeux Tapestry shows rudimentary flamethrowers, made of torches tied to the ends of long spikes and used to ignite the siege towers and engines, which were nearly always made of wood. During the attack on Jerusalem the chroniclers reported the absolute deluge of burning matter flung down by those who were besieged: "The men within threw fire most thickly upon the siege castles. We could see a great quantity of blazing arrows, firebrands of brimstone, oil, or pitch, and anything else that would feed the fire."

Greek fire, however, was more formidable than the pitch or firebrands familiar to the Westerners. It is known that it was made of oil of naphtha, or paraffin, sealed into porous clay pots. These were thrown at the place to be set on fire; breaking as they fell, they allowed the oil to run out. It was then ignited by means of splinters of hard stone, made white-hot in a brazier and thrown by sling or catapult. The terror produced by this fire, capable of traveling even on water, has been described by the chroniclers.

Greek fire was actually borrowed from the Greeks, who first made use of it during their wars with Islam in the seventh century. Its invention was attributed to the engineer Kallinikos (678). Nicetas, the historian, speaks of "the fire that slept in closed pots and could flash out suddenly like lightning, enfolding everything that it touched".

Supplies of naphtha oil were plentiful in Arabia and in the conquered countries. The Muslims in their turn could easily obtain it, and they seem to have kept immense reserves. At the time of the attack brought against Egypt by the Franks and the Byzantines in 1168, the Muslims stacked twenty thousand pots of naphtha at Foustat, near the gates of Cairo. They later threw ten thousand torches into the town to set it on fire and prevent it from falling into the hands of the Franks. Saladin started a blaze in the same way in the camp of his Nubians in order to stamp out a revolt among the guards. His method was effective. When the rebels saw their camp, which held their possessions, their wives, and their children, go up in flames, they dispersed and fled.

An eyewitness has described the effect produced at the siege of Damietta, during the same expedition, by the spreading sheets of Greek fire: "Greek fire coming like a flood, from the river tower below, and from the city above, spread terror everywhere. But people came to the help of the stricken with vinegar, sand, and other materials that smothered it."

For even if the Crusaders obviously did not own oil wells, they soon learned how to gain protection from 'liquid fire'. They draped their siege engines with newly flayed hides and learned to put out the fires, not with water, but with vinegar or sand, or even with the talc that the Arabs had long used to ensure their own safety.

The activity of the Crusaders as builders cannot be discussed without at least some mention of the castles they built in Greece. They were not so strong, generally speaking, as those of the Holy Land—conditions of life were not the same— but they are not less attractive. Some of them, like those at Bodonitsa, Mistra, Kalamata, and Salona, are surrounded with double walls like Krak des Chevaliers. Most of them, like those at Beauvoir, Passavant, and Carytaena, had only one. In Greece also the castles formed part of a defensive system. Chains of fortresses, like Quelmo over the valley of the Eurotas, or Carytaena, Crève-Cœur, Saint Helena, Bucelet, and Saint George along the northwest route toward Ilia, guarded the mountain passes.

The coastal road from Corinth to Kalamata was studded with castles. Some, like the Acrocorinth, were built upon ancient fortifications. Some, like Mistra, were entirely new. This was the castle of the Villehardouins, begun in 1249 after the seizure of Malvoisie. Another new building was Clermont (Khlemoutsi), defending the town of Andravida, where the Franks had made their capital. It is still standing and includes a great vaulted gallery, 150 feet long by 25 feet wide, inside the large hexagonal keep. This rises in the center of the encircling walls, which are crenellated and protected by high towers. The ruined chapel and the cistern that provided the inhabitants with water can still be seen. The castle of Passavant stood at the end of the Le Magne peninsula; Le Grand Magne watched over the Slavonic peoples of Taygetes, who were particularly warlike. Mategrifon (bearing the significant name of "curb on the Greeks") dominated the valley of the Ladon, and Carytaena that of the Alphios. Finally, the maritime towns were also defended by such places as Beauvoir, Kalamata, Patras, and Arcadia.

The most important grouping was that within the town of Rhodes, which was for two hundred years the refuge of the Knights of Saint John of Jerusalem. They made themselves masters of the place in 1309, and it capitulated to the Turkish fleet after its third siege in 1523. During this time the opposition put up by Rhodes had prolonged Christian resistance in the Mediterranean for seventy years after the fall of Constantinople.

The ramparts built during the final period, between 1478 and 1521, are therefore among the last constructions of their kind. They are surrounded by an external ditch, cut out of the rock, 52 to 65 feet deep by 97 to 140 feet wide. It was provided with scarps and counterscarps. The ramparts were divided into sections whose defense was entrusted to the various *langues* or provinces of the order. On the northern side, men of the French tongue were in charge of the section stretching from the tower of Naillac to the gate of Amboise. Then the men of Dalmatia took over, as far as the bastion of Saint George. The tongue of Auvergne commanded between the bastion of Saint George and the tower of Spain, and that of Aragon as far as Saint Mary's Tower. Then the tongues of England, Provence, Italy, and Castille were responsible for the wall between the gate of the windmills and the tower of Naillac. The *auberges* or hostels where the members of the different provinces lived can still be seen today in the famous Street of the Knights. The auberge of France is one of the best preserved and still bears the name of the Grand Prior Aimery of Amboise and the date 1492. The palace of the grand masters, in spite of the restorations from which it has suffered, stands today within the citadel, the highest point in the town. It is a splendid example of military construction of the fourteenth century. The various churches in the town stand as examples of religious art, each bearing the stamp of its age. The cathedral of Saint John, dating from 1310, in the early years of the overlordship of the knights, shows the influence of Catalan builders. The church of Saint Catherine, built about 1330, is reminiscent of the Gothic style of France, while that of Saint Anne, with its network of flamboyant tracery, recalls the architecture of England.

CHAPTER IX

FINANCE AND PROPAGANDA

Among the preparations normally made by a Crusader before his departure there was one that is worth particular attention, for it emphasizes the difference in outlook between the world of the Middle Ages and our own. A man gathering together his equipment and faced in consequence with the enormous cost of his expedition would generally begin by distributing gifts to churches and monasteries. Some of these were endowments to ensure the saying of Masses for his soul after death; others were various legacies to abbeys on his domain. Sometimes he would enfranchise his serfs or perform some other work of Christian mercy. At the same time, if his conscience was troubled by some extortionate act, he would confess it and make amends. In one celebrated case, the vidame of Chartres, before setting off on Crusade, made due reparation before the chapter of the Holy Father at Chartres for violence and injustices committed against the abbey.

To us these donations seem to run contrary to all man's instincts of prudence. They were made by people who were gathering together all the resources at their disposal and were about to submit themselves to the dangers and suffering of an uncertain expedition. Yet such gifts were a normal part of the preparations for departure. In much the same spirit the

Crusaders would fast the day before a battle, even though they would need all their strength for the attack they were to make. They considered that spiritual force was as necessary to the winning of battles as material might.

All this is nothing less than the *opus Dei*, or the putting into practice of the three essential works of Christianity. That is, prayer, through which a man appeals to God; fasting, the personal asceticism that allows him to share the sufferings of Christ; and, lastly, almsgiving, by which the community, represented by the poor, benefits from the efforts made through the operation of grace.

A record of many of these gifts and alms made by Crusaders before they set out has been kept in abbey cartularies, and several details are known about the principal Crusaders. Godfrey of Bouillon and his mother, the pious Ida, made many gifts to the churches. Raymond of Saint Giles made the equipment of the poor his responsibility.

Later on a whole series of actions of this kind are recorded for the Villehardouin family. Each departure was the occasion for some new gift, made either by the Crusader himself or by the family. In 1198 John of Villehardouin founded a chapel in honor of Saint Nicholas when his brother and his son, the two Geoffreys, were about to set out on Crusade. The chronicler in his turn made a gift of land to the abbey of Quincy. Further gifts followed in 1202 when he was ready to leave. In 1205, when it was learned that Geoffrey the younger had been shipwrecked on the coast of Morea, another chapel was dedicated to Saint Nicholas, the patron saint of seamen. Another donation was made in 1214, when old John of Villehardouin, at the age of seventy, himself took the cross. He assigned a quantity of cereals annually to the abbey of Saint Lupus at Troyes when he left in the following year.

Once these charitable duties had been performed, it was necessary to consider the costs of the expedition and to make sure of one's financial resources. With this in view, Godfrey of Bouillon, who was later to play so great a part, sold his domains of Mouzon and Stenay to the church of Rheims and pledged the duchy of Bouillon itself to the monastery at Liège. Robert Curthose handed over Normandy to his brother, the King of England, as surety for ten thousand marks. Many pledges of this kind were made later. For instance, Theobald of Marly, who was once believed to have written the splendid stanzas of the *Vers de la Mort* now credited to Hélinand, the monk of Froidmont, on his departure overseas in 1173 made a gift to his brother of all his possessions in Gonesse and Montmorency in return for a sum of 140 livres.

In fact, according to feudal usage, each baron raised and equipped men at his own expense, demanding aid for this from his vassals. The time was not far off when in most of the domains, in France at least, departure for a Crusade would be considered one of the four occasions on which a baron could levy an "aid". The other occasions are well known to students of legal history: the marriage of the lord's eldest daughter, the knighting of his eldest son, and when he himself was taken prisoner and it was necessary to gather money for his ransom. The term *aid* was to become synonymous with tax—a tax strictly exceptional, as can be seen, throughout the whole feudal period. Taxation under the same name and used for the profit of the King was not to become a regular feature until the fifteenth century.

Some unspecialized funds were supplied by the Church from the imposition of a twentieth on its possessions. In special cases permission was obtained to levy tithes in the West when a Crusade was being prepared. Over and above this, the military orders, the Templars and the Hospitallers, had the right to make a collection annually in every church in Christendom for the upkeep of their armies and their strongholds. The Church also received gifts from more unusual sources. These often came from Crusaders who had been unable to leave and who were released from their vow on the payment of a large sum in alms. It did not take long for this practice to be abused. Remorse on this account is frequently revealed in wills, and the most striking case is undoubtedly that of King Philip Augustus.

He had not fulfilled his Crusader's vow until he was compelled to do so, and immediately after the siege of Acre, he had made haste to strike camp, leaving the whole burden of military operations on Richard Cœur de Lion. In 1122, the year before his death, he redrafted his will. It was written in his own hand and is still in existence.

> We give and bequeath three thousand silver marks to the King of Jerusalem, two thousand marks to the house of the Hospital in Jerusalem, and a similar sum to the Templars of Outre-mer for their next expedition in the spring. . . . [This gift was important for its consequences.] Further, we give and bequeath to this King, to the Templars, and to the Hospitallers 150,500 silver marks for the succor of the Holy Land, so that they may provide three hundred soldiers more than the trained men of their own following, for three years after the truce between themselves and the Saracens is broken. Out of this sum, the King of Outre-mer may claim sufficient to pay one hundred soldiers, that is to say, one-third of the money. Another third is to go to the Hospital, and another to the Temple.

Comparing these huge sums with those that the King bequeathed elsewhere, for example, ten thousand livres to his wife Ingeborg—and in fact she held only a small place in his affections—and a similar sum, more significantly, to his natural son, Philip Hurepel, one can conclude that the King wished by this act to make amends for the lack of enthusiasm he had shown, thirty years earlier, for involving himself personally.

These lines show exactly how much it cost to keep soldiers in the Holy Land. According to the King, the sum of 150,500 marks was intended to provide for three hundred soldiers for three years. Therefore, at the beginning of the thirteenth century, 165 silver marks would keep one soldier for one year. This, then, was the cost of maintenance. A Crusader who was about to set out had first to consider his equipment, and it was probably very expensive. Even a plain coat of mail involved a great deal of work for the blacksmith and the engraver. So we find, for instance, a humble Crusader from Boulogne making his will at Damietta in 1219 and leaving his armor to the Hospital of the Germans, where he wished to be buried, in order that it might be of use to some other soldier.

The list of legacies included in this will make it a touching document and leave us with a fair idea of the kind of stores and small belongings which these ordinary Crusaders were likely to possess. This man left gifts to the priests for Masses to be said for him. He left all that would be found on him at Damietta to his wife, Guilliette, who had gone with him overseas, and all he possessed at Boulogne to his mother and brother. A friend who had taken the cross with him was to receive his shirt, two sacks of biscuits, two of flour, two measures of wine, and a side of bacon that he possessed.

A deed dated 1248, that is, from the time of Saint Louis' Crusade, is equally significant. It shows a citizen of Gaëta who, wishing to equip himself for the next "passage beyond the seas", hired a set of iron armor for seventeen sous. It is stated in the deed drawn up that if through the fault of the

borrower the armor was lost on the journey, its value—
seventy sous—was to be repaid in full.

After equipment had been dealt with, there came the cost of
transport. There is no doubt that as long as he journeyed in
a Christian land the pilgrim could count on receiving hospitality wherever he went. There is nothing in our own age
to give us an adequate idea of what medieval hospitality was
like. Youth hostels probably come nearest to the *maisons-
Dieu*, places of refuge that could be found practically everywhere along the way. A pilgrim, whether a Crusader or not,
could rely on being given his food and somewhere to rest,
not only at the monasteries, but in case of need in the homes
of ordinary people. Some customaries of the time mention
expressly that a pilgrim on his journey was entitled to take
sufficient to keep himself and his horse. The accounts of pilgrimages that have come down to us, although they date
mostly from the fourteenth, fifteenth, or sixteenth centuries, by which time the meaning of hospitality had considerably weakened, nevertheless mention that, from the moment
when a man found himself beyond the seas, it was well to
have a fat purse, for "one was not going among kindly people who would do anything for charity".

It must be remembered, too, that much of the journey, at
least after the middle of the twelfth century, was made by
sea. The barons who took an army with them had to charter
ships. Several examples are extant of contracts similar to those
drawn up for "general passages", like the ones which Villehardouin negotiated with the city of Venice.

At the time of Saint Louis' Crusade, some of the lords,
including Joinville himself, did not join the main part of the
expedition but made their own arrangements with shipowners (mostly at Marseilles or Genoa) to transport their men

and their horses. A contract, which still exists, was entered
into by Count John of Dreux with two Marseilles shipowners, William Suffren and Bernard Loubet, who hired their
nef La Bénite to him and agreed to reserve it entirely for the
arms and baggage of the count and his followers. This was to
cost him 2,600 *livres tournois*. At about the same time Count
Guy of Forez hired the *nef La Bonne Aventure* for 975 silver
marks. It was stated that the ship could provide stabling for
sixty horses and had a crew of forty-one men. This suggests
that it was fairly large.

The humble pilgrims who traveled on their own were
given places on the ships according to the amount they
could afford to pay. Some details of the voyage of James of
Vitry are to be found in a letter dated from Genoa in 1216.
It is true that, since he was at the time bishop of Acre, he
was a man of some importance. Nevertheless he had his
troubles:

> As soon as I set foot in Lombardy it happened that the devil
> threw and cast down into a river, swift, turbulent and terri-
> bly deep, all my arms, that is to say, my books, with which I
> had decided to fight against him, and together with these all
> the other things I needed. The river was enormously swol-
> len through the melting of the snows, and bridges and rocks
> had been swept away. One of my chests, full of books, was
> carried away by the waters of the river. Another chest, con-
> taining a finger of my mother, Mary of Oignies, upheld my
> mule and saved him from being completely drowned. When
> my poor beast had only one chance in a thousand of escap-
> ing alive, he came safe and sound to the bank with the chest.
> The other chest was caught up in some branches and, by a
> miracle, was later found. What is still more miraculous is,
> that although my books are somewhat spoiled, they can all
> still be read.

He then goes on to describe the arrangements he had made for the crossing itself:

> There is a new ship that has never before put to sea. It is just finished, at a cost of four thousand pounds. I have taken five *loca* [places] on her for myself and my people, that is, the quarter of the upper castle.[1] There I shall eat, study my books, and remain throughout the day, unless there are storms at sea. I have reserved a cabin where I shall sleep at night with my companions, another for storing my clothes and the food needed for the week. I have paid for another cabin where my servants are to sleep and prepare my food and a place for the horses that I am taking with me. My bread, biscuit, meat, and the other food necessary for three months have been put in the hold of the ship.

But these were exceptionally comfortable conditions. The ordinary Crusader had to be content with a place in the steerage, between the first and second "covers", or decks, where he slept rolled in his cloak. The statutes of the town of Marseilles laid down that a place of this sort should be at least two and a half measures wide and six and a half or seven long.[2] The statutes add that to allow a little more room it was always permissible to arrange the pilgrims end to end when they were lying down, "the head of one touching the feet of the next". Each pilgrim was entered in the ship's register. The clerk responsible for this list gave each man a ticket, such as we have today, bearing his surname, first name, and the number of the place he was to occupy in the ship. For his food, the pilgrim had to come

---

[1] This castle, in the forepart of the vessel, was the part that contained the most comfortable berths, the equivalent of our "deluxe cabins". They were normally reserved for the shipowners or for important passengers.

[2] That is, about two feet by five feet in modern measurements.

to an arrangement with a man known as the *cargator*, who
was in charge of provisions for the ship. It may give a rather
depressing idea of the way in which he carried out his
job to mention that some people find in this word the
etymological origin of the term *gargotier*, which means a
bad cook.

We have as an example a contract concluded with Andrew of Vintimille, one of these *cargatores*. It is dated March
25, 1248, and in it he undertakes to carry out his duties on
the *buss Saint Francis*, belonging to Raymond of Rhodes. It
would therefore be a Greek ship. For providing food for the
pilgrims until they reached port he was to charge nineteen
sous in mixed currency, or thirty-eight *sous de raymondins* for
each person. He could bring four servants for each group of
one hundred people, but if there were over four hundred
travelers, he was to have fifteen.

The reports of pilgrimages—though it must be remembered that the greater number of them are much later than
the time of the actual Crusades—suggest that it was wise to
take certain precautions when embarking on the sea. A certain Greffin Affagart recommended those who were going
to sail to the Holy Land, as he had done, to take a straw mat
with them on the ship "because of the pitch"—a reminder
that ships' timbers were coated with pitch. They should also
take "two small jars, one to carry the soft water of Saint
Nicholas, which keeps sweet longer at sea, the other for Padua
wine, which is good to drink in a hot country as it is not too
heady". He also suggested carrying "salt meat, like ham or
ox tongue, cheese, butter, some little cooking pots for use
when necessary, enough fresh bread for seven or eight days,
some biscuit, figs, raisins, almonds, sugar, and, most important of all, a little bottle of the dark syrup of preserved roses,
or something of the same sort, to take on the advice of a

doctor. This is good for restoring the stomach after an attack of diarrhea." [3]

Then, when he had reached the Holy Land, a poor pilgrim could enroll in the army of one of the lords or could win some profit through plundering or the fortunes of war. Often enough Crusaders who were wealthy when they set out were only too happy to receive occasional help of this kind. The chroniclers mention this sort of thing as far back as the First Crusade, when dealing, for example, with the work on the walls of Antioch:

> The laborers who could not afford to work for nothing received wages taken from the offerings made by people at the church services. None of the princes, in fact, was now sufficiently wealthy to pay the salaries of the men he had to employ, except for the count of Toulouse, who was always much better off than all the others. He was able to pay all the expenses of the men who worked for him out of his own treasure, without needing to ask the people for anything. There were, moreover, many noblemen who had lost all their supplies for the voyage and were paid by the count.

> For long now we have heard the echoes of your sane doctrine and this has made us very happy.... So that you may follow your calling as a preacher with even greater success, and especially so that you may help the province of Jerusalem, we have decided ... to give you full powers to attach to yourself as helpers those among the black or the white monks and the canons regular whom you know can preach well.

In these terms Pope Innocent III, under the mandate of his legate Peter of Capua, authorized Fulk of Neuilly to preach and to obtain help in his task.

[3] Greffin Affagart, *Relation de Terre Sainte*, published by J. Charanon.

Peter the Hermit had shown how much a preacher's word could accomplish in the age of feudalism. But Peter the Hermit was not the only one. He himself, Robert of Arbrissel, and the other preachers of the First Crusade were followed by many more, among whom some great names are outstanding. That of Saint Bernard is preeminent, and his cross at Vézelay keeps his memory green in our generation. Unfortunately, none of his crusading sermons has survived, and the words attributed to him are entirely apocryphal. But we have some information about the activities of other preachers and some idea of the way in which their sermons were composed.

On the first Sunday in Advent in 1199 a great crowd poured into the small canton of Asfeld, once called Écry-sur-Aisne, near Rethel in the Ardennes. Count Theobald III of Champagne had organized a great tourney, which was to be attended by all the lords of his domain and of the neighboring baronies.

The illuminations in several manuscripts show us vividly what these tourneys must have been like. The most celebrated, those of the *Tournois du Roi René*, were two centuries later than this, but they provide brilliant evidence for the riot of color at these meetings. The streets along the route of the procession were hung with tapestries; glowing surcoats covered the riders' horses as well as their armor, and on them the coat of arms identified each champion, or at least his lineage, as he passed by. The whole dazzling rainbow of medieval colors was unrolled: or, argent, azure, gules, sable, purpure, vert. They were displayed in the stands draped in scarlet cloth that were erected at either end of the lists; in the pennons fluttering from lance tips, in the standards flapping in the wind, and above all in the gowns of the *dames et damoiselles* bidden there as spectators of feats of valor. Days such as these were also days of popular rejoicing, and the crowds too are shown in the miniatures, no less brightly clad than the seigneurs themselves. Along with all this, trumpet notes and the shouts of the people created a scene of exuberant joy.

All the nobility of Champagne from the Count downward met at the tournament of Écry. He was the husband of Mary of France, and she, whose mother was the lovely Eleanor of Aquitaine, was the sister of both Philip Augustus of France and Richard of England. Geoffrey of Villehardouin, one of those present, lists in his chronicle the names of the others who were there. Among the most renowned were Count Louis of Blois and Simon of Montfort.

Gradually silence crept over the crowd as the time came for the first knights to enter the lists. On that day the waiting was longer than usual. Suddenly, instead of that idolized pair, which at that time the rider and his horse formed, both adorned alike and both groomed with the same care, people saw in amazement a venerable priest come forward into the lists. His glance was lively, his bearing resolute, "and he preached such a sermon there that many hearts were touched and turned toward our Lord". He made a profound impression on the populace as well as on the barons. One by one, moved by the words this unexpected preacher had spoken, the knights removed the helmets of state they had donned for the tournament and came to kneel before the priest to take the cross.

Fulk of Neuilly, who had interrupted the festivities and brought the tourney at Écry-sur-Aisne to this unexpected end, was a rather unusual person. As an ordinary man of lowly origin, he took orders and went to minister to the parish of Neuilly. He was a bad priest, depraved and dissipated;

then he suddenly experienced a change of heart—it was always the unforeseen that happened with him—and from then on dedicated himself with enthusiasm to the affairs of his parish.

At that time Maurice of Sully, bishop of Paris—the man who built Notre Dame—was stirring up the zeal of his clergy and had begun to urge them to preach every day instead of reserving their homilies for Sundays and holy days. Fulk bowed his head to the episcopal ordinance and put his mind to the making of sermons. However, his first essays into the career of preacher proved difficult. His parishioners, who at that period had no inhibitions about letting their priest know what they thought of him, reproached him with his lack of culture.

Fulk did not need telling more than once and went off to study theology at the neighboring University of Paris. He worked so hard, under the direction of Peter le Chantre, that he took his master's degree in the growing university. He then went back to preaching. He found the parishioners of Neuilly as hard to please as ever. For two more years the crowd went on interrupting him, pelting him with insults. Then once again things changed with startling suddenness. He received the gift of influencing souls. "His words struck the hearts of wicked men like sharp arrows and brought them to tears and to repentance", wrote his contemporary, Ralph of Coggeshall. On several occasions, at the invitation of Peter le Chantre, the masters of the University of Paris came to Saint-Séverin to listen to this curé of Neuilly who had become the greatest preacher of his time.

It was not long before he was in demand everywhere. He preached not only at Neuilly and Paris, but also in Flanders, Brabant, Normandy, Picardy, Champagne, and Burgundy. According to the fashion of the day, he spoke in public places and at crossroads, and the crowds flocked around him as they had done earlier around Peter the Hermit. He succeeded as well with ordinary people as with educated men. "God in his mercy has chosen this priest to be a star shining in the darkness, and to be rain in time of drought, so that his vine may be tended", wrote James of Vitry, bishop of Acre, himself a celebrated preacher. Many miraculous acts were attributed to Fulk. A rich man invited him to dinner. There was stupefaction when the covers were taken off the dishes and there was nothing in them but toads and serpents. Another time, a usurer, smitten with repentance, confessed to him where his treasure was hidden. They went there together and found that the place held nothing but snakes.

Occasionally he drew the anger of the audience down upon his own head, for he thundered mercilessly, chiefly against usurers and misers. He was insulted, and even, at Lisieux, thrown into prison for reproaching the clergy of the town, in his usual violent language, with corruption. "The whole of France felt the lash of his sermons."

They had an effect even beyond the boundaries of France, if one can credit the unlikely tale that he rudely upbraided Richard Coeur de Lion, exhorting him to "get rid of his three daughters". "You lie, hypocrite, I have no daughters." Fulk replied that the King had indeed three daughters: pride, gluttony, and sensuality. Richard was not easily taken aback. "Good", he retorted, "I give my pride to the Templars, my gluttony to the Cistercians, my sensuality to all churchmen."

To complete the portrait, drawn by his contemporaries, of a vigorous preacher, quick to wrath, it must be added that he was most charitable. He founded the Cistercian convent of Saint Anthony, near Paris, for prostitutes who wished to

redeem themselves, and with gifts he had received he provided a dowry for those who wanted to marry.

We possess some other accounts of preaching. One of them
is particularly interesting as it comes from the preacher himself, James of Vitry. It is a letter dated from Genoa in October 1216. He was on his way back to his bishopric of Acre in
the Holy Land after a stay in Rome. He had allowed himself
some time to rest in Genoa before he embarked, and he tells
how he made use of it to recruit more Crusaders.

When I arrived from France it was wintertime, and I had
soon to continue my journey, from which I had had little
respite and much trouble. As I felt very tired, I chose to rest
a little so that I might be able to work all the better in Outre-
mer, especially as many thousands of Crusaders have already
set out, and I shall have to welcome and comfort them. I
intended to preach the word of God to the men of my own
diocese and to the others from Outre-mer before the great
crowd [of these Crusaders] came, so that I could warn and
exhort them to receive these pilgrims well and to keep from
sin so that they would not draw the strangers into evil ways
by their example. When this huge crowd does arrive I shall
be so busy with their affairs that I shall hardly be able to
spare time for the men of Acre, who are my special charge,
unless I do something about it beforehand. . . .

And so I set out for Genoa. . . . When I arrived, the citizens welcomed me kindly but took my horses willy-nilly for
an attack on some stronghold. It is the custom there for them
to take horses, wherever they may find them and whoever
may be their owner, when they are setting off on some expedition. The women had remained in the city. During that
time, I did what I could and preached the word of God to
many women and a few men. A great number of noble and
wealthy ladies took the cross. The men had taken my horses,

and I induced their wives to take the cross. They were so fervent and so devout that they barely left me a moment to rest from early in the morning until nightfall. They either came to glean some edifying words from me, or they wished to make confession. When the citizens came back from their expedition and found that their wives and their sons had taken the cross after listening to my preaching, they also received the sign of the cross with much fervor and love. I stayed in this city of Genoa for the whole of September and often preached on Sundays and feastdays to the people of the city. Even though I could not speak their language, thousands of men turned toward God and took the cross.

For the taking of the cross, a ceremony had gradually evolved. Psalms recalling the captivity of Babylon were sung and were usually followed by a sermon. Then, to the chant of the *Veni Creator* or the *Vexilla Regis*, the preacher distributed the crosses. They were as a rule small crosses cut out of cloth and fastened to the right shoulder. The Crusader thereafter wore one always. Crosses like these are outlined on the stone figure of the returned Crusader that can be seen in Nancy. Sometimes a noble might have a "deluxe" cross made for him. Baldwin, count of Flanders, received a cross made of linen embroidered with gold on Ash Wednesday, February 25, 1200, when he took the Crusader's vow in the church of Saint Donat at Bruges. His wife, Mary, was the sister of Theobald of Champagne.

During the course of the thirteenth century, as time went by, the activity of the preachers increased in inverse proportion to the amount of enthusiasm for a Crusade. It is significant that the same age that fixed the status of a Crusader from a juridical point of view also turned the preaching of a Crusade into a sort of institution. In the same way, feudal customs were first put into writing at the time when they were beginning to decline. There was felt an instinctive need to protect them, but instead it changed them into an administrative shell—the very opposite of living custom. The thirteenth century was the time when the crusading movement lost its enthusiasm and became an institution.

From this time comes the curious *Manuel du Prédicateur* written by Humbert of Romans, who was master general of the Dominican order from 1254 to 1277. He was an expert on preaching and belonged to an order of men that had made it their special study. He was already the author of a less specialized work intended for preachers in general. The manual was probably written at the end of 1256. The whole of Christendom had just heard with horror the news of the capture of Saphet and the massacre of its garrison of about two thousand men. This had been done at the command of Sultan Baibars, although when the surrender was negotiated he had promised to spare the lives of the knights.

Humbert wrote no less than forty-six chapters for the benefit of preachers of Crusades. First, for those priests charged with the work, he makes clear their responsibilities. Above all, it was essential that they should have taken the cross themselves. They should not dare to exhort others unless they had themselves first set the example. This reminds us of James of Vitry's reflection that showed him to have been vividly aware of the reciprocal responsibilities that in those days linked the pastor and his flock:

> I did not wish to return [to my bishopric of Acre] without doing something to protect the Crusaders who are everywhere oppressed by taxes and other exactions. Otherwise they would not accept my preaching, but would be more likely to spit in my face if I were unable to shield them as I promised in my sermons.

Obligation, it seems, was no empty word at that time.

It is surprising to note the amount of theoretical and practical knowledge that Humbert demands of his preachers. They are expected to know thoroughly everything contained in the Old and New Testaments relating to the Holy Land. They should have studied the globe and be conversant with the geography of Palestine. Above all, they must have studied the history of Muhammad and *have read the Qur'an*. It is difficult for us today to realize that such an obligation was laid on preachers of the thirteenth century. Moreover, they are expected to know, even if only in outline, the history of the establishment of the Christians in the Holy Land. The *Historia Transmarina* by James of Vitry is the book chiefly recommended for this. Finally, they have to have some idea of ecclesiastical law on such subjects as the privileges of Crusaders, the effect of indulgences, the cases in which they may grant dispensation or absolution, etc.

Once he has established these essential points, Humbert gives the preachers a whole series of themes that they can develop in their sermons. He then proceeds, as usual in compilations of this sort, of which there were many at the time, to give examples by way of illustration, drawing them arbitrarily from history and legend and ranging from the victories gained by the Emperor Constantine to the visions of Turpin in the *chansons de geste*. He builds up also a picturesque list of the various reasons that could turn people against a Crusade and offers the preachers arguments with which to refute them. Some do not wish to go for reasons of health, some for lack of money, others through fear. Some are like fat and heavy palfreys that want to spend all their lives in the stable; others are like domestic fowls that prefer to sleep in their own roosts at night; others are like the cows in Flanders that spend the whole day close to their sheds with a rope tied around their necks; or again there are those who are like freshwater fish that have no wish to leave their bowl and turn back as soon as they smell the sea. The true knight looks on the country where the Savior lived as his real homeland and does not hesitate even to tear himself away from his family in order to follow the word of the Gospel.

There are others who hesitate to commit themselves for fear of what people might say; they do not want to be laughed at. This clearly suggests that at the time feeling was not unanimous. Those who set off as Crusaders were often encouraged, but they might also have to contend with the mockery of their neighbors. Many of them went "to be the same as the others"; some did not go because they were afraid of public opinion. We have some verification of this, and, moreover, from a time when, in the words of a modern writer, going on Crusade had become a "fashionable sport". Some years earlier, in 1264, the scenes at the tourney of Écry had been repeated at the tourney of Meaux. Many knights, seized by enthusiasm, responded to the appeal of the archbishop of Tyre and took the cross. But these vows often remained unfulfilled, and there began to develop a disquieting tendency to redeem the vows for a sum of money, by making an offering to the Church proportionate to the expenses that would otherwise have been incurred.

The preacher makes allusion also to another feeling that was gaining ground. This was discouragement, fed on the persistent lack of success of the later Crusades:

> There are no longer any spiritual fruits or temporal advantages. The Saracens are not being converted, the victims of the war mostly end up in Hell, and we cannot even keep the lands we conquer. Saladin takes everything back instantly. The Emperor Frederick was drowned in a pool of water at

the beginning of his campaign; Saint Louis was taken prisoner over there with his brothers and all his nobility. . . .

The Saracens are without number and endlessly renew
themselves because they are on their own ground.

The emphatic words of Joinville when he refused to follow
Saint Louis on Crusade for a second time hold an echo of
this feeling:

> When I was in Outre-mer, and since then, the men of the
> King of France and of the King of Navarre have ruined and
> impoverished my people. If I did not stay to defend them, I
> would be angering God who did all things to save his people.

The time was no longer right for the lost cause that the Crusades had become. In order to conquer, the fiery spirit of the
early Crusaders had been essential.

But there is no doubt that something of that first enthusiasm comes through in the "invitatory" that Humbert of
Romans suggested that the preacher should use at the end of
his appeal:

> Dearly beloved, you see to what the wars of the world, so
> often unjust, can lead, and you see where the war of Christ,
> the most righteous of all, can lead. Into the former many
> people are dragged by ties of friendship with one of the world's
> great men. May you be persuaded by friendship for Jesus to
> undertake the latter. Those others are prompted by the de-
> sire for an empty glory. May you be led by the desire for the
> heavenly kingdom. . . .
>
> I promise you in the name of the Father, and of the Son,
> and of the Holy Spirit that all those who take part in this war
> and die while bearing arms, if their hearts are contrite and if
> they have been confessed, shall enter into possession of that
> kingdom that the Lord has conquered for us by the Cross,

and here and now I invest you with that kingdom by that same cross, by the cross that I offer you. Come therefore, and may no one of you refuse to accept so glorious an investiture, so formal a warranty of the throne that is waiting for you above.

The preacher, however eloquent, could not have been fully successful in his work of inspiration and propaganda entirely on his own. Another person took on part of his task and deserves a place beside him—the poet. The thread of poetry was woven through medieval life. It would have been surprising to find it absent from the great epic of the Crusades.

The epic poetry of France belongs to exactly the same time as the First Crusade, and it has been said that the one cannot be understood without the other. Reto Bezzola[4] has analyzed profoundly the impulses that moved men in that age of feudalism at the end of the eleventh century, at a time when the King of France was preoccupied with matters quite different from the defense of Christianity, to recall longingly the mighty figure of Charlemagne as he fought against the Saracens in Spain. The dominating concern of the period was to recapture the holy places from Islam, and this feeling is reflected in all the epics, from *La Chanson de Roland* to the cycle of *Guillaume d'Orange*.

At the same time, or very shortly afterward, some traces of this great concern are apparent also in the poetry of the *langue d'oc*, then just beginning to unfold. William IX of Aquitaine, the first of the troubadors, wrote one of his finest poems as he was about to leave for the East:

---

[4] See in particular *De Roland à Raoul de Cambrai in Mélanges Ernest Hoepffner* (Paris, 1949).

Now from my home to lands afar
In danger and in dread I go,
And leave my son harassed by war
While evil neighbors work him woe.

Gladness of mind and strength of limb
Are over now, and I am bound
Upon a pilgrimage to him
In whom the sinner's peace is found.

Once I was blithe and debonair,
But God has chosen to impose
A load well nigh too great to bear
As life is drawing to its close.

All that I loved I now resign,
Forsake my prowess and my pride;
But 'tis God's will and shall be mine,
And may he keep me at his side.

The oldest of the crusading songs is also to be found in Provençal poetry. Here the voice of the poet joins that of the preacher in exhorting those who may hear to take up the cross. Its author, Marcabru, calls the poem *Le Chant du Lavoir*. He compares the Crusade to a beautiful "washing place" like that in which Christians are plunged at the time of their baptism and that will wash them clean at the end of their days:

Now by our heavenly Father's grace
A wondrous font is close at hand,
Such as was ne'er in any place
Beheld, save in the distant land
Where lies the vale Jehoshaphat . . .
Wherein, as seemly is, we may
Cleanse ourselves both night and day:
And thus I say.

At the other side, as one might call it, of the world of the Crusades, in that second half of the thirteenth century, which saw the end of the kingdoms of Outre-mer, there rises the voice of Rutebeuf, the greatest medieval poet of France. Eleven of his crusading songs are known. That pressure of public opinion that impelled the movement to the Holy Land and that is clearly revealed in the preachers' sermons can be detected in his verses. It is displayed throughout the whole of his *Debat du croisé and du décroisé*, in which arguments for and against the Crusade are opposed. At every opportunity he soundly berates the men whom he holds responsible for the loss of the crusading spirit—the kings and princes who were concerned only with their private quarrels and the prelates who thought only of their own well-being:

> Ye holy prelates, who would save
> Your bodies both from wind and wave,
> Nor join the matin song whereto
> My lord of Sergines[5] summons you
> In regions far beyond the sea—
> But much I think to blame is he
> Who dares to ask that you should think
> Save on rich food and costly drink
> And spice to whet your appetite.
> But is not this your cause, your fight?
> Your God, your good, for which we strive?
> Alas, what answer will you give
> When God shall ask the land again
> Where, for your sakes, his Son was slain?

In the intervening time the Crusades found some echo in almost every form of literature, whether in prose or poetry.

---

[5] A Crusader celebrated for his exploits.

They inspired epics such as *La Chanson d'Antioch* and *La Chanson de Jérusalem*, histories like the first French prose work, Villehardouin's *La Conquête de Constantinople*, and innumerable pieces of folklore. The *Legende de Saint Géraud* tells of the founder of the Hospital in Jerusalem, who, during the siege of the city, fed the Christians battering it from without by throwing to them stones which changed into bread. Another tale concerns William of Villehardouin, a man born in Greece who became a hero of the folklore of that country and hence the ideal of the perfect hero, as is seen in the second part of Goethe's *Faust*.

Almost all the events of the Crusades were made the occasion for poems, written often by the Crusaders themselves. Only one by King Richard is left to us. It expresses his misery when he was held captive in Austria on his return. More surprisingly, Philip of Novara, besieged in the tower of the Hospital by the followers of the Emperor Frederick II, sent for help in a hastily written little poem with the delightful ending:

Caged like a nightingale, what can I do but sing?

The names of many of the Crusaders were often those of the best poets of the day, whether they were troubadors like Peire Vidal, Gaucelm Faidit, Raimbaut of Vacqueyras, and Elias Cairel—the last three were certainly in either the Holy Land or Greece—or *trouvères* of the north like Theobald of Champagne, Conon of Béthune, Huon of Oisy, and many others.

By the thirteenth century, moreover, the Crusades had revived the essential theme of courtly love. Now it is the departure for overseas that separates the poet from his lady, arousing his anguish and despair. She will only despise him if he remains at home, and that will mean losing her love.

> For there it is our knighthood we must prove,
> Where heaven and honor may at once be gained,
> And wealth and worship, and our lady's love.

And if he goes, it will be at the cost of a broken heart, as Huon of Arras laments:

> Thither I'm bound, to suffer pain and woe,
> Where God himself travailed in human clay,
> And sad my thoughts will be, because I know
> That my dear lady will be far away.

The delightful Châtelain of Coucy takes up the same theme, and sighs, before setting off in Villehardouin's company on the Crusade during which he was to die:

> To you, O lovers, most of mortal race,
> This melancholy verse I dedicate,
> As now to foreign lands I set my face,
> And from my sweet companion separate. . . .
> But wheresoe'er under God's hand I go,
> Lady, may you beneath his care remain;
> I dare not speak of my return; we know
> 'Tis but a chance if we shall meet again.
> Wherever I may be, in God's great name,
> Keep troth with me, whether I go or stay,
> Remembering, if I return, sweet dame,
> The holy cause for which I went away.

Other poets, like Guiot of Dijon, sing of the despairing wait of the ladies who have seen their *bel ami* depart:

> When the gentle breezes blow
> From that country far away,
> Where my dear one fronts the foe,

Thither all my longings stray,
And his clasp I seem to know
Underneath my cloak of grey.

When the exile cries to thee,
Father, send the pilgrim aid:
How I fear the cruelty
Of the hostile paynim's blade.
Very soon he will return,
Setting all my fears at rest;
On this tunic he has worn
Meantime let my lips be pressed.
When at night with love I burn
Let me snatch it to my breast,
And my heart shall cease to mourn
By its loving folds caressed.

Toward the end of the twelfth or the beginning of the thirteenth century the theme of courtly love saw the birth of the pleasant legend of the faraway princess as an explanation for the refrain *amor de lonh* that rings through the poems of the troubador Jaufre Rudel. Without ever meeting her, he had fallen madly in love with the Princess Mathilda of Tripoli, and, in order to see her, he braved all the perils of the seas and the Crusade and came at last to fall dead at her feet.

Thus were merged together the departure for the Crusades, which was for the knight his supreme moment, and that concept of courtly love that was perhaps the greatest poetic invention of the Middle Ages.

PART THREE

THE SPIRIT OF CONQUEST

CHAPTER X

THE KINGS AND THE MERCHANTS

The second phase of the history of Frankish Syria—one of reconquest—is marked by the emergence of two powers that had until then played a merely subsidiary role. These were, first, the temporal powers—kings and emperors who either supplanted the barons of earlier days or imposed their will upon them—and, second, what one may term economic powers—the merchant cities, chiefly those of Italy.

It is true that these two powers had already been seen in action. When Saint Bernard preached the Crusade at Véze-lay, the Kings of France and England and the Germanic Emperor all took the cross. The thirteenth century saw a new trend when they began to claim the baronies for themselves on behalf of their "nationals". The time was coming when the crown of Jerusalem, although it was then little more than a symbol, was to be the ambition of one princely family or another, and even of the Emperor himself. The Kings of the West were to consider that they had "interests" in the East. When John of Brienne came, full of enthusiasm, to report that the Emperor, Frederick of Hohenstaufen, was seeking the hand of his daughter, the heiress to the Latin kingdoms, Philip Augustus received him coolly, for the news did not please him. It would be absolutely wrong to talk about "the rise of nationalism" at the beginning of the thirteenth century,

but certain tendencies can be noted that were to bring about
that rise a hundred years later. The people of the time were
aware of them:

> When Syria, in the last Crusade,
> Was lost, and after repossessed,
> And Antioch so sorely pressed . . .
> In former days, what soldier said
> He was of French or Norman seed,
> Of Poitiers or of Brittany,
> Of Maine, perchance, or Burgundy,
> Of Flemish or of English breed? . . .
> Each brought home honor, proud to bear
> The name of Frank, whether his hair
> Were red or white or dark or fair . . .
> Could we but shape our lives by these,
> And cease our foolish rivalries!

In his rhymed Chronicle, almost contemporary with these
events, Ambroise expresses matters thus as he records and
deplores the divisions among the Crusaders.

It has been noted that from a political point of view the
merchants played little part in twelfth-century Syria, yet there
is no doubt that there were many Western traders established
in the country. The great expansion of Mediterranean commerce dates from this time, although similar commercial relations between some Italian towns and the Muslim countries
can be proved in the eleventh century, perhaps even earlier,
and certainly before the Crusades. The cities of Bari and
Amalfi in particular had built a connection with Syria, but
they were to be eclipsed later by Genoa, Pisa, and, above all,
Venice. The merchants of Amalfi had a street in Antioch
that antedated the First Crusade, and they owned a hostel in
the same town. Later on, there were in Jerusalem many traders

and artisans who had come from the West. Baldwin III granted exemption from town dues and tolls to all the merchants who frequented the city, which included Syrians, Greeks, Armenians, and Saracens as well as the Latins. Queen Melisende ordered the building of a market in the town, and according to the chroniclers twenty-seven bakeries could be counted there in the twelfth century. The population included some wealthy burghers like the man who had a cistern dug during a drought to increase the people's water supply. It was called the Pool of Germain after him. Many of the others were certainly poor, for when Saladin entered Jerusalem there were more than twenty thousand who could not pay their ransom.

The new development was the way in which the commerce of the "foreign" cities began to expand and the care that these cities took from the moment of reconquest to ensure themselves privileges in the coastal towns, the only ones that really interested them. These merchant communities had already made their presence felt. The Genoese fleet had brought help to the Crusaders from the time when they first came within sight of Jerusalem, and in 1123 the Venetians suggested that their ships anchored at Jaffa should be used to help in the capture of one of the ports. There was difficulty in deciding between Ascalon and Tyre, and an orphan child was given the task of drawing lots between them. As a result Tyre was captured and the Venetians took up their quarters within the city on July 7, 1124.

The merchant cities, however, were to find themselves directly interested in the reconquest of Frankish Syria. Their business instinct impelled them to share in all the feats of arms, making sure beforehand that they would have considerable privileges in Tripoli, Tyre, and Acre. The role these merchants played was to be of vital importance. René Grousset has summed up the situation: "In the last years of the eleventh century the Latin East, from a moral point of view, was created by faith. In the thirteenth century, it was the search for spices that kept it going."

As a result of this outlook and these new conditions, though the Franks won back the coastal towns, they never recovered Jerusalem itself, for, commercially speaking, it was of no interest. The reconquest would perhaps have been impossible without the military aid provided by these cities, but later their economic rivalries caused endless troubles in Outremer. Immediately after the siege of Acre, which was one of the main towns retaken, the Pisans, who had adopted the cause of Guy of Lusignan, and the Genoese, partisans of Conrad of Montferrat, came to blows. These quarrels were to become more frequent and more bloody as the thirteenth century wore on. This same town of Acre was the scene of a pitched battle, the "war of Saint Sabas", which lasted for two years, from 1256 to 1258.

In the arrangements made between the merchants and the princes at the time of the reconquest, whole districts of the towns were sometimes allotted to the former. A district of this sort was known as *fondouk*, from an Arab word coming from the Greek term *pandokheton*. Warehouses for merchandise were set up there, and the traders built their houses, grouping them by "nations". A town hall, which contained a court of justice, was nearly always included, together with a church, an oven, and baths. The Venetians set up the figure of a boar in their *fondouk* to annoy the Muslims. The merchants generally put to sea early in spring, in March, laden with the goods of the West. These were usually fabrics, for weaving was the most important medieval industry. Woolen cloth from Flanders or Languedoc, linens from Champagne or Normandy, were bought up at the great fairs in the Île de

France or in Champagne and used to win the treasures of the East. These had often been brought great distances by caravan: silks from China, muslin from Persia, perfumes and carpets from central Asia, the highly valued spices of the Indies—pepper, cloves, nutmeg, camphor—with perfumes and dyestuffs—indigo from Cyprus or Baghdad, and scarlet. The products of Syria itself were also there, from the finely worked weapons of Damascus to the sugar canes of Lebanon, the silks and the brocades of Tripoli and Antioch. In Tripoli in the thirteenth century four thousand people were employed in weaving silk, and other industries—tapestries, soap, glass, ceramics, and so on—also flourished. It was not without reason that the Venetians diverted the Crusade of 1204 toward Greece, for the silk industry there was of great importance. In Thebes alone, two thousand Jews as well as many Greeks were employed in it.

This explains why the merchant cities, particularly the Italian ones, attached such great importance to the reconquest of Frankish Syria, and why the merchants were granted many privileges in the edicts of the kings of Jerusalem or of those who aspired to that position, including Conrad of Montferrat as well as Guy of Lusignan.

The Crusader who dominates this time of reconquest is, for his bravery and for the brilliance of his deeds, worthy to stand beside the leading barons of the First Crusade. He was Richard Cœur de Lion. While they were overseas, he outshone Philip Augustus of France, who was his rival as well as his ally in the reconquest. The English King, who was, after all, an Angevin and spent only a few months of his life in England, was extremely popular even with the Frenchmen of France. In the Muslim world he played the part of the bogeyman, for Arab mothers would threaten their children with "King Richard" when they wanted a little peace.

His Crusade began in a burst of glory with the capture of Cyprus. It was a possession of the Byzantine Empire, but two of the King's companions had been wrecked in sight of the island, and the Emperor was accused of seizing their property. A battle between the Greeks and the crews of the wrecked ships followed. King Richard's own sister had been traveling on one of the ships, and when he heard of the battle he hurried immediately to the port of Limassol. The Latin translator of Ambroise's chronicle reports what happened:

It was on a Monday morning that God had prepared the business that he wished the King to perform. He wanted him to succor the shipwrecked men, to rescue his sister, and to take to safety his betrothed [Berengaria of Navarre, who was accompanying the King's sister]. These two were both cursing the day they had reached those shores, for the Emperor would have seized them if he could. When the King decided to capture the port there was no lack of men to oppose him, for the Emperor himself had come down to the shore with every soldier he could bribe or command to be there. The King sent a messenger in a boat to shore, courteously asking the Emperor to return their belongings to the people who had been wrecked and to make reparation for the wrongs done to the pilgrims, which had caused the tears of many orphans. The Emperor mocked the messenger like a madman. He could not control his fury and spat at him: "Troupt, sire!" [We would probably translate this "Pish!"] He would not give a more sensible answer, but growled derisively. The messenger immediately went back and reported this to the King.

When the King realized that he was being mocked, he said to his men, "Arm yourselves!" They set to at once and did not take long about it. Then, in their armor, they climbed down into the ships' boats, the fine knights and the brave bowmen side by side. The Greeks too had crossbows, and their men came down close by the shore. They had also five armed galleys. But when they saw the arms of their opponents, they did not feel so safe. Everything movable in the town of Limassol, where the battle had begun, had been carried down to the beach to use in the attack on the pilgrims. They did not leave one door or window in the place, or anything that could be thrown, not a cask or barrel, shield or targe, old galley or old boat, beam or plank or staircase. The Greeks stood armed upon the shore, more arrogant than anyone else in the world, with pennons and banners of precious stuffs and rich colors. They were mounted on big horses, strong and swift, and on powerful, fine-looking mules, and they began to bay at us like hounds. But their pride was soon humbled. We were at a disadvantage since we were coming at them from the sea, piled into narrow little boats, dazed with weariness, worried by the tossing of the waves, and borne down by the weight of our armor; moreover, we were all on foot. They were on their own ground. But we knew better how to fight.

At this point the chronicler Ambroise, who was apparently a member of this expedition, slips in a little story that illustrates King Richard's sense of humor. He was lying in ambush in an olive grove waiting to attack the Greek army when:

> A cleric, Hugo de la Mare,
> Came to the King, attired for war,
> And with advice the monarch cumbered:
> "Sire, we are fearfully outnumbered;
> Let us retreat at once!" whereto
> The King replied, "Sir Clerk, for you
> A pulpit were a fitter post
> Than here amid an armored host:
> For God's sake and his Mother's, then,
> Leave the affairs of war to men!"

Having thus put the unfortunate priest firmly in his place, he charged, overthrew the Greeks and the "Ermins"—the Armenians who had joined forces with the Emperor—and took the town: "What more can I tell you?" says the chronicler. "In fifteen days, and I do not lie, the King, under God's direction, had Cyprus at his mercy and in the power of the Franks."

That done, King Richard went on with his fleet to join the French Crusaders before Acre. The siege of this town had been begun in August 1189. He arrived in June 1191, when both besiegers and besieged were reduced by famine to a state of great distress. Yet from then on operations must have proceeded briskly, for the town capitulated on July 17. The decisive assault was carried through by the greatly increased number of mangonels, which were brought up to batter at the walls, and by mines, which toppled them down. It was marked by picturesque incidents, mostly arising out of the rivalry between the two princes, Philip and Richard. Philip proclaimed that knights who had fallen on hard times might join his forces for one gold bezant a day. Richard immediately let it be known that he would pay two gold bezants to those who would sign up on his side. There was also the incident of the meeting of sappers from the opposing armies under the Accursed Tower at Acre, which was the first objective to be chosen:

> When the sappers [from the Frankish forces] hacked their way in under the Accursed Tower . . . they shored it up, for it was already very shaky. The besieged, for their part, prepared a countermine in the hope of wounding our men. Eventually the two parties met, and made a truce among themselves. Among the men making the countermine against the Christians were some in irons [prisoners of war, probably themselves Christians]. They talked to our men and

allowed them to get away. When the Turks in the town learned of this it gave them great sorrow.

Philip Augustus left the Holy Land as soon as the town fell, not without causing among his barons "tears and groans. . . . So discontentented were they that they almost repudiated their lord and King." The success achieved by the capture of Acre would in fact have gone for nothing if Richard Cœur de Lion had not personally assumed the leadership of the Crusade. We have noticed elsewhere how his magnificent feats of arms and the unforgivable faults springing from the violence of his nature made him at once feared and loved in both camps. Ambroise tells us of a curious discussion that, according to him, took place between Saladin and the bishop of Salisbury about King Richard:

> So they remained in company,
> Conversing long and earnestly,
> And oft to learn the Soldan sought
> Those deeds the English King had wrought,
> And what renown the Saracen
> Bore in the minds of Christian men.
> "Sire," was the bishop's steadfast word,
> "I truly can affirm my lord
> The doughtiest knight and man of war
> In all the world, both near and far. . . .
> And he who rightly shall compare
> Your worth with his, may truly swear
> That never, though the utmost bound
> Of earth were searched, could there be found
> Two other princes who could claim
> Such valor and attested fame."
> The Soldan heard the churchman out,
> Then said, "Your King, I do not doubt,

Is strong and fearless, but may yet
His rashness all too late regret.
To whatsoever rank I rise,
I wish that I may rather prize
The wisdom of a balanced soul
Than hardihood that lacks control."

This is surprising homage to pay to the complementary qualities of the two adversaries. Richard might have been superb had he possessed "all the wisdom of Saladin". As it was, he went so far as to suggest a romantic solution to the problem of Syria. He proposed that his own sister should marry Saladin's brother!

The project came to nothing—one condition was that the Saracen should accept Christianity—and the Crusade itself, in spite of the prodigies of valor performed in its cause, failed to achieve its true goal—the deliverance of Jerusalem. Richard, in vexation, denied himself the pilgrimage to the Holy City, a right that was now granted to the Christians. It is significant that it was personal misunderstandings between two Western sovereigns that had brought about this semi-defeat in the struggle against the Eastern world.

CHAPTER XI

THE CORONATION OF AN EMPEROR

And so the Emperor was led to the monastery of Saint Sophia. When he arrived he was taken away into a chamber, and there his clothes and his shoes were removed. He was then attired in hose of scarlet samite and shoes decorated on the uppers with precious stones. A rich tunic was then put on him, fastened at the back and front, from shoulder to chest, with golden buttons. Then they dressed him in the pallium. This was a kind of garment that fell to the instep in front and at the back was so long that it was girded round him and then thrown back over the left arm. This pallium was extremely rich and fine, and it was embroidered all over with costly precious stones.

After that, he was robed in a splendid mande covered with jewels and embroidered with eagles. These were sewn with jewels that glittered so that it looked as if the mantle were on fire.

When he was thus vested, he was led before the altar. The Count Louis [of Blois] carried his imperial standard, the count of Saint Pol bore his sword, and the Marquis Boniface [of Montferrat] his crown. Two bishops supported the arms of the marquis as he held the crown, and two other bishops escorted the Emperor. Every one of the barons was most richly dressed, and there was no one there, Frenchman or Venetian, who was not wearing clothes of samite or of silk.

The "monastery" was the basilica of Saint Sophia, built in
the sixth century, the greatest age of Byzantine splendor, and
a source of wonder to the visiting tourist even today. The
procession that was making its way there was that of the first
Latin Emperor of the East, who had been borne by completely unforeseen circumstances to the throne of Justinian.
Baldwin of Flanders, count of Flanders and of Hainault, was
the knight on whom this honor had fallen. All-powerful lord
though he was, he must have felt a quite unique emotion at
finding himself risen to such an unexpected eminence. In
the eyes of the men of the West, the Emperor of the East was
the only true descendant of the Roman Emperors, and, as
we have seen, he represented supreme power. From the earliest days of the Crusades, Christendom had shown a respect
for the occupant of the throne of Constantine that had never
been accorded to the Holy Roman Emperor, and this in spite
of all the difficulties that arose between Constantinople and
the West. Now a succession of events, beginning with the
diversion of the Crusade, but precipitated by the Byzantines'
own internal discords, had culminated in the crowning, on
Sunday, May 16, 1204, of a Frankish knight, one of those
"barbarians" whom the Greeks affected to despise.

The detailed account of the ceremony was written by Robert of Clary, an unimportant knight from Picardy. His "fief",
at Clary-lès-Pernois in the bishopric of Amiens, covered almost exactly fifteen acres. He was one of the lesser members
of the company of which Geoffrey of Villehardouin was the
star. Fortunately they have both left us an account of what
happened, so for the same series of events we have the parallel points of view of the general and of the plain soldier.

The latter is by far the more interesting in his account of
the coronation. Villehardouin only mentions in passing how
Baldwin of Flanders was chosen by his companions in arms

with the common consent of both Venetians and Franks. After a midnight proclamation to the army, he was crowned "with great joy and great honor in the Church of Saint Sophia", and "many splendid robes were made for his coronation". But Robert of Clary, an ordinary soldier who had the good fortune to be present at a unique spectacle, was enchanted by it. When he set down his recollections he revealed all the qualities that we expect today in a reporter. His account is almost cinematic in its quality and in its succession of actions and gestures, and little transposition would be required to give it the appeal of a direct broadcast version of the ceremony. Something of this can be judged from the following passage:

> The Emperor comes up to the altar and kneels there; first his mantle is removed and then the pallium, leaving him only in his tunic. The golden buttons at the back and front of the tunic are undone, and when his chest is bare, he is anointed. When this has been done, the buttons are refastened, he is dressed again in the pallium, and the mantle is clasped on his shoulder. [When he is thus] robed, two bishops lift the crown from the altar, the other bishops join them, and they all take hold of the crown. Then, all together, they bless it and consecrate it and put it upon his head. Around his neck is laid an exceedingly costly jewel mounted in a clasp, a jewel for which the Emperor Manuel paid sixty-two thousand marks.
>
> Now that he is crowned, he is taken to sit upon a lofty throne, and there he stays while the Mass is sung. In one hand he clasps his scepter, in the other a golden orb surmounted by a cross. The ornaments that are upon him are worth more than a mighty King's treasure. When the Mass is finished, a white horse is brought up to him, and he mounts. The barons then lead him to his palace of Boucoleon, and he is seated upon the throne of Constantine. And there, upon the throne of Constantine, he, as Emperor, receives homage

from everyone. The Greeks who are there also pay honor to him as their holy Emperor.

A count of Flanders was seated on the throne of Constantine. This was the fact that must have seemed so striking to the crowd of Franks and Greeks, to the barons as well as to the ordinary folk. All the prestige of Rome and Greece, of Justinian and of the centuries of culture and civilization that his name symbolized, and even the incarnation of the temporal sword, the hope and the temptation of Christendom since the days of Constantine, were concentrated in the crown that the bishops had just placed upon the head of Baldwin of Flanders.

The previous state of affairs was now reversed. From the coming of the Crusaders at the time of the First Crusade, the Byzantine Emperor had intended to make use of them for the recovery of his realm. There was no other reason for the delays imposed on Godfrey and his companions under the walls of Constantinople than the diplomacy of Alexius Commenus, for he was concerned above all else that the profit of future expeditions should accrue to him without any accompanying risk. For more than a hundred years the Byzantines, disappointed in their calculations, had proved themselves to be unreliable allies who missed no opportunity to do harm to the Christian army. The initial misunderstanding only worsened as time went by. The Byzantine Emperors had thought all the lands that had once belonged to the empire would be returned to them. The Crusaders refused to hand over to a power that had not known how to guard them conquests that they had won by bitter fighting and paid for with their blood. The Byzantine rulers had not only failed to retain the sympathies of their own subjects—there were, for instance, profound disagreements between the Armenians and the Greeks—but had also created a schism within Christendom. "We have driven out the pagans but not the heretics", wrote the barons in 1098 at the beginning of the First Crusade in a letter to the Pope.

A century later the capture of Constantinople gave them the satisfaction of driving out the "heretics". This stroke was none the less serious for being dictated primarily by the commercial calculations of Venice and perhaps also by the veiled personal ambitions of some of the barons, such as Boniface of Montferrat. For the first time Christians had taken arms against Christians. When the Pope learned of their intentions, he opposed them: "Use your forces only to deliver the Holy Land and to avenge the sufferings of him who was crucified. If you must look for spoils and conquest, seek them rather among the Saracens, your real enemies. By staying in the Greek Empire you run the risk of despoiling your own brothers."

The Crusaders could have given him a thousand reasons for what they did. At the outset the Venetians, who certainly knew what they were up to, literally held a knife to their throats and forced them "to work for them" by threatening, since they knew their lack of resources, to refuse to carry them across the sea. Other factors involved were the discords flourishing in Constantinople; the sorry flight of the usurping Emperor, Alexius III; the broken promises of Isaac Angelus and his son, whom only the Crusaders' intervention had restored to the throne; and finally, the rebellion of a new usurper, Murzuphlus. All these events had led up to the second siege, which Villehardouin describes in such vivid fashion.

At Constantinople, the Crusaders revealed even more than elsewhere their bravery in combat and their weakness once the battle had been gained. They found themselves in the most celebrated of all cities, known as far away as China as "the city of cities", confronted by an enormous accumulation of riches. Robert of Clary states that "the Greeks testified that two parts [two thirds] of the wealth of all the world was in Constantinople." In the eleventh century the revenue from the customs and markets alone was estimated at 7,500,000 gold sous, equivalent to a thousand million prewar francs.

Some fifty years earlier, at the time of Louis VII's Crusade, a story was told that showed the fascination that the riches of Constantinople held for the soldiers of the north. A Flemish Crusader had found his way into the market in the business center of the town. It was in the street called the Mésé, which was lined with two-storied porticoes on either side and led from the forum of Augustus to the Golden Gate. The part of this street between the Grand Palace and the forum of Constantine was the place for dealings in gold. There the money changers had their tables, heaped with coins of all kinds, and there the goldsmiths and silversmiths had their shops. The soldier, dazzled by such mountains of riches, lost his head and with a shout made a sudden charge, sweeping up everything within his reach. The terrified money changers fled, and the ensuing uproar was enough to cause the King of France to claim the guilty man from the count of Flanders and have him hanged. Half a century later, as far as the Byzantines were concerned, much the same thing happened again on a larger scale—the same "barbarians", with greedy eyes upon their treasures, came scrambling for the spoils.

The chronicles are in fact full of marveling descriptions of these riches. They were to be distributed ultimately throughout Europe—France, Germany, Italy all benefited, but Venice, naturally, had the lion's share. Even today tourists stop in Saint Mark's Square to look at the group of bronze horses that were brought at that time from Constantinople to the city of the lagoons. They had previously decorated the imperial gallery at the Hippodrome, where they had been installed by Constantine, who, in his turn, had brought them from Alexandria—a curious symbol of the fragility of empires. Their wanderings did not end with the thirteenth century. Napoleon, after his Italian campaign, took them to Paris, where they adorned for a time the Arc de Triomphe du Carrousel. However, they were sent back to Venice after the Congress of Vienna.

> There were so many rich vessels of gold and silver, so much cloth of gold and so many costly jewels, that indeed a great marvel of wealth had been brought to that place. And never since this century came in has there been wealth as great as this, so noble and so rich, either seen or taken as the spoils of war, either in the time of Alexander or in the time of Charlemagne, either before or since.

Robert of Clary gives an awed description of the palace of Boucoleon. He puts it into the mouth of the marquis of Montferrat:

> In this palace there were easily five hundred rooms, each one opening out of another, and they were all covered with golden mosaics. There were certainly thirty chapels, some big and some small. One of them was called the Holy Chapel, and it was exceedingly rich and fine. There was no hinge or ring in it made of iron; all were of silver. The columns were all made of jasper or porphyry, or of costly precious stones. The floor of the chapel was paved with a white marble so polished and so limpid that it seemed to be crystal. This chapel was rich and fine beyond description.... Within this chapel many valuable reliquaries were found. There were two pieces of the True Cross as thick as a man's leg and half a fathom long, also the head of the lance which pierced our Lord's

side and the two nails that were driven through his hands and through his feet.

The relics stood high among the splendors that most attracted the Crusaders. The taking of Constantinople was the occasion for the scattering throughout the West of a quantity of Eastern relics. Villehardouin sent a vase reliquary back to Saint Remi at Rheims, and Robert of Clary left in his own district a reliquary in the form of a crystal cross. It still forms part of the treasure of the abbey of Corbie and bears the following inscription: "Let all those who read these words know that the holy relics that are sealed within this vessel were brought from Constantinople. They were taken from the Holy Chapel in the Emperor's palace of Boucoleon, and Robillart of Clary brought them here in the time when Count Baldwin of Flanders was Emperor."

There are many local holy places that date from that time. Among them are Saint Étienne at Châlons-sur-Marne, Saint Mammés at Langres, and Saint Victor at Sens.

There is no doubt that dishonest dealers exploited unscrupulously the veneration that the various relics aroused, and from that time on the authenticity of some of them was challenged. A great deal of importance was attached to the letters of warranty that certified their origin—in the same way as today we require proof that valuable antiques or the paintings of the masters are genuine.

As early as the beginning of the twelfth century Guibert of Nogent had written a treatise protesting against the use of unauthenticated relics. This is sufficient indication that the critical faculty was alert in spite of certain abuses. As far as the True Cross was concerned, the fragment that had been preserved at Jerusalem had been hastily buried in the sand on the eve of Hattin, and therefore the other pieces that were in Constantinople aroused the covetousness of the Crusaders.

Various pieces of the Cross were shared among the churches of the West. Many of them were later challenged, and it became a well-worn joke to say that enough was left of the True Cross to build a ship—until the day when the learned Rohault of Fleury had the patience to measure all the existing relics. He found that their volume [1] would not have made up a third of that which would normally be needed for a cross capable of bearing the weight of a man.

The most astonishing story about the relics found at Constantinople is probably the one told about the Crown of Thorns. The Emperor Baldwin, at the end of his resources, pawned it to the Venetian merchants. When Saint Louis heard of this, he redeemed it, and in 1239 the relic was sent to Paris, where the King built the Sainte Chapelle to enshrine it.

Writers who describe scenes of pillage are fairly plainly suffering from uneasy consciences. Villehardouin is foremost in saying that once again the Crusaders did not know how to live up to their own ideals after their victory: "Thus one brought good and the other harm, for covetousness, which is the root of all evil, was never idle. Henceforth covetous men began to keep things for themselves, and our Lord began to love them less."

The dividing of the spoils caused all sorts of disputes, and the avariciousness it aroused sowed trouble and discord among the Crusaders. Robert of Clary was the first to break out in complaint against the "great men" who shamelessly allotted themselves three-quarters of the spoils when they were divided up:

[1] 3,941,975 cubic millimeters.

> The very men who should have guarded [the treasures] seized the golden jewels and anything they wished for . . . and every rich man took either golden jewelry or lengths of silk, and whatever he liked best he carried away . . . and no one gave any of it to the men in the ranks. There was nothing for the poor knights, or for the soldiers who had helped to win it.

He spoke from experience, for in another passage he tells at length how his brother Aleaume, distinguished for his deeds in battle and one of the first into the town, was most unfairly treated at the division of spoils. The pretext given was that, being a cleric and not a knight, he had no right to anything.

When everything is taken into account—and Villehardouin is the first to realize this—the conquest of Constantinople is one of those events that can be explained, but not justified.

Even so, it had its happier aspects, at least from a material point of view. The establishment of the Franks in Greece was accomplished fairly smoothly. Only a few years after the conquest Villehardouin could say that the lands between Constantinople and Salonica were so well pacified that the road was safe enough "for anyone to travel along who wished to do so". Yet it was a good twelve days' journey between the two cities.

Jean Longnon has brilliantly described the establishment of Frankish knights in the peninsula. On the whole, they had an easy way of life diere and discovered affinities with the Greek population that the subordinate race were not to find again with any of their successors, from the Catalan mercenaries to the savage Turkish conquerors. The provinces had represented tedious exile for the Byzantine officials, whose one ambition was to live in "the City". They were roused for a while to brilliant life by these barons who took pleasure in making their homes there.

It remains to say that the break between the Greek and Latin churches worsened from this time, thus compromising one of the designs that the papacy had cherished for the Crusade. Further, it has been noted that the capture of Constantinople had the result of turning the knights away from the Holy Land and scattering their forces, for it attracted them to the more fertile and pleasant lands of Romania and the empire. The vital impulse died away before the covetousness that Villehardouin continually denounces:

> Then they began to divide up the lands. The Venetians had their share, and the army of pilgrims had the rest. And when each one heard himself nominated to his land, the covetousness of the world, which was to do such harm, gave him no rest. Each man began to do evil in his land, one more and another less, and the Greeks began to hate them and to bear them a grudge.

For the Crusaders, the Byzantine Empire had always been a stumbling block on the way to the Holy Land. That obstacle had now been removed. But it is questionable whether easy solutions are the best. The capture of Constantinople, which brought unexpected prosperity to the barons and at the same time led to the loss of the crusading spirit, proves that they are not.

CHAPTER XII

THE TEMPTATION OF EGYPT

Frankish Syria was a minute kingdom, surrounded by immense Muslim territories extending from Persia to Morocco, from the shores of the Caspian to those of the Atlantic, and it would be easy to imagine that its existence had been one endless battle. Jean Richard has, however, shown that during the century between 1192 and 1291 the kingdom of Syria knew eighty years of peace.[1] Fairly soon after their arrival, the Franks realized that it was in their interest to form alliances, since, by very reason of its enormous size, the Muslim world was far from presenting an unbroken front. Throughout the history of the kingdom of Jerusalem, the biggest contrast between the mental attitude of the *poulains*, those born or settled in the country, and the newly arrived Crusaders, was shown in regard to the practice of negotiation with those Muslims with whom it was known that alliances could be made against the rest of Islam. The former had learned to fathom the subtleties of the Oriental world, but its complexities escaped the latter. Hence Louis VII's Crusade launched an ill-considered attack against Damascus, although the first Crusaders had soon learned that it was better to deal with the city more tactfully.

---

[1] *Le Royaume latin de Jérusalem* (Paris, 1953), p. 161.

However, it must be said that the *poulains* themselves were quick to understand that this was a task that had to be done over and over again. They were in a world where alliances were not to be depended upon, where a man might be a friend one evening and an enemy by morning, and where internal upheavals were always a threat.

Thus, throughout the history of the Crusades, the Egyptian question, in one or other of its many changing forms, was always being raised. For the men of the West, Egypt was veiled in a light that made it almost as attractive as Palestine, although for different reasons. Even if, in the Gospel stories, it was only the temporary refuge that concealed the Savior from the massacres of Herod, in the Old Testament, on the other hand, it held an important place. Pilgrims to the Holy Land never failed, if circumstances permitted, to round off their visit to the holy places of Palestine with a pilgrimage to Egypt. To this we owe, from the fourteenth and fifteenth centuries particularly, wondering descriptions of the land where flowed the river supposed to be one of the four that sprang from the earthly paradise. On its banks stood the Pyramids, tremendous monuments of Egyptian antiquity, which were called at that time "Pharaoh's granaries". ("That is false, for they are not hollow within, but are the sepulchres of the Kings of Egypt", states Greffin Affagart, a pilgrim at the beginning of the sixteenth century, in his account.) There the memory of Moses was particularly venerated—there was a convent on Mount Horeb—and also that of Saint Catherine. It was told of her that she had had long discussions with the Alexandrian doctors and that her body was carried away to Mount Sinai, where there is still an ancient monastery that bears her name.

It only needs a glance at the map to understand the great interest the Christians had in separating the kingdom of Egypt

from the rulers of Aleppo or Damascus and from the Meso-
potamian power. This was the policy invariably followed during the thirteenth century, at least on all those occasions during
this period when a policy is discernible. But the outlines of
this policy had been laid down during the earliest phase of
Frankish Syria. The whole reign of Amalric I, one of the
most active and best-informed rulers of the kingdom of Jerusalem, had been dominated by this Egyptian question, which
was resolved most favorably for the kingdom by Egypt becoming for a time a Frankish protectorate.

The circumstances in which this protectorate was established have been described with his usual mastery by William of Tyre. He witnessed the negotiations conducted by
the King and wrote his personal story as well as that of his
campaigns. At that time the terrible Nur ed-Din, the atabeg
or governor of Aleppo, a Turk by birth, had just captured
Damascus, on April 25, 1154, and had achieved as a result
the unity of Muslim Syria. Egypt, on the other hand, was
under the control of the last degenerate descendants of the
Fatimite dynasty, and conspiracies and tragedies followed one
another in the heart of its court, "perhaps the most corrupt
there has ever been".[2] Furthermore, most Muslims looked
on the Fatimids as heretics. In 1153 a drama more violent
than the others was played out in Cairo, when Dhirgam, one
of the palace officials, drove out the Vizier Shawar and, it is
said, had more than seventy emirs massacred. This, as the
Eastern chroniclers observed, contributed more than a little
to the weakening of the Egyptian army. Shawar had at first
sought the help of Nur ed-Din, but meanwhile Amalric,
the King of Jerusalem, had sent forward a reconnaissance

---

[2] René Grousset, *L'Epopée des Croisades* (Paris, 1939), p. 195.

expedition as far as the valley of the Nile, and this was to prove useful later.

Shawar, restored to his position with the help of Nur ed-Din, soon found the protection of the Syrian power unwelcome. Nur ed-Din's lieutenant, Shirkuh, uncle of the famous Saladin, who was probably making his first expedition in arms with him, treated Egypt like a conquered country. He levied tribute as he pleased and stayed there with his army. In order to get rid of him, Shawar made haste to appeal to the King of Jerusalem. A first campaign in Egypt, in 1164, was effective and had as its result the evacuation of Egypt by Shirkuh's armies. In 1167 the latter, still under Nur ed-Din's orders, made a second attempt, and Shawar again appealed to the Franks. Thus the Frankish king found himself the arbiter of a situation where the two opposing poles of the Islamic world carried on between themselves not only a political war but also a religious one, between the orthodox Sunnites and the heretical Shi'ites.

This situation was the cause of an unusual incident in the history of the Crusades. Two Frankish knights, Hugh of Caesarea and a Templar named Geoffrey, under the patronage of the Vizier Shawar, were received by the caliph in Cairo. The caliph of Egypt was quite a young man, "extremely dark, tall, fair of feature and most liberal, who passed his life among an infinite number of women". He received them in a room in his palace that made a great impression on the Frankish barons:

> They saw fountains of marble filled with clearest water, and flocks of birds unknown in our world were heard singing. . . . There were galleries intended for walking that were lined with marble columns sheathed in gold and adorned with carvings. The floors were made of various materials,

and all the surroundings of these galleries were truly worthy
of the royal power.... The chief eunuch led them farther
still, and they passed through other buildings even more el-
egant than those they had already seen. There was a most
astonishing variety of animals. The hand of an artist would
have delighted to paint them; poetry alone could have described them, or the imagination of a sleeping man might
have invented them in his dreams at night. Yet they are actually to be found in the countries of the East or of the South,
although the West knows nothing like them.

In this Arabian Nights setting the Vizier Shawar presented
the envoys of the King of Jerusalem to his lord:

> Curtains of cloth of gold, adorned with an infinite variety of
> precious stones, were hanging in the center of the room and
> enclosing the throne. These were drawn apart with extraor-
> dinary rapidity, and the caliph came into view, revealing his
> face to beholders. He was seated on a golden throne, clad in
> garments more magnificent than those of kings, and at-
> tended by a small number of servants and eunuchs of his
> household. Then the vizier went forward humbly, with ev-
> ery sign of respect, and kissed the feet of the sovereign on his
> throne. He explained the reason for the arrival of the del-
> egates, reported the tenor of the treaties that he had con-
> cluded ... and ended by declaring what the lord King was
> pleased to do for them.

A characteristic episode took place during this reception.
Hugh of Caesarea had obviously retained his sangfroid in the
face of this display of luxury and the appearance of a caliph
before whom his people constantly prostrated themselves with
every mark of respect. He demanded that the latter should
shake him by the hand as a mark of good faith. The poten-
tate's entourage "were apparently horrified at this suggestion, as though it were an unheard-of thing". In the end the

caliph offered his hand, but held it out covered with a veil. The imperturbable Hugh insisted, "My Lord, good faith is straightforward. It is essential that everything be laid bare in making the contracts that tie one prince to another. . . . Thus, unless you offer your hand uncovered, I shall be obliged to think that you are holding back something and that you are less sincere than I should like." The caliph smiled indulgently at this request, and with his bare hand he clasped the hand of the envoy.

Another curious episode in Franco-Egyptian relations was the entry of the Franks into Alexandria after besieging the town, which had been defended by the young Saladin. This took place in August 1167, after the forces of Shirkuh and Saladin had capitulated. Egyptian and Frankish soldiers had fought side by side against them. On this occasion, King Amalric showed how a Frankish knight could behave when by his own efforts he obtained a full amnesty for those who had been Saladin's auxiliaries in Alexandria. Saladin himself had fled as a refugee to the King of Jerusalem. Furthermore, Amalric offered the use of his own ships to carry the wounded of the Kurdish-Arab army back to Syria. William of Tyre describes the sort of fraternization that existed between the two opposing camps:

> The inhabitants of Alexandria, emaciated and disheartened by the weariness of a long siege, . . . came out of the town to soothe their troubles and to amuse themselves by talking in a friendly fashion with the men whom so short a time before they had feared as the messengers of danger and the ministers of death. Our people, for their part, hastened to go into the town that had been the object of their desires. They walked freely about, visiting the streets, the harbors, the ramparts, examining everything with care so that when they got back to their own camp fires they could discuss it all at length

with their countrymen and divert their friends with interesting tales.

From then on the government in Cairo undertook to pay a yearly tribute of one hundred thousand pieces of gold to the King of Jerusalem and became, as it were, the vassal of the Frankish kingdom. However, the situation worsened the following year, and an expedition, led this time against Shawar, ended by annulling the effects of the previous treaty.

Then, on January 18, 1169, a new revolution shook Egypt. Shawar was assassinated by Saladin, who remained in Egypt and in 1171 deposed the last descendant of the Fatimite caliphs, so that a military government now replaced the decadent court. It would not have been difficult to foresee that sooner or later this energetic man would achieve the unity of the Muslim world. The chance for this occurred when Nur ed-Din died in Damascus on May 15, 1174, leaving only a child of eleven, Malik es-Salik, to succeed him. To crown this disaster King Amalric died of typhus on July 11 of the same year, at the age of thirty-nine. The situation in which his Egyptian policy had for a time made him the arbiter of the Muslim world was now violently reversed.

Throughout the thirteenth century the endeavors of John of Brienne, then of Frederick II, and finally of Saint Louis show that Egypt appeared to provide the key to the position of the Franks in Syria. On two occasions it was suggested that Damietta, besieged by the Franks, should be exchanged for Jerusalem. The first time, the city had in fact cost the Crusaders enormous losses. Therefore, when in 1249 Saint Louis led his forces against this same city of Damietta and at one blow assured his hold on it by the striking success of his landing on June 6, the news of the victory stupefied Egypt. The sultan of Egypt immediately had fifty of his emirs executed in reprisal, and around him, more now than ever before, murder and revolution followed one another at the court of Cairo.

Joinville has told a touching story of the horrible manhunt that ended in the death of the Sultan Turanshah, the last descendant of Saladin. He was killed by the Mamelukes at the instigation of the Sultan Baibars, a man whose name quickly became famous as a series of assassinations carried him up to the supreme command of the Turco-Arab forces. The chronicler had been taken prisoner with a large number of his companions and was being held in a galley from which he watched part of the barbarous execution. Turanshah had built "a tower of pine wood, hung about with painted cloths" that stood by the camp gate. As he came out from a banquet that he had given he realized that the Mameluke guard were going to attack him, and his first thought was to take refuge there:

> The sultan, who was young and lightly built, ran with three of those who had eaten with him to the tower that he had had made. They called to him to come down, and he asked to be given some surety. They replied that they would make him come down and that he was not in Damietta. They threw Greek fire at him, and it caught on the tower, which was made of pine planks and cotton cloth. The tower quickly caught fire, and I have never seen flames go up so fine and straight. When the sultan saw this he came down in a hurry and began to flee toward the river along the path that I have mentioned before. . . . [The Mamelukes] had smashed up the path with their swords, and as the sultan went by toward the river one of them drove a lance into his ribs, and the sultan fled on toward the river dragging the lance after him. And they went down after him as he tried to swim away, and they slew him by the river, quite close to our galley, where we all were.

After this appalling manhunt, one of the Mamelukes presented himself before Saint Louis, who was a prisoner, "with his hands all bloody and said to him, 'What will you give me? I have killed your enemy; he would have put you to death if he had lived.' And the King said nothing to him." The prisoners could well fear the worst in the terrible state of disorder that reigned in the Egyptian camp: "Thirty men came to our galley with their naked swords in their hands and Danish axes on their shoulders. I asked my Lord Baldwin of Ibelin, who understood their tongue, what the men were saying. He told me that they said they had come to cut off our heads."

We shall see how Baibars, followed by the Sultan Al-Ashraf who succeeded in his turn to the throne of Egypt, would in the end deliver the final blow to Frankish Syria with the capture of Acre. This did not prevent the Venetians in 1304 from entering into commercial treaties with their successor, Sultan Nasser, who with alacrity granted the Venetians the right to set themselves up on Egyptian shores. Egypt had never been wealthy in wood or metals and was obliged to rely for armaments on foreign powers. Trading in arms was certainly forbidden and subject to excommunication, since, sooner or later, these would be turned against Christians. But we have seen that at that time, as far as the Italian merchants were concerned, economic interests took precedence over the interests of Christendom.

PART FOUR

MYSTICISM AND POLITICS

CHAPTER XIII

THE MONK AND THE SULTAN

The situation in Frankish Syria at the beginning of the thirteenth century no longer resembled anything that had been
known there before. Everything there was paradoxical. "The
kingdom of Jerusalem" was still the phrase used, but Jerusalem in fact was no longer part of the kingdom. On the other
hand, the territory that its king was now called on to administer, although reduced to a narrow strip, formed a base
for reconquest that could have become dangerous for the
Muslims since it consisted of a coastal margin, allowing liberty of access and easy provisioning for the Crusaders. From
this point of view, they found themselves on the whole in a
better position than their predecessors in the eleventh century. Ultimately, the conquest of Cyprus on the one hand
and of Constantinople and the Morea on the other made
possible a whole range of operations that in the previous
century the ill will of the Byzantines prevented, or at least
delayed.

Conditions were therefore radically different from what
they had been during the first hundred years in the existence
of the overseas kingdoms. But in Christendom as well the
situation had changed. It was perturbed by many movements, by currents of economic and social change, but chiefly
by currents of intellectual activity. Among these it was difficult

to choose which one to follow. In matters of religion, it was possible to discern already the split between those who wished to remedy the ills of the Church by working within her and those who sought to work against her. Everyone was to some extent aware that the Church might well be stifled beneath her own wealth—but who was to deal with the problem? Was it to be one of the many heretical sects or members of the mendicant orders? This problem was characteristic of the turmoil of ideas and interests that was agitating the West. Passionate controversies were springing up between the universities; rivalries that soon became embittered grew up between merchant cities, and opposing mental attitudes divided the townspeople and the barons.

This was to be another occasion when the West would see itself most clearly revealed in the East. The new tendencies growing up in the Christian world were to be put to the test there in a quite empirical fashion and perhaps without thought for the consequences of unfinished gestures. This was the implication of certain outstanding events in the history of the Crusades, whose significance was all the greater because they foreshadowed new ways of existence and of action. We shall watch the complete mystic and the complete politician at work in turn. The former is a man who rejects every weapon and every skill and, excluding every human agency, prefers to put his trust in grace alone. The latter looks for nothing but efficiency and brings a total scepticism to bear on an enterprise that previously had been justified only by faith. Finally, combining the mystical and scientific extremes, comes the man who sets patient and methodical preparation to serve his belief.

Two men, wearing tunics of rough homespun belted with rope, were walking quietly through the brush. Any watcher who caught sight of them probably assumed at first that they were lunatics, or renegades, perhaps coming to seek protection in the Muslim ranks—a thing that happened occasionally in those troubled times. The men must be one or the other, for, a little while earlier, it had been proclaimed that by order of the sultan any Christian captured would be beheaded on the spot. Be that as it may, once they were caught, Francis of Assisi and his companion, Brother Illuminato, repeated their surprising request with calm assurance: "We are Christians; take us to your master." They repeated it to such good purpose that, unbelievable though their adventure seems, in the end they were both brought before the sultan of Egypt himself, Malik al-Kamil.

This episode actually took place in Egypt outside the town of Damietta. It was at a time when the organization of the Holy Land was breaking down, along with the moral forces that had brought it into the possession of the Franks.

From a strictly military point of view, however, the events of the year 1218–1219 might have encouraged the Franks, since they spread terror through the Islamic world. John of Brienne, the King of Jerusalem, had decided to carry out the old plan of attacking the Muslim powers in Egypt. When they reached Damietta, a series of lucky raids had given the Franks first the Chain Tower, which defended the passage of the Nile (August 1218), then the Muslim camp (February 1219), and finally the town of Damietta itself (November 1219). This was at the cost of an arduous siege, for the great mercantile city, the key to the whole of Egypt, with its double enceinte, thirty-two huge towers, and a highly perfected system of fortifications, had been thought to be impregnable.

It was, however, from the moral point of view that the situation of the Crusaders was endangered. The author of *L'Histoire d'Héraclès* writes, "The Pope sent two cardinals to the army at Damietta—the Cardinal Robert [of Courson], who was English, and the Cardinal Pelagius, who came from Portugal. Cardinal Robert died, and Pelagius lived, which was a great pity, for he did much evil."

Certain writers have tried without much success to restore the good name of this sinister individual. Pelagius had already distinguished himself by causing the failure of the negotiations between the Greek and Roman churches. He was now to become the evil genius of the expedition that had started so well and that he was to destroy. The Sultan Malik al-Kamil, like his brother, al-Mu'azzam, King of Damascus, was panic stricken to see the Christians set foot in Egypt, and he offered the King of Jerusalem in exchange for Damietta nothing less than the cession of Palestine—an unhoped-for chance that should have been seized immediately. The King, in fact, had the upper hand, but he had been almost ruined by the effort that he had put into the Crusade. While he mobilized most of the available knights, the Sultan al-Mu'azzam increased his deadly raids into Frankish Syria, where his men carried out a methodical devastation of the countryside, burning the houses, cutting down trees, and tearing up the vines.

Cardinal Pelagius refused to listen to the King's advice and saw himself already as the master of Egypt. He acted as an absolute despot and opposed all John of Brienne's counsels, brandishing the threat of excommunication at every turn, until the weary King left Damietta and retired to Acre. For eighteen months the army was immobilized and looked on while the sultan's forces were consolidated. At the same time it provoked a series of reprisals that, as a rule, took the form of the persecution of Syrian and Coptic Christians. One hundred and fifteen churches were destroyed, notably the Cathedral of Saint Mark in Alexandria, heavy taxes were levied, and countless vexations were practiced against these Christians. This continued until Cardinal Pelagius, eternally sure of himself, on his own authority and without even telling John of Brienne, directed an attack against Cairo. It rapidly turned to disaster, and the Franks were then only too happy to give up Damietta in exchange for the liberation of their army, now completely encircled by the Muslim forces. Meanwhile, among the Frankish forces, all sorts of quarrels flourished in this atmosphere of disagreement and depressing inactivity, dividing the Franks from the Italians and setting the latter against the Knights of the Temple and the Hospital.

The incident recalled earlier took place during this time of discord, but well before it had brought the Christians to the edge of disaster. Damietta was taken by assault on November 5, 1219, and in September, during the last phase of the siege by the Crusaders, Saint Francis, accompanied by Brother Illuminato, arrived among them. He resolved to present himself at the sultan's camp and preach the Christian faith to him. Historian James of Vitry thus describes the occasion:

> When the army of the Christians was before Damietta in the land of Egypt, Brother Francis, strong in possession of the buckler of his faith and unafraid . . . marched off to the sultan of Egypt. When the Saracens seized him on the way be said, "I am a Christian. Take me to your master." When they had taken him there, the wild beast was quietened by the sight of the man of God and listened attentively to the sermons about Christ that he preached for several days to him and his followers. Then he began to fear lest, through the power of the preaching, some of his soldiers might be converted to a belief in our Lord and go over to the Christian army. So, with every mark of respect and in complete safety, Brother Francis was brought back to our camp. The sultan said to him at the end, "Pray for me, that God may

deign to show me the law and the faith that are most pleasing to him."

The chronicle of Brother John Eleemosyna adds further details to this story. He suggests among other things that Francis told the sultan that he was willing to submit himself to the judgment of God by undergoing the ordeal by fire:

> It is said that he went before the sultan and that the latter offered him many gifts and precious things. When the servant of God did not wish to take any of them, he said, "Take them and give them to the churches and to the poor Christians." But the servant of Christ, disdaining earthly things, refused, affirming that the Divine Providence looked after the needs of the poor. When the blessed Francis began to preach, he offered to go through the fire with a Saracen priest and thus to prove to him completely that the law of Christ was the one true law. But the sultan said, "Friar, I do not think that any Saracen priest would wish to go through the fire for his faith."

Other chroniclers state that the sultan had a counselor at his side, *un vecchio santo*, who got up and went away when he heard Saint Francis' proposal. The episode has been studied recently by Louis Massignon, who has identified this person. "He was Fahr ai-Din al-Fanisi. I do not think that this ascetic, this disciple of Hallaj (the Muslim mystic), would have withdrawn through fear. He did not accept the ordeal because a man must not tempt God."

The scene inspired Giotto, who painted it in the church of the Santa Croce in Florence. Among the Christians the legend grew up that the sultan was converted before his death, through the efforts of a group of Friars Minor who had been sent to him.

When reduced to its essentials—Saint Francis standing before the sultan of Egypt at the very time when persecutions of the Christians in that country were on the increase—the episode is still sufficiently striking. It has a share in that gleam of golden legend that casts its light over the whole story of the Poor Man of Assisi. Sultan al-Kamil, at a time when feeling against Francis' coreligionists was at its height, was captivated by the gentleness of this little man who had passed unarmed through the no-man's-land that separated him from the opposing camp and who had aspired to come and preach his faith to the very person whom his own side were fighting. The appeal to faith at a time when the appeal to arms alone seemed to command respect—this corresponds exactly to the spirit of mystical poetry that is the familiar atmosphere of the Poverello.

This gesture, the mere presence of Francis at Damietta, indicates a cloud of aspirations that were to take shape as time went on. Saint Francis embodied both the poor man and the knight—the two forces that had set out together in olden times along the road to the Holy Land and had retaken Jerusalem. The chivalrous ideal exercised a great attraction over Saint Francis. He wished to be God's *jongleur*, then God's knight. And, for someone who took the Gospels literally, there is nothing surprising in the magnetism of the land of the Cross.

For him, as for those who had been stirred years before by Pope Urban II's appeal, the taking of the cross had to be understood in a literal sense. But this is where, with his marvelous intuitive mysticism, he opens up a new way, and, if he is always attracted by the idea of sending his Friars to the Holy Land, it is primarily so that they may experience martyrdom. When he heard that five of them, in repeating his own gesture, had been killed by the crowd, he exulted, "Praise

be to Christ! I know now that I have five Friars Minor!"
James of Vitry, who has been quoted already, recalls the early
days of this evangelizing mission:

> The Saracens listen willingly to the Friars Minor when they
> speak of the faith of Christ and the teaching of the Gospels.
> But when their words openly contradict Muhammad, who
> appears in their sermons as a perfidious liar, they strike them
> without respect, and if God did not protect them marvel-
> ously, would almost murder them and drive them from their
> cities.

The attraction that the Holy Land held for the Saint of Assisi
was partly the attraction of the Manger. We aré familiar with
the story of how he reconstructed for the first time the scene
in the stable at Bethlehem for the faithful of Greccio, and
how the devotion for the Holy Child was to go on growing
side by side with that for the Way of the Cross, the latter
becoming particularly important from the fourteenth century onward. This feeling, which was to regenerate so profoundly Christian compassion, sprang from Saint Francis' first
journey to the Holy Land, from the shock of battle and the
tumultuous riots dividing the Christians. It needed this one
outpouring of love, this one act of heroic folly to shatter
forever the original conception of the knight in arms whose
taking of the cross was to be expressed in the reconquest of
Jerusalem. The solutions that the eleventh century had worked
out were no longer acceptable in the thirteenth. From that
time on hints can be caught of the way in which the ideal of
the *militia Christi* was to be entirely reshaped. The first step
toward the inner comprehension of the meaning of the Cross
was taken by Brother Francis, between the two opposing
camps at Damietta.

The Crusaders meanwhile carried on with their own warring concerns without any understanding of the sublime gesture that had been made under their very eyes. Cardinal Pelegius believed at first, and throughout the whole time Francis spent in the sultan's camp, that the little mendicant Friar had renounced Christianity. The attitude of the other prelates can be guessed at from James of Vitry's reservations in his *Histoire orientale* and in his letter written from Damietta in March 1220:

> We have seen the first founder and head of this order whom the others obey as their grand master. He is a simple, unlettered person, beloved of God and man. His name is Brother Francis. . . .
>
> The master of the Friars Minor, who instituted the order, came to our army. Then, burning with the zeal of his faith, he went across to the Saracens' army and, after preaching the word of God to the Saracens for several days, had a great deal of success. The sultan, the King of Egypt, begged him to pray to the Lord that he might choose the religion that was the most pleasing to God. Our cleric, Colin the Englishman, and two more of my companions, Master Michael and Sir Matthew, to whom I had given the charge of the Church of the Holy Cross [at Acre], joined this same order. I had difficulty in keeping back the cantor and Henry and some of the others.

The prelate could not understand the impulse that drove his companions to join the little man in rough homespun. Some lines earlier he notes with ecclesiastical circumspection the fears which the saint inspired in him: "This man seems to me very dangerous, for not only mature men, but also those who are young and unformed and need conventual discipline for some time to mold and prove them, are sent out two by two throughout the world."

This is certainly a properly prudent point of view for a man with a regard for the ways of the Church, but it is too curt a dismissal for the wonders that were to result from the "folly of the Cross". It is a forerunner of the criticisms that are sometimes brought today against the Little Brothers and Little Sisters of Père de Foucauld.

However, Brother Francis' approach was to bear unsuspected fruit. There followed certain events of the same nature that some years earlier no one could have foreseen. First there were the letters which Pope Gregory IX himself sent in 1233 to the sultans of Morocco and Egypt urging them in moving phrases to embrace the Christian faith:

> We are praying as best we can to the Father of Light that he will consider with his habitual goodness the love that is our guide, and that he will listen with pity to our supplications . . . and think us worthy of his mercy. May he open your ears and your minds so that with devoted hearts and humble spirits you may come to us who thirst for grace in this life and glory in the life to come. . . . May he reveal to you his only Son, the one true Light, and may you, when brought into the Christian faith by baptism, be able, by leading a completely new life, to please, as adopted sons, the Lord who desires that his faithful followers shall reign with him in Heaven.

These letters were entrusted by the Pope to the sons of Saint Francis, for he had already planned for them the role of guard of honor for the holy places that was ultimately to be entrusted to them. The age of missions had not yet arrived. It was not until almost the end of the same century that Raymond Lull outlined for the first time a real program of missionary work. But frequent attempts were already being made to effect a complete change in the Crusade, to approach the world of Islam with no other weapons than those of the gospel.

Saint Francis himself had sent two of his Friars, Brother Giles and Brother Eli, to Tunis. Their preaching failed, but it was due more to the hostility of the Italian and Provençal merchants, who feared that their attempt would prove harmful to current commercial treaties, than to that of the Muslims. Further, in 1257, another mendicant, Brother Philip, the provincial of the preaching brothers in the Holy Land, was able to list for this same Gregory IX the results of their work among the recently schismatic Eastern Christians. The Jacobite patriarch had rejoined the Roman faith and become a Dominican. The Maronites of the Lebanon had been restored to the fold. Talks had been started with the Nubians, and many members of the Nestorian Church had announced their intention of reentering the Roman Church. At that time, in fact, preachers were already at work, particularly in Egypt, and the Minorites had reached Aleppo, Damascus, and Baghdad.

CHAPTER XIV

THE CRUSADER WITHOUT FAITH

An unusual Crusader sailed from Brindisi on June 28, 1228. The short bald man who embarked that day with a fairly small army—only fifteen hundred knights and about ten thousand infantrymen—was the head of the Holy Roman Empire, Frederick II of Hohenstaufen. He had united the crown of the King of Jerusalem to his own imperial crown a short time before. But, King and Emperor though he was, Frederick II was nevertheless an outlaw in Christianity, for he had been excommunicated. This was the first time that a Crusader had set off on Crusade against the formal wish of the Pope.

Frederick had taken the cross thirteen years before, on July 25, 1215, the day of his coronation at Aix-la-Chapelle. He had been crowned Emperor with the full support of the Papacy, after Otto of Brunswick had been defeated in battle the year before by the armies of Philip Augustus at Bouvines. Frederick II of Hohenstaufen, who was then King of the Romans, had been brought up by Innocent III as a ward of the Church. But during the past thirteen years he had let no chance go by of disappointing the hopes which the Pope had placed in him and of demonstrating that he intended to continue the traditional policy of the Germanic Emperors of enmity to the priesthood. Through his father, Henry VI, he was the grandson of Barbarossa, and as his father had done, he was to turn his armies against Rome. But through his mother, Constance, he was the heir of the Norman Kings of Sicily, and from the very beginning of his rule, he had shown what importance he attached to his fine Sicilian fiefs. Breaking the promises he had made to Pope Innocent III, he reaffirmed on his son's head, as well as on his own, the union between his possessions in Sicily and in Germany. Meanwhile the sovereign, who displayed an "intelligence without equal", made no secret of a scepticism that scandalized the age. Quite casually he put off from year to year the accomplishment of his Crusader's vow, until in 1227 the Pope, exasperated by his procrastination, excommunicated him.

During these years the contempt that he openly showed for the defense of Christianity in the East had brought about a real catastrophe. At the Lateran Council of 1215 it was decided to send off an expedition that, as we have seen, took Egypt for its objective and resulted in the capture of Damietta in 1219. But it could not succeed, and indeed lacked any purpose, unless Frederick launched against Palestine the parallel attack expected of him. Frederick had dispatched some help, but he himself did not set out, and the offensive mounted after the capture of Damietta ended in disaster. The Crusaders were forced to surrender the town, and in the eight years' truce that was eventually concluded, it was specifically stated that this truce would not be broken except by the arrival in the Holy Land of a crowned King. Clearly, Frederick II was the one who was expected. Pope Honorius III wrote to him, "Does not the very situation of your kingdom mark out you above all others for the struggle for the faith?" For Sicily was becoming more than ever, as the Normans had envisaged, the main base of departure for operations in the East.

The Emperor had not the conscience to feel himself bound by an oath. Yet all the circumstances should have made it easy for him to accomplish it. After the defeat at Damietta, John of Brienne, King of Jerusalem by right of his wife, came to the Pope and the Christian princes to explain why he thought the King of Jerusalem himself should take the lead in future operations and hold all forces gathered for that purpose under his own authority. He argued that the disaster of Damietta had been caused by the unfortunate leadership of the infamous Pelagius, the pontifical legate, who acted without consulting the barons. Taking it all in all, John of Brienne realized the need to put an end to that state of latent anarchy that till then had marked the history of the kingdom of Outre-mer. Their conquests, threatened as they were, could no longer be retained without a solid basis of agreement, which implied the unification of all forces under one leader. Honorius III, replying to this appeal, saw a chance of rousing the personal interest of Frederick II, in whom he still rested his hopes, in the reconquest of the Holy Land. The plan to get him to marry John of Brienne's daughter Isabella, the heiress to the kingdom, was formed at once. Frederick II was quick to welcome this chance to add another crown to those he already possessed and to strengthen the sovereignty over the kingdoms of the East that had been claimed by his predecessors, particularly by Barbarossa. As for John of Brienne, he was dazzled by the prospect of having an Emperor as his son-in-law, and he joined with enthusiasm in the Pope's project. The *Gestes des Chyprois* tells us:

> The marriage was agreed and all things arranged on both sides, with the result that the Emperor fitted out and armed twenty galleys to go to Syria and bring back the lady [Isabella], Queen of Jerusalem.... He ordered knights and

servants to go in these galleys to accompany the said lady, and the Emperor sent costly presents, beautiful jewels to the lady and to her uncles [John and Philip of Ibelin] and to her other relatives. . . . All the barons and knights, the commons and townsmen and the others, prepared wonderful robes and other things in keeping with celebrating such a fine wedding and such a magnificent coronation. And they brought the lady to Tyre, and there she was married and crowned by Simon, archbishop of Tyre.

This marriage, celebrated by proxy, was made between a little princess of fourteen—no older than Juliet—and the Emperor, who had no trace of Romeo about him and a reputation that was already more than disquieting. The chronicle quoted, which was written by Philip of Novara, a brilliant historian and sensitive poet, allows us to share the fears of the young girl, standing sadly among the rejoicing crowds.

And the celebrations lasted for fifteen days with jousts and dances and sermons . . . and when the day of July 8 in the year 1224 arrived, the said Queen went into the galleys that the Emperor had provided for her. At her going, Queen Alice, her sister, the Queen of Cyprus [she was the daughter of Isabella of Jerusalem and Henry of Champagne], and the other ladies who had accompanied her to the shore wept many tears as if they knew well that they would never see her again, and they did not. And, as the said Isabella was leaving, she looked down at the ground and said, "I commend you to God's keeping, sweet Syria, for I shall never see you again." She spoke prophetically, for thus it was.

A brutal violation of promises ended the story. On the very evening when the wedding was celebrated at Brindisi, Frederick II told his father-in-law that he regarded the agreements reached between them as null and void and that he was now taking the crown of the Latin kingdom. John of

Brienne, as Isabella's guardian, had exercised till then a power that, according to the arrangements made with his future son-in-law, should have been left to him until his death.

Two years later the unfortunate little Isabella ended a life that had been filled with tears when, at the age of sixteen, she gave birth to a son, Conrad. According to the chronicles, "This lady lived only a short while in the Emperor's company; it came about that she had a son, and his birth was so difficult that she died. And the child lived and was named Conrad." Frederick had not dealt kindly either with an adolescent's weakness or with a woman's feelings. He had no scruples in being openly unfaithful to her and had kept quite a harem, whose members were mostly Moorish women. This advertisement of his lack of religion, together with his bonds of close friendship with the Muslims, gave rise to a suspicion that he had secretly accepted Islam. The accusation does not seem to be well founded, and it may be that, as René Grousset remarks, "It was the ease of Muslim morals that he appreciated more than anything else in Islam." [1] But a harem is not enough to make a Muslim, and eventually Frederick scandalized Arabs as well as Christians by his total lack of belief.

This thirteenth-century Emperor, who, it has been said, behaved like a Renaissance prince out of the pages of Machiavelli, presents a remarkable figure. Some present-day writers have praised him with the greatest enthusiasm. They have been delighted to recognize in him a forerunner of the "enlightened despot"—sceptical, tolerant, cultured—a sovereign, in short, with "modern" ideas, out of place in the feudal world. But if the acts that marked his reign are examined individually, it becomes necessary to make some corrections

---

[1] René Grousset, *Figures de Proue*, pp. 130–31.

to the picture. He was certainly a man of brilliant intelligence, and he had received a wide education in his Sicilian home. Here, by a tradition going back to the time of the Norman kings, the civilization of the Muslims was welcomed as eagerly as that of the West, and the island benefited from the contributions of both cultures. The claim that he was a scholar seems nevertheless exaggerated. His scientific work is limited to the composition of a treatise on falconry similar to many others written at the time. The breadth of his tolerance and the attraction he felt for Islam were not enough to keep him from beginning his rule with a four-year campaign—a real "war of extermination"[2]— against the Muslims of Sicily. Under the rule of the Normans these people had enjoyed a very real toleration similar to that extended to the Christians living under Muslim authority in Spain, and now they were degraded to the condition of serfs beneath the Christian landowners. Most of them were deported to the Italian mainland, mainly to Lucera, and in 1233 Frederick confiscated the goods of many members of the Italian nobility who had not provided sufficiently large contingents for use against the Muslims.

It was in the well-defined sphere of the Inquisition, more than elsewhere, that the action of this "enlightened" monarch was a decisive factor. The Inquisition was actually set up only between 1231 and 1233, and it was in the famous compilation the *Constitutions of Melfi*, that monument of imperial law, that death was for the first time decreed as the punishment for heretics. Frederick had already, in 1224, laid down that in his Lombard provinces their penalty should be the stake. Needless to say, he was concerned less with the

<hr />

[2] Édouard Jordan, *L'Allemagne et l'Italie aux XIIe et XIIIe siècles*, p. 205.

fight against heresy as such than with its use as a tool of government. In this matter also, Frederick was a forerunner of some of the Renaissance rulers. The Emperor intended to use his own officers to judge the heretics, and in connection with these same *Constitutions of Melfi*, Pope Gregory IX, the Pope of the Inquisition, called Frederick II "the destroyer of public liberty". Nevertheless, the increasing severity of the sentences carried out against those who were persecuted for their faith, punished previously by exile or imprisonment, was to exercise a profound influence on the character of the age.

Frederick II was able to take this action by reviving certain ancient clauses of Roman law and by extending them gradually to cover the whole of the Holy Roman Empire. It seems indeed that the sole passion of this "modern" sovereign was to restore an absolute imperialism on the Roman pattern. It has been said that the *Constitutions of Melfi* are the only product of all the Western Middle Ages that even approximate to the great Roman compilations, by which after all they were directly inspired. René Grousset writes, "From this body of laws emerges the abstract idea of the sovereign and universal Roman state, of which the Emperor was but the universal and sovereign emanation." [3] In 1226 Frederick II had founded the University of Naples as a center for the study of Roman instead of feudal law. From that time on imperial officials were to be trained there. In accordance with the spirit that had inspired its foundation, students were absolutely forbidden to go abroad to study, even though the imperial university was the only one in the realm. By such means it was assured that their minds should be formed in

[3] Grousset, *Figures de Proue*, p. 137.

ways approved by the Emperor. Himself a born jurist, and moreover a jurist on the Roman pattern, he adorned his least phrase with expressions culled from antiquity. In the announcement of his march on Rome in 1240 he proclaimed that he was going "with the cooperation of the Roman people, to raise again in his capital the victorious eagles, the ancient fasces of the empire, and the laurels of triumph". His letters are peppered with such terms as "trophies", "quirites", "capitol", and so on.

Those writers who see in him a personality directly opposed to the feudal and customary way of life have summed him up well. He embodies the irreconcilable opposites of feudal man and legist, of monarchical state and medieval kingship. Even in a physical sense this little man with his bald head and bent back has nothing in common with the knightly ideal personified a little later by Saint Louis.

Nowhere do these opposing forces show themselves better than in the opening acts of Frederick's strange "Crusade", beginning with the scene in Cyprus when the man who had come to claim the crown of Jerusalem met the barons of the kingdom. The story has been told in extraordinarily moving terms by Philip of Novara.

The Emperor disembarked at Limassol in Cyprus, and the first thing he did was to summon John of Ibelin, lord of Beirut, who was acting as regent of the island during the minority of the young King, Henry of Lusignan:

> He sent courteous letters to my lord of Beirut at Nicosia, asking him and requesting him as his dear uncle to come and have a talk with him, and to bring the young King, his own three children, and all his friends. He sent another word to him, which by the grace of God was prophetic, saying that he and his friends and his children should be enriched and

honored by his coming. And so they were, thank God, but it was not the way he wanted it.

John of Ibelin, according to custom, called his council together when he received the letters from the Emperor. Philip says of him, "No lord was ever more dearly loved by his men." John of Ibelin, the ideal of knighthood, had most of the barons of Palestine on his side. Those whom he called to his council at Nicosia begged him to defy the Emperor and to find some pretext for avoiding the meeting. John of Ibelin was anxious to do what seemed best for the interests of Christianity and went nevertheless, with all his "*mesnie*". But Frederick had prepared a real trap for him. Philip of Novara writes:

> That same night, in secret, he had a door made in the wall of a room that led into the garden of the fine house where he was lodged and that had been built in Limassol by my Lord Philip [of Ibelin]. At night, through this false postern, the Emperor secretly let in three thousand armed men, together with sergeants, archers, and seamen, until almost the whole complement of his ships was inside. He hid them in the stables and in the chambers, with the doors closed upon them, until the time for dinner came, when the tables were set and the water poured out.

Meanwhile he had received John of Ibelin and his suite with great ceremony and every appearance of joy. He had even asked that the lords, in honor of the occasion, put off their black mourning clothes, donned for the recent death of Philip of Ibelin, and instead wear scarlet as a sign of rejoicing. At the banquet he made the lord of Beirut and the constable of Cyprus sit beside him. The two sons of John of Ibelin served before him at table, "the one with the cup and the other with the bowl". That is, one acted as cup bearer and the other as carver, according to the custom of the time.

When the meal was almost over and the last course was being served, the men at arms came out of hiding and stationed themselves in front of the doors. The Cypriot barons "said not a word and strove to appear unconcerned". Then the Emperor showed his true colors. To the lord of Beirut he said, "I require two things of you. First, that you hand over the city of Beirut to me, for you have no right to have it or to hold it. Second, that you give me all the sums that have accrued to the bailidom of Cyprus and all that the regality has been worth and has brought in since the death of King Hugh, that is, ten years' revenue, for such is my right according to the custom of Germany." In other words, the Emperor was demanding not only possession of Beirut but also the considerable revenues of the kingdom of Cyprus.

The lord of Beirut remained for a moment speechless: "Sire, you must be making game of me; you are not serious." The Emperor laid his hand on his head and replied, "By this head, that many a time has borne a crown, I shall have my way over the two things I have asked of you, or you will suffer for it."

This brutal demand—not the only one in the history of the German Empire—left the company open-mouthed. But the lord of Beirut pulled himself together, and in front of the silent and dumbfounded assembly he rose and said "loudly and with great composure": "I have and I hold Beirut as my fief by right. It was given to me by Queen Isabella, who was my sister and the rightful heiress of the kingdom of Jerusalem, when the Christians recovered it. Then it was in ruins and in such a state that the Temple and the Hospital and all the barons of Syria refused it. I have strengthened and maintained it through the charity of Christendom and my own toil, and always I have applied and assigned to it all my revenue from Cyprus and elsewhere. If you contend that I hold it wrongfully, I will show you the rights of the matter before the court of the kingdom of Jerusalem. As for your demanding the income of the bailidom of Cyprus, I never had any of it. My brother held the office only for the sake of the Cross and for the work and the government of the kingdom. But Queen Alice, my niece, had the revenues and did with them as she pleased, as she was the one who had the right to the bailidom, according to our usage among ourselves. . . . And you may be sure", he added, "that no fear of death or prison will make me do otherwise unless I am forced to do so by the verdict of a true and loyal court."

"The Emperor was furiously angry", writes Philip of Novara, and swore and threatened and finally said, "Before I crossed the sea I certainly heard a long time ago that your words were fine and courteous and that you were very wise and skillful in speech, but I am going to show you that all your wisdom and shrewdness and all your words will be useless against my strength."

There could not be anything more annoyingly Hunnish than that reply, or anything more "imperial", and, on the whole, more normal coming from someone who intended to reestablish the former absolutism. This was the "divine Augustus" speaking to a baron from the world of saga, and adding weight to his words with the three thousand armed men who guarded the gates. But this was not the end of the scene:

> The lord of Beirut spoke out so firmly that all who were present marveled, and all his friends were seized with fear. He replied in this fashion: "Sire, you have already heard of my courteous speech, and I have indeed often heard of your deeds. When I was making ready to come here my council warned me that you would do as you have done. And I did

not wish to believe it. It was not that I was not suspicious. I came knowing full well how things stood. I would far rather accept prison or death at your hands than allow anyone to say or think that the work of our Lord and the conquest of the Holy Land had been neglected by me or by my family or by the men of the land where I live.... I told my council this when I left Nicosia to come to you. I came away prepared to accept all that might befall me, as I ought to do for love of our Lord who suffered death for our sakes and who will deliver us if it so pleases him. And if he wishes or is pleased to allow us to suffer death or imprisonment, I thank him for it. And I stand fast by him in everything." Then he ceased speaking and sat down.

This was the Christian hero defying the pagan Emperor.

The latter was very angry, frequently changing color, and people eyed the lord of Beirut and growled threats at him. Then the men of religion and other good men tried to reconcile the two, but they found it impossible to get the lord of Beirut to alter anything that he had said he would do. As for the Emperor, he made most strange and perilous requests.

In the end it was decided that they should have recourse to the arbitration of the High Court of Jerusalem. The Emperor demanded John's two sons, Balian and Baldwin, as hostages and had them immediately chained up and thrown into prison, where "they were fastened to an iron cross so that they could not bend their arms or their legs. When night came, other men were put in irons along with them."

As soon as John of Ibelin had withdrawn with his followers, he was urgently pressed by two barons of his court, who suggested, "Sire, go back to the Emperor and take us with you. Each of us will hide a dagger in his breeches, and as soon as we get to him we will kill him, and our men will be

by the gate, armed and on horseback." But, as Philip of Novara tells, the lord of Beirut was extremely angry and threatened to strike them and kill them if they ever suggested such
a thing again. "The whole of Christendom would cry out,
'The traitors of Outre-mer have killed their Lord Emperor.'
And afterward, with him dead and ourselves alive and well,
our right would be turned to wrong, and no one would
believe the truth. He is my overlord. Let him do what he
may; we shall keep our faith and our honor." Upon this,
John of Ibelin left Limassol, and, to quote the chronicler
again, "there was such an outcry at his going that the Emperor, hearing it, was afraid and left the manor house where
he was staying and went to the tower of the Hospital, which
was strong and nearer to his fleet".

This dramatic action had a comic epilogue. After treating
the Ibelin party thus, the Emperor received a visit from the
prince of Antioch, who had come to Cyprus to join forces
with the Crusade. Frederick II instantly demanded of him
an act of faith and homage on behalf of the men of Antioch
and Tripoli similar to that which he had exacted from the
barons of Cyprus. "The prince imagined himself dead and
disinherited. So he pretended to be stricken both ill and dumb,
and constantly cried out, 'Eh, ah, ah.' He continued to do
this until his departure, but as soon as he reached Nephin
(one of his castles) he recovered completely", says the chronicler with some humor. By thus making out that he was mad,
the old prince of Antioch had succeeded in hoaxing the
Emperor.

The Crusade begun under such auspices was to go on in
a fashion quite unlike any of the others. Even if he had brought
with him only a handful of men, Frederick II had carefully
prepared a diplomatic offensive. For some years he had been
in communication with Malik al-Kamil, the sultan of Egypt,

although the first overtures had actually been made by the
sultan and not by Frederick. The Palestinian kingdom was
profiting from the extraordinary circumstance that al-Kamil,
at enmity with his brother al-Mu'azzam, sultan of Damascus, was seeking aid from the Christians. He had sent Fakhr
al-Din, one of his emirs, to the Emperor to get his help against
the Damascenes, who were threatening to let loose against
Egypt the bands of the terrible sultan of the Khwarismian
Turks, who were everywhere feared for their barbarity.

Unfortunately, in the event something happened that occasionally befalls those diplomats who are so clever that they
wreck their own plans. Frederick, convinced that "time was
on his side", continually deferred, as we have seen, his departure for the Crusade. A few years earlier he had thus missed
another valuable opportunity; in 1225 the Georgians, who
were Christians, had offered themselves as allies for the coming Crusade, but in the following year these people, whose
help would have been appreciable, were attacked and beaten
by these same Khwarismians who were now being feared by
the sultan of Egypt. The new delays over the Egyptian proposals were to lead Frederick into remarkable difficulties, for
while all this was going on al-Mu'azzam died (in November
1227). When this happened the sultan of Egypt was no longer so anxious to conclude his treaty with the Emperor, for
he knew he had nothing to fear from the young al-Nisir, the
new sultan of Damascus, who was considerably less formidable than his father. Thus, when in the end Frederick was
driven at last to keep his word and embarked at Brindisi, he
was at the same time in trouble with the Pope, who had
excommunicated him for his delays, and very awkwardly
placed as far as the sultan was concerned. Further, since he
was excommunicated, he could no longer claim help from
the Knights of the Temple or from the other military orders,

and we have seen how his first act was to alienate the Frankish lords, over whom the Ibelins exercised a kind of moral
overlordship. A few Cypriot barons were his only allies.

The friendly relations that he had maintained with the
Muslim world finally enabled Frederick to get himself out of
trouble. He wrote a pleading letter to the Sultan al-Kamil.
In the end, through the mediation of the same emir Fakhr
al-Din, who had the year before (1227) been made a knight
by Frederick II himself and who bore the Emperor's arms
upon his banner, the negotiations resulted in the Treaty of
Jaffa in 1229. There had also been a display of military force
along the coast that had convinced the Sultan of the wisdom
of showing a conciliatory spirit. This demonstration had been
made by the tiny imperial troop, followed at a distance as a
guard against disaster by the Templars and Hospitallers, who
always rode separately to prevent their soldiers associating
with those of an excommunicated man. By the terms of the
treaty al-Kamil handed back to the Christians the three holy
places—Jerusalem, Bethlehem, and Nazareth—and also the
seigneurie of Toron and the lands belonging to Sidon that
had just been partly reconquered by the English and French
Crusaders. Moreover, in order to ensure access to the holy
places by pilgrims, the sultan also ceded a "corridor" running through the posts of Lydda, Ramleh, and Emmaus. It
was also laid down that, though the Franks had recovered
Jerusalem, the Muslims were to retain within the city the
Mosque of Omar and the Mosque al-Aqsa (the former Temple of Solomon), that is, the area of the Haram es-Sherif,
where they could come without hindrance to make their
devotions.

Thus the three towns whose possession was essential to
Christianity were won back without a blow being struck.
Even if the Treaty of Jaffa did not, properly speaking, restore

the kingdom of Jerusalem, it did at least make it possible to envisage an entirely new era for the Christians in the East. From a political point of view, it was a master stroke.

Unfortunately, it turned out that the treaty satisfied no one. The Muslims reproached the sultan for handing over to the "polytheists" the place that they too looked on as a Holy City. The Christians could see only too clearly the weaknesses of the treaty. The Templars were annoyed that their house in Jerusalem had been given to the Muslims, and there was general criticism of the way in which one vital point had been left vague—whether the fortifications of Jerusalem were to be restored. If this was not done, it would be impossible to defend the Holy City, and the treaty would leave it lying open to any sudden attack by the Muslim princes.

This point has remained obscure, even for present-day historians. The Arab chronicles state that the secret clauses in the treaty forbade rebuilding the walls of the town. In fact, however, some restoration work seems to have been at any rate begun. But as early as 1229 certain Saracens living in the district took it upon themselves to demonstrate the weakness of the Treaty of Jaffa on this point. They carried out a raid that claimed some victims among the people of Jerusalem, who had no alternative but to seek refuge in the citadel and await the arrival of help from the Christians.

A final point was that Frederick was an excommunicated man, and he conducted himself in a way that could only alienate sympathy. He was determined to go to Jerusalem, to the Holy City, to be crowned. The ceremony developed along unusual lines. There was no religious celebration. The Emperor walked into the Church of the Holy Sepulchre, took the crown from the high altar, and placed it on his own head. One of his predecessors had done the same thing in Saint

Peter's in Rome, and some centuries later Napoleon was to follow their example in Notre Dame. Hermann of Salza, the grand master of the order of Teutonic Knights, was the single representative of a religious power to stand beside the Emperor. At about this time he accepted from the Hohenstaufen a mission with a political bias. This was the conquest of the Prussian people, a goal far removed from the true intention of the Crusade.

His presence on this occasion was significant for more than one reason. The Teutonic knights had been formed into a military order about the year 1190 with the help of the Hohenstaufen, of whom they showed themselves to be the devoted servants. It was the first time in history that the constitution of a religious order had been thus linked with a particular nationality. Contemporaries were surprised, even scandalized, by this. Foundations of this kind had shared hitherto the international character of Christianity itself. The Hospitallers, who recruited men from every country, were content to group the members of their order, for convenience, into "*langues*", or "tongues", a term that corresponded roughly to the "provinces" to which the mendicant friars were assigned.

On the day following this "secular" coronation, Gerold, the patriarch of Jerusalem, laid the Holy City under his interdict. Frederick in fury went back to Acre, where the first thing he did was to authorize an attack on the house of the Templars and on Chastel Pelerin, which belonged to them. He tried to regulate the government of the kingdom in such a manner that power should remain in the hands of the German barons and the Teutonic order; then he set sail from Acre on May 1, 1229. The tale of this embarkation deserves to be retold in the words of the chronicler of the *Gestes des Chyprois:*

His departure was a shabby affair. The Emperor made the preparations for his passage in secret, and on the first day of May, without telling anyone, he set out before dawn, going through the butchers' quarter to reach his galley. Now, it came about that the butchers in these streets ran after him and pelted him shamefully with tripe and entrails. The lord of Beirut and Messire Odo of Montbeliard heard the tumult, ran to the place, and chased and arrested the men and women who had assaulted him. Then from the shore they called out to him in his galley, commending him to God. The Emperor replied in a low voice, and I do not know whether his words were good or ill . . . And in this way the Emperor left Acre, hated, accursed, and reviled.

There is no doubt, however, that if achievement alone were taken into account, Frederick would have deserved the gratitude of Christendom. But these achievements belonged to a time when men were aware of spiritual values as well as material results, when, to put it in another way, the end did not justify the means. And Frederick's conduct had seemed shameful from beginning to end.

The feudal barons thought it shameful; so did the Christians, and so, on the whole, did the Muslims. It is the Arab historians who, in spite of the numerous demonstrations of friendship that he had lavished on members of their faith, make the most unfavorable comments on the Emperor. One of them writes, "This red-headed man, with his smooth face and short sight, would not have been worth two hundred dirhems[4] in the slave market." Another says, "To judge by his conversation he was an atheist and made game of the Christian

---

[4] The usual currency in the Muslim world. Its normal weight in silver was a little less than three grams. The name, like that of the *dinar*, the *denier*, was derived from the Greek *drachma*.

religion." One might well ask whether the Muslims did not prefer their former enemies, whom they could at least respect, to this friend whom they despised. Frederick's goodwill, which extended to permission to continue the muezzin's call to prayer over the Holy City and to a slap in the face for a priest caught begging near a sanctuary, showed, the Muslims felt, a kind of dilettantism that was far from agreeable to people who were themselves deeply religious.

Generally speaking, the Treaty of Jaffa did not, even in its practical results, produce the hoped-for peace. The Frankish barons could not accept the German overlordship implied in Frederick II's arrangements. He had hardly set sail when, to borrow René Grousset's phrase, the "seeds of civil war" that he had left in the Orient began to bear fruit. The disagreements, latent until now, between the Frankish barons and the followers of the Emperor had been merely worsened by his conduct.

In the years that followed the Westerners were to offer the Muslims the spectacle of internal warfare in the Holy Land, which could have been saved only by the closest unity among them. Cyprus, rather than Acre or Tyre, was the battleground for the struggle between the Ibelins and the Imperialists. In 1243 the last traces of imperial domination were finally destroyed, but in the very next year an attack by the Khwarismian Turks robbed the Christians forever of Jerusalem.

Frederick II lived until 1250. He was again excommunicated by the Pope, then deposed. Gradually he had lost all his supporters and was left alone. He had driven his own son, Henry VII, and Peter de la Vigne, who had been his most trusted counselor, to kill themselves. He had stirred up quarrels and rebellions wherever he went, and his doings were eventually to bring about the ruin of the Hohenstaufen. From a political point of view, none of his work had any permanence except for one outcome that he could not possibly have foreseen—the establishment of Prussia. This was at first a sort of monastic state under the aegis of the Teutonic Knights, who had been turned aside by this conquest from their original vocation, and later a military state, "an army that has a country", according to the popular saying. But the history of Prussia is another story.

CHAPTER XV

THE PERFECT CRUSADER

When Saint Louis in his turn decided to set out on Crusade his first move was to build a port of embarkation. To put it another way, this mystic, whom some people like to imagine lost in prayer, did not do things by halves. Yet such an enterprise was difficult enough to discourage even the boldest. Along the Mediterranean coast the only land that belonged to the kingdom of France was the region of the Petit-Rhône, and here, although some of the waterways in the delta were navigable, there was nothing that could be remotely compared to the excellent anchorage at Marseilles or even to the outer harbor of Lattes, which served Montpellier. In spite of this, a town rose, by the King's will, between the wasteland and the marshes. A witness, questioned fifty years later as to what he had seen there in his childhood, declared that there was "neither tower nor stones" on this barren tract, which belonged to the abbey of Psalmodi. The place was a bay of slack water where a few fishing boats sheltered, until a day in the year 1241 when the construction materials began to arrive, wagonload by wagonload.

A causeway and a bridge were built almost at once between the sea and the cluster of houses at Psalmodi so that traffic could move. At the same time men began work on the splendid foundations of what was to become the Tower of Constance. When the King set sail eight years later, this tower had already risen to its full height and carried a beacon as a guide to mariners. At that point of time, the town too was born. In 1246 the King had had recourse to the classical procedure of the age for attracting inhabitants—he had granted a charter. All the people who came to settle in the new city of Aigues-Mortes not only were to have liberty of person and protection for their goods, but also were to be exempted from many obligations, both military and financial. No tax, toll, or loan could be levied on them; in legal matters they were to answer before the royal judge, and if need arose, the castellan of the Tower, appointed by the King, would ensure the safety of the town. But the inhabitants were to be administered by consuls chosen by themselves, though under the control of the royal provost. They could bring in free of tax the materials needed for building their houses, and later on their personal supplies were to be similarly free of all charges. They could hold a weekly market and, better still, an annual fair where all the merchants enjoyed the King's protection.

The inhabitants of this town were mostly fishermen, paying their dues as in the past to Psalmodi Abbey, but commerce was to bring them new conditions of life. It was not long before these people of Aigues-Mortes claimed the same advantages as those already enjoyed at Acre by other merchants, such as the Venetians, Genoese, and Pisans. This proves that they had attained a certain standard of prosperity at home as well as overseas. Some of them worked at the nearby salt pans of Peccais; others brought part of the neighboring forest of Silve under cultivation and pastured their animals there, although they got little enough return from it. But above all, their livelihood depended on the business of the port. And from this port, on a summer's day in 1248, August 25, the

King embarked with his retinue on the two *nefs, Montjoie* and *Paradis*, that he had chartered.

At that time everyone was well aware that Aiguës-Mortes was "a real miracle of the Crusade", as one of its historians has said.[1] At one stage the inhabitants decided that the name of their city was too mournful and drafted a petition suggesting that it should be called *"Bonne par force"*, "Good through fortitude". This name, which was never used, must be understood with all its medieval overtones. "Good" suggests, as well as its actual meaning, "valorous, courageous, prosperous", while "fortitude" carries all the implications of the Christian virtue of that name.

However that may be, Aignes-Mortes was for more than a century the one French port trading with the East. The town grew quickly, becoming a typical example of the work of the time. The streets were straight, and wide green spaces were left between the houses to allow for family vegetable plots. The church and the town hall stood in the center of the town within a square where the markets were later held. The whole foundation was completed later by ramparts and by a breakwater, still known today as the Peyrade, built of fine bossed stones. Both were constructed in the time of Philip the Bold, the son of Saint Louis. The city was never besieged, so the ramparts have remained undamaged to this day, presenting the most perfect surviving example of thirteenth-century town walls.

The reason Saint Louis was preoccupied with the problem of a port of embarkation to such an extent that he built one for his Crusade was that the sea route, first adopted nearly a hundred years before, had become by this time—the middle

---

[1] Jean Morize, in *Annales du Midi* (Paris: Picard, 1914).

thirteenth century—the normal way of travel for Crusaders. The sea routes, more rapid and less costly, had proved to be the most practical. On the other hand, the Crusaders using them were at the mercy of the shipowners, and from the time of Villehardouin's expedition onward it had become apparent what difficulties the Crusaders could be drawn into by the rapacity of the merchants to whom they were obliged to entrust themselves and their goods. It was probably in order to avoid falling into the power of these people that Saint Louis made sure of his own port at the outset. At the same time he was concerned with gathering a fleet. That implies preparations on such a scale that several dockyards had to be set to work at the same time.

A letter from the grand master of the Hospital, Fulk of Villaret, gives some idea of the scope of these preparations:

> We have had seven galleys made in Catalonia, three at Narbonne, sixteen at Marseilles, twelve at Genoa, together with one *nef* over and above the other large *nef* that we bought there, four at Pisa, six at Venice. And, further, five at Genoa and two at Venice are being armed at this moment and will be ready to go to those regions by next spring or earlier if possible.

Thus the dockyards of six great Mediterranean cities, from Barcelona to Pisa and Venice, were used for the building of his fleet. Every preparation for a Crusade during the course of the thirteenth century had meant more or less the same sort of activity. Although a good many barons were in fact satisfied to hire for the purpose a *nef* for which they drew up a contract with a shipowner, important convoys like those bearing a royal army required that new vessels be specially constructed. And this activity manifested itself on more than one occasion in places other than the Mediterranean. The count of Saint Pol, for instance, had ships built for him at

Inverness in Scotland. For his first Crusade Saint Louis gave half the orders for his ships to Genoa and half to Marseilles. In the latter town he had twenty *nefs* built at a price of thirteen hundred silver marks each. The town also agreed to provide him with ten galleys as escort vessels. At Genoa he signed a contract for twelve *nefs* at thirteen hundred marks and for four rather smaller ones at twelve hundred marks, as well as for the three ships intended for himself and his retinue—the *Saint-Esprit*, the *Paradis*, and the *Montjoie*.

The preparations did not end there. Two years earlier, that is, in 1246, the King began to gather together the supplies he considered essential for his troops. He used as his base the island of Cyprus, which had been the usual base for the Crusaders since 1191, when Richard Cœur de Lion had seized it in a moment of bad temper.

Joinville, who took part in this Crusade at the King's side, writes in his excellent account:

> In Cyprus we found great abundance of the King's provisions, namely, his cellars, his treasures, and his granaries. For the King's cellars, his men had piled up, in the middle of the fields beside the seashore, huge masses of wine barrels, which they had purchased during the two years before the King arrived. They had stacked them one on top of the other in such a fashion that when a man stood before them they looked like barns. The men had heaped the wheat and barley in the middle of the fields, and they seemed like mountains when one looked at them, for the grain had been left open to the weather for so long that it had sprouted on the top, and there seemed to be nothing there but green grass. But when the time came to take the grain to Egypt, the top layer with the green shoots was lifted off, and the condition of the wheat and barley was found to be as good as when they were first piled there.

Joinville himself had made an arrangement with John, the lord of Apremont, who was sailing at the same time as six other knights, to hire a vessel at Marseilles. He embarked there in August 1248 and has described the occasion in memorable fashion:

> In the month of August we embarked in our vessels at Marseilles.
>
> The same day that we embarked in our vessels, the gates of the ship were opened, and all the horses that we were taking overseas were led within. Then the gates were closed and well sealed, as a cask is sealed, since the whole of the gateway is below water when the ship is at sea.
>
> When the horses were on board, our master mariner shouted to his sailors at the prow, "Is your work all done?" And they replied, "Yes, sir. The clerics and priests may come now." As soon as they had come, he called to them, "Sing, in the name of God!" And they cried with one voice, "*Veni, Creator Spiritus.*" And the master shouted to the sailors, "Make sail, in the name of God!" And so they did.
>
> The wind quickly filled the sails, and we lost sight of land. We could see nothing but sky and water, and each day the wind carried us farther from the country where we were born.
>
> And I tell you that the man who dares put himself into such danger when he is responsible for the welfare of others or when he is in mortal sin is a feckless madman. For when he lies down to sleep in the evening, he does not know whether or not he will find himself at the bottom of the sea in the morning.

Someone has called Saint Louis' Crusade an "engineers' Crusade". When it is considered in detail it becomes clear that the technical problems did not end with the preparations. The royal army included bridge builders who were capable of setting up across the Bahr as-Saghir, one of the branches of the Nile, a barrage that served both as a causeway for the soldiers and as a dam to deflect the waters back toward the junction with the Nile. The work was carried out under a hail of Egyptian arrows, since the sultan's forces were massed on the south bank of the river. A sort of covered gallery called a "cat" was erected beforehand to protect the men as they worked; this was itself protected by a battery of eighteen catapults directed by Master Joscelin of Cournault, the engineer. Unfortunately, the Saracens, based upon Mansourah, had greater resources at their disposal. They replied to the eighteen catapults with even stronger siege engines. These hurled "stones, darts, arrows, arbalest quarrels, and Greek fire, all of which flew as thick as a storm of rain". As protection against the Greek fire, the labourers stretched the hides of newly slaughtered oxen over the "cat".

Joinville writes, "The manner of Greek fire was thus: it came straight forward as big as a barrel of verjuice, and the tail of flame that issued out of it was fully as big as a large sword. . . . It made such a noise as it came that it seemed like a thunderbolt; it looked like a dragon flying through the air. It cast such a great light that in the midst of the army a man could see as well as if it were day."

He adds that Saint Louis, who was present with the laborers working on the embankment, fell to his knees every time he saw the fire coming and cried, "O, good Lord God, look after my people!" In command on the opposite bank was the emir Fakhr al-Din, the man who had been knighted by Frederick II, so that the Crusaders had for opponent a knight who bore the Emperor's arms upon his banner.

Along with this carefulness in technical preparation, Saint Louis' Crusade displayed a spirit whose purity of purpose was equal to that of the first Crusaders. From the point of view of general organization, the acts and achievements of the King and his entourage bear witness to the most remarkable aspects of feudalism. The astonishing speech made by the King to his company when their ships were in sight of Damietta is preserved for us in a letter from a man who was a member of the expedition. It reveals the spirit in which the King approached the problems of leadership:

> My faithful friends, we shall be invincible as long as we are undivided in our love. It is surely with divine permission that we have been brought as far as this, to disembark in a powerfully protected land. I am not the King of France; I am not the Holy Church. It is all of you who are these two things. I am but a man whose life will end like that of other men when God wills it. Whatever can happen to us will be for our good. If we are conquered, we shall be martyrs; if we triumph, the glory of God and of France, and of all Christendom, will be exalted.

He said also, "This is God's cause; we shall conquer for Christ's sake. He will triumph in us; he will give the glory, the honor, the blessing, not to us, but to his name."

This magnificent definition restores to the word *Crusade* its real meaning of a people's pilgrimage. Never for one instant did Saint Louis deny by his actions this conception of power, the very opposite of the monarchical ideal. Throughout the period of the Crusade, councils of war were frequent, and no decision was ever taken until it had first been discussed by the barons and, moreover, discussed with absolute freedom.

The most dramatic of these councils took place when the Crusaders met after the royal defeat. Most of them thought it would be best to return to the West without delay, while others, including Joinville, considered that it was their duty to stay in Outre-mer to help and console the Christians who remained there and to free the prisoners. It is worth recalling Joinville's summary of his motives:

> I would willingly have gone from the country but for my recollection of the words of Monseigneur de Bourlement, my first cousin, when I was leaving to go overseas : "You are going now to Outre-mer", he said. "Be mindful of the way in which you return, for no knight, rich or poor, can return without disgrace if he leaves in the hands of the Saracens the little people of our Lord in whose company he set out."

Joinville had to overcome his own feelings in order to remain faithful to these remembered words. At the council of war he found himself almost alone in opposition to the other barons, whose sole thought was to get back to their own land. The King had previously explained the situation to them:

> My lords, Madame the Queen, my mother, has begged me as strongly as she can to go back to France, for my kingdom is in great peril. I have neither peace nor truce with the King of England. Those people of this country with whom I have spoken have told me that if I go, this land will be lost. They will all follow me to Acre, for none of them will dare to stay here with so few men. So take careful thought, I do beg of you, and since this is an important matter, I will give you until a week today to bring me the reply that seems best to you.

The barons consulted together during that week, and they chose Guy Mauvoisin to speak for them before the King. When the formal council was held, he made his speech:

> Sire, your brothers and the barons who are here have considered your position and have perceived that you cannot remain in this land with honor to yourself and to your king-

dom, for of all the knights who came in your company, and of whom you led 2,800 into Cyprus, not one hundred remain in this town. Therefore they advise you to go back to France and to collect troops and money with which you may quickly return to this land to take vengeance on the enemies of God who held you in prison.

In a similar way, the King sought the advice of each of the knights. He paid particular attention to the count of Jaffa, the holder of one of the frontier fortresses and also of one of the ports through which the country could be entered. The count refused to reply because, he said, "My castle is on the frontier, and if I advise the King to stay, people will think I do so for my own benefit."

But when pressed to give his opinion as a native of the country with special knowledge of the situation, the count of Jaffa added that if the King "indeed wished to continue the campaign for one year, he would achieve great honor". Joinville was the fourteenth to give his advice and said that he was in agreement with the count of Jaffa. Immediately he was taken up: "How is it possible for the King to campaign with the few troops that he has?" Joinville was nettled and went on to explain more clearly:

Sire, it is said (though I do not know if it is true) that the King has not yet spent his own treasure, but only that of the clergy. Let him now lay out his money and send out for knights from Morea and overseas. When men hear it said that the King is giving lavishly, knights will come to him from everywhere, and he will continue the campaign for a year if God pleases. And in this time he will be able to free the poor prisoners who have been taken in the service of God and himself and who will never be released if the King goes away.

The assembly was silenced. "Everyone there had some close friends in prison," says Joinville, "so nobody replied, and they all began to weep." Messire William of Beaumont, marshal of France, was the first to speak, and he proclaimed that the seneschal had spoken well. Another member of the Beaumont family, his uncle, was furious. Joinville says that he was desperately anxious to get back to France. "He shouted at him most abusively and said to him, 'You filthy scum, what are you saying? Sit down at once!' The King was obliged to intervene: 'Messire John, you are behaving badly. Let him speak.' 'Indeed, Sire, and I will not.' The marshal was forced to keep quiet, and "nobody else spoke up for me," continues Joinville, "except the lord of Châtenay." Then the King brought the discussion to an end: "My lords, I have heard you well, and I shall tell you a week today what I shall be pleased to do."

At the next meeting the King let them know what he had decided:

> The barons of this land tell me that if I go, the kingdom of Jerusalem is lost, as no one will dare to remain here afterward. I have thus decided that I cannot desert the kingdom of Jerusalem, which I came to guard and protect. I have therefore resolved that I will stay here for a time. So I say to you, my lords, here present, and to all other knights who wish to stay with me, come and speak to me boldly, and I will give you so much that the fault will not lie with me but with you if you do not want to remain.

There were many who heard these words, adds Joinville, and who were astounded, and there were many who wept.

They were left completely free to make up their own minds, and several of them, including the King's two brothers, Alphonse of Poitiers and Charles of Anjou, reembarked. But the rest of the Crusade remained in the Holy Land.

This interpretation of government, which was that of all medieval Kings, did not exclude acts of authority when these were required. Joinville's account tells later how the King severely punished six young men, the sons of Paris burghers, who had endangered their traveling companions. The fleet had put in at Pantellaria, and they had wandered off on the island, delaying the rest of the convoy. He had them sent to the boat where murderers and thieves were held and, in spite of the stormy weather, left them there until the next port of call, not allowing himself to be swayed by any entreaties, not even those of the Queen.

All the acts and achievements reported by Joinville, who made himself the chronicler of the Crusade as well as of the King, give us a remarkable impression of the spirit that animated it. There was a profound sense of mutual responsibility, and one of his stories illustrates the importance the Crusaders attached to the feeling of love that they felt should rule them. In Joinville's own escort there were "two most valiant knights, Monseigneur Villain of Verfey and Monseigneur Guy of Dammartin", and he says that they hated each other bitterly. They had, as he puts it, "seized each other by the hair in Morea", and "nothing would induce them to make peace." But when the fleet neared Damietta and they were about to give battle to the Saracens, Joinville swore upon the relics that "we would not go in to land with their hatred." In the end the two knights were moved to mutual pardon and "embraced each other".

To this profound sense of the love that ought to preside over Christian relationships must be added the binding force of a promise. No menaces were sufficient to extort from captured Crusaders the surrender of the fortresses on which depended the safety of the kingdom in the Holy Land. These prisoners were condemned to terrible suffering and threatened with death, yet to all the attempts of their enemies, who offered them freedom in exchange for the castles, they returned answers full of the most tranquil heroism. The following dialogue is an example. It took place in "a courtyard surrounded by a mud wall where the knights were held captive":

> These were the words: "Messires, the sultan has sent us to you [the sultan of Egypt's interpreters were speaking] to find out if you would like to be set free?" The count [Peter of Brittany, Joinville's companion] replied, "Yes." "And what would you give the sultan in return for your freedom?" "As much as we could do and bear within reason", he replied. The others asked, "Would you give us for your freedom some of the castles of the barons of Outre-mer?" The count replied that he had no power over these castles as they were held from the Emperor of Germany, who was still alive. They then asked whether we would hand over the castles belonging *to* the Temple or to the Hospital in exchange for our freedom. And the count replied that that could not be. When the castellans were appointed they were made to swear on the relics that they would not surrender any one of these castles for the release of a man's body [that is, even in exchange for their freedom]. Then they replied that we did not seem particularly anxious to be released and that they would go away and send some men to us who would play with us with their swords, as they had done with others. And then they departed.

Now that happened after a terrible scene in which the Saracens had lined up a group of prisoners and asked each one, "Will you deny your faith?" And, says Joinville, "those who would not abjure were made to go to one side, and their heads were cut off. Those who abjured were moved to the other side."

There were similar scenes when the sultan's envoys talked to the King:

> The sultan's counselors questioned the King, as they had questioned the others, to find out if the King would promise to hand over to them some of the castles belonging to the Temple or to the Hospital, or the castles belonging to the Kings of the country. And God so willed it that the King gave them the same answer that we had done. And they threatened him, saying that if he were not willing to do this, they would torture him. To their threats the King replied that he was their prisoner and they could do what they would with him. When they realized that they could not beat down the good King with their threats, they returned to him and asked him how much money he would give the sultan and with that whether he would hand back Damietta. The King then replied that if the sultan wished to accept a reasonable sum of money from him, he would ask the Queen to pay it for their release. And they said to him, "Why are you unwilling to pledge your own word?" The King told them that he did not know whether the Queen would be willing to do it, because she was the boss.

Once Saint Louis was free, he ordered the counting out of the bezants that he had promised to hand over to the sultan as his ransom. Someone gave him to understand that ten thousand bezants too few had been counted without the Saracens noticing. At once the King grew angry and gave the order to recount the money in front of him, to ensure that exact payment of the whole sum had been made. Thus do the actions of these knights bring to life the outlook of the age.

We catch a vivid impression of this mentality with its greatness and its weaknesses, from Joinville's account. Setting aside for a moment the historical interest of an eyewitness' report of things as they happened, we can appreciate too its great importance as a human document. It gives us those typical reactions that form the secret of an age; it is stripped of all literary effect and unconscious of the impression of nobility which becomes apparent. Its heroes seem to be familiar with the spiritual world to a degree that makes their outlook profoundly different from our own, and different too from any outlook that might have seemed normal in a less fervent or less generous atmosphere. There was, above all, that calm affirmation of their faith in the worst possible circumstances that earned them the admiration of the Muslims themselves.

One day, after Joinville and his companions had refused to hand over their fortresses and when they were hourly expecting to be killed, "a great crowd of young Saracens girded with swords rushed into our tent. They brought with them a white-haired man of great age who asked us if it was true that we believed in a God who had been taken for our sakes, wounded, put to death for us, and on the third day had risen again. And we answered yes."

In such circumstances that "yes" might have cost them their lives. But the exchange was to have a different ending from the one they expected: "For the old man told us that we ought not to be perturbed if we had suffered persecution for him, for he said, 'You have not yet died for him, although he has died for you. If he had the power to raise himself, you may be sure that he will deliver you when it pleases him.' "

"Then," says Joinville, "he went away, and all the young men went with him. I was very happy at this, for I had been convinced that they had come to cut off our heads."

There is another moving story that reveals how much more the spiritual world in which they believed mattered to them than the visible world. It tells of something that happened in the Christian camp at a time when the army, badly placed, was held up by Saracens on the bank of the Nile and was ravaged by an epidemic. Joinville himself fell ill:

Because of the wounds that I had . . . the sickness took me in the mouth and the legs. I had a high fever and a cold in the head so heavy that the cold ran out of my head through my nostrils. Because of these maladies I went to bed, sick, at mid-Lent, and my priest sang Mass for me at my bedside in my tent. And he had the same sickness [typhus, which was raging in the camp]. It came about that he fainted when he reached the Consecration. When I saw that he was about to fall, I jumped out of bed, just as I was in my shirt, and, without putting on my shoes, I took him in my arms and told him to make the Sacrament slowly and softly and said that I would not leave him until he had quite finished. He came back to his senses and made his Sacrament. And he completed the singing of the Mass and afterward never sang it again.

This episode, which nears sublimity in its quiet telling, is characteristic of the age. Our reaction if a priest fainted at the altar would be to fetch a doctor. For a thirteenth-century knight the important thing was that the Mass should be said and the sacrifice consummated.

One last story reveals how far the miraculous seemed to be part of daily life and also gives us some idea of the atmosphere of the time. One of the secrets of the age, and perhaps the fundamental reason for its dynamism, was the belief that the natural play of cause and effect, even when most inescapable, could always be modified by divine intervention. The chronicler has this to say:

Another adventure befell us while we were at sea. Monseigneur Dragonet, a wealthy man from Provence, was lying in bed one morning on his ship, which was a good league ahead of ours. He called his squire and told him, "Go and shut that opening, for the sun is shining on my face."

The squire realized that he could not shut the opening unless he climbed over the side of the vessel. So he climbed over the side of the vessel. As he was going to shut the opening, his foot slipped, and he fell into the water. Now this ship was small, and it had no dinghy, and it was not long before the squire was far away.

Those of us who were in the King's ship saw him, and we thought it was a tub or a cask since the boy who had fallen into the water made no effort to help himself. One of the King's galleys picked him up and brought him to our ship, and he explained how this thing had befallen him. I asked how it was that he did not try to help himself to be saved, by swimming or in some other way. He replied that there was no need or necessity to try to help himself, for as soon as he began to fall he recommended himself to our Lady, and she upheld him by the shoulders from the time that he fell until he was picked up by the galley. In honor of this miracle I had it pictured in my chapel at Joinville and also in the stained glass windows at Blécourt.

These few anecdotes are enough to show how in the Crusade of Saint Louis we may perceive in the King and his companions a mysticism that is identical with that of chivalry in its purest form. The hero of the time is characterized by fidelity to his promise, by a feeling for solidarity, and by this kind of familiar dealing with another world. We may look at his carved figure on the famous retable of the *Knight's Communion* behind the great doorway of Rheims Cathedral. There is no doubt that among men such beings stand out as does a sculpture of this quality in the realm of art. It is indeed thus that we imagine a civilization that was able to conceive of the cathedrals and the quest of the Grail. Moreover, these people brought to the service of their mysticism technical skills that themselves represented a peak of achievement in their age.

A Crusade begun under such auspices could not fail to achieve success. It started in fact with what was perhaps the most brilliant feat of arms in all the history of the kingdoms of Outre-mer—the capture of Damietta. This was the city before which so many armies had wasted away some decades before. Now it was taken as the men came from their ships, at a single bound. The story is to be found in a letter from John of Beaumont, the chamberlain of France, to the grand baker, Geoffrey of La Chapelle:

I doubt if so great a fleet as that which sailed from the port of Nicosia in Cyprus with the Lord King had ever before been assembled in convoy. On the Friday after Trinity [June 4] there were actually more than 120 of the large *nefs*, while the smaller vessels were put at 800 or over. So we reached the port of Damietta happy and joyous for the most part. Early on Saturday morning, when they had heard the hours and divine service, the Lord King, his brothers, the barons, the knights, and the others, infantry as well as ballista men, climbed down from the big *nefs* into the smaller vessels, galleys and other boats, to come near the shore and set foot on land. When they neared the land, the boats were unable to come right in to the shore, so the Lord King, the barons, the knights, and all the others threw themselves joyfully and without any fear breast-deep into the water. They carried lances and ballistas and like courageous athletes of God bravely faced the enemies of the Cross. The armed Saracens waited on horseback upon the shore to keep us from the land and to protect it according to their strength, and they defended themselves by discharging arrows and thick javelins at our forces. But our men, whose bows were directed with greater strength by our Lord, scrambled ashore and attacked the Saracens, and with the help of God they swiftly seized the victory and put the infidel Saracens to flight. Most of them were killed or mortally wounded. By the grace of God few or none of our men were killed. Thus the Saracens by their confusion were forced to leave the seashore, and God put such fear in their hearts that the next day, Sunday, they all, great and small, began to flee. They set fire to the houses and to the gates of the city in various places, and by the smoke that arose we were made aware of the flight and the rout of the Saracens.

But this extraordinary success was not to be followed up. Or, rather, its results were to be slowly whittled away by a series of circumstances that again throw a light on the mentality of Saint Louis' companions, and disclose the other side of the medal. For the knighthood of France was to commit here its own particular fault, one that was to be committed more and more frequently as time went on and that gradually brought the whole kingdom of France to the verge of ruin. The Crusade of Saint Louis was thus rather like a summit from which the downward slope could be seen as well as the path by which the ascent had been made. It was the King's own brother, Robert of Artois, who best personified this fault among the knights, the fault that led them to prefer the isolated exploit rather than the cooperation that had been their strength, to substitute recklessness for gallantry, and to indulge their taste for panache at the expense of true glory.

Robert of Artois was the evil genius of the expedition. It was his insistence that decided the King, against the advice of the barons, to carry out an attack against Babylon (Cairo), instead of first besieging Alexandria, whose port would have made it easier to take in fresh stores for the army. As well as this, the King's prearranged order of battle was quickly disorganized by his brother's foolish temerity. Joinville, describing the beginning of the battle of Mansourah, writes, "The

Templars had been ordered to form the advance guard." In order to join battle, the army had first of all to ford the Bahr As-Saghir, which was of necessity a lengthy business and one that compelled the soldiers to wait for a time until their forces could be regrouped. The count of Artois was to command the second group and follow the Templars.

> Now, as soon as the count of Artois had crossed the river, he and all his men threw themselves upon the Turks, who were fleeing before them. The Templars sent to tell him that he had offered them a gross insult, since although he should have followed them, he had gone before, and they asked him to allow them to pass through into the front rank as had been ordered by the King.

But Robert of Artois firmly intended to acquire for himself all the honors of the day. He spurred his horse, and the Templars, flicked on the raw, chased after him, each one "driving in his spurs and striving to outdo the others".

Thus the whole battle order was thrown into confusion. The advance guard was involved in a madly imprudent melee inside the city of Mansourah, while the bulk of the army was still on the other side of the river. The move condemned the whole enterprise to complete disaster, although for a little while the attack made by Robert of Artois seemed likely to succeed. It caused panic in the Egyptian camp, where no one was aware of the maneuver of the royal army. The emir Fakhr al-Din was surprised in his bath and had barely time to leap on his horse before he was struck dead by a blow from a lance. If Robert of Artois had had the good sense to stop then, he would indeed have been credited with all the honors of the battle. At exactly that moment there arrived ten knights sent by his brother with an order for him to halt. He did not want to listen to them and, refusing to obey, continued his charge, sweeping madly on into the streets of Mansourah. Then the renowned Baibars, whose name was soon to be celebrated in Frankish as well as Eastern annals, came up at the head of the Mameluke cavalry. The handful of French knights, together with the Templars who followed them, were swept away, and the narrow lanes of the town became so many ambushes in which they were slaughtered like wild animals caught in a trap. Presently the victorious Mamelukes themselves began to attack, and the larger part of the royal force had to endure their assault under the most unfavorable conditions, before they were able to form up in battle order, and while the rearguard, under the duke of Burgundy, was still on the other side of the river. A moment of indiscipline had thus wiped out the effect of the crossing, which was quite unexpected by the Egyptian army, and brought the Crusade to the verge of defeat.

"One might say that we would all have been lost that day, if the King had not ransomed us with his own person", writes Joinville. It was, in fact, only the King's personal bravery that saved the situation. The chronicler sketches for us this memorable portrait of him in that moment: "And the King came up with all his array with much shouting and a great noise of trumpets and drums, and he halted upon a high road. I have never seen a knight who looked so fine, for he towered head and shoulders above his men, with a golden helmet on his head and a sword of Germany in his hand."

"Physical valor and spiritual goodness", the ideal of chivalry, is here perfectly personified in the King. That day, it was in actual fact his personal courage as much as his deeds that saved the situation.

Everything so admirably described on this page by the chronicler is worth remembering—so too is the good humor displayed by the King and his companions in these desperate circumstances. Joinville tells us how at that moment, which was perhaps the most critical of all, he recalled that a little bridge over a stream had been left unguarded and suggested to the count of Soissons that they should make it their business to defend it. "If we leave it alone, the Turks will advance upon the King by that way, and if our men are assailed on both sides, they may well be overcome." So the pair of them defended the bridge and held it heroically, attacked sometimes by streams of Greek fire, at other times by showers of Saracen arrows. (The seneschal calmly relates, "I was wounded only five times by their arrows.") At the same time he adds, "The good count of Soissons, in the straits that we were in, joked with me, saying, 'Seneschal, let us make this rabble howl. By God's hat (that was his oath), we'll talk of this day when we are with the ladies!'"

In the end victory remained with the royal army. It was dearly bought, but it allowed them to stay in Mansourah. It was then that these heroic beings became human again, displaying those sensitive feelings that we find so moving in the sober account given in Joinville's chronicle. He tells what happened when he again came into the King's presence:

> I had his helmet taken off and gave him my iron hat so that he could get some air. Then there came up to him Brother Henry of Rosnay, the provost of the hospital, who had crossed the river, and he kissed his armed hand. The King asked if he had heard any news of his brother, the count of Artois; and he told him that he had indeed some news, for he was certain that the count of Artois was in paradise. . . . And the King replied that God should be worshipped in all he brought to him, and great tears fell from his eyes.

The army had been decimated by its hard-won victory, and now, under the implacable sky, it fell a victim to disease.

Saint Louis himself became ill with typhus. The army tried desperately to cling to its position—a most critical one, between two branches of the Nile—but, blockaded by a flotilla that intercepted every food convoy passing between Damietta and the Christian camp, it was forced at last to capitulate. We have already seen how Queen Margaret of Provence had maintained the defense of Damietta and saved a situation that was more than difficult. Now the city was handed over in exchange for the King. A ransom of five hundred thousand *livres tournois* was promised for the release of the army.

But this was not the end of the Crusade of Saint Louis. He was released from prison in Egypt on May 8, 1250, and for four years more he stayed in Syria, where his activity was the reverse of that of Frederick II. He unified where the other had divided, and strengthened where he had enfeebled. He restored discipline in Frankish Syria, where anarchy was the evil to be most feared; he inflicted public humiliation on the grand master of the Templars, who had followed a policy opposed to his own; and he reconciled the principality of Antioch with the Armenians of Cilicia. Moreover, he fostered the old alliance with the notorious Assassins, sending to the Old Man of the Mountain as a present "many jewels, lengths of crimson cloth, cups of gold and silver", while the latter, not to be outdone in politeness, presented him with a crystal elephant and a splendid set of chessmen. Finally the King sent as a delegate to the Mongols the Franciscan friar William of Rubruck, to whom we owe a detailed account of that hitherto unknown race.

Such defeats befalling a Crusade that seemed bound to succeed—a Crusade of saints and heroes as well as of engineers—apparently suggested some discouraging conclusions to its contemporaries: How was it that the exploits of his knights had not been sanctified by the blessing of our Lord?

The conclusions which the King himself drew can be found in Joinville's account:

> During the return voyage, after the King and his family had almost been lost in a tempest, he was talking to his seneschal and said to him, "Seneschal, God just now showed us part of his power. One of those little winds, so small that we hardly know what to call it, almost drowned the King of France, his children, his wife, and his men. Now," he said, quoting Saint Anselm, "these are the threats of our Lord. The saint says, 'O Lord God, why do you threaten us? For if you threaten us, it is neither to your benefit nor to your advantage. If you had lost us all, you would not be any the poorer, and if you had gained us all, you would not be any the richer. Hence' the saint argues, 'we can see that these threats that God makes toward us are not made in order to increase his profit or to defend himself from harm; instead, on account of the great love that he bears for us, God is awakening us by his threats to see clearly our shortcomings and put away that which displeases him.' Now," said the King, "let us do likewise, and we shall do wisely."

Historians have, in fact, noticed the change that came over the King after his Crusade. His life was already an example to all; now he began to lead an increasingly chastened existence. His regard for justice and charity was revealed in every action, from the Treaty of Paris of 1259 whereby he handed over part of his lands to the King of England, "to engender love between my children and yours since they are cousins-german", to the famous anecdotes of the oak of Vincennes or his sensational almsgiving, which, according to Joinville, aroused protests among his courtiers. To these he replied, "I prefer that any excess in my great expenditure be poured out in alms rather than in ostentation or in the world's empty glory." It does appear that, whatever may have been the reasons given for his second Crusade, it was actually an offertory on his part, a sacrifice similar to that which half a century later was to be made by Raymond Lull in the same land of Africa. At the time when the King took the cross, Joinville tells us, "his weakness was so great that he allowed me to carry him in my arms from the Hotel of the Count of Auxerre to the Greyfriars, where I took my leave of him." The King was ill when he embarked, and he fell an immediate victim to the plague that was raging in the Tunis district.

Two moving items from his last voyage have been preserved. One is his will, which was dictated off the coast of Sardinia, and the other is the codicil, added a few days before his death, which replaced among his testamentary executors two of the barons who had already died of the sickness that was taking hold on him. The return journey became a real Way of the Cross for his escort, for it was marked by the deaths of eight members of his family. One thing survives as its testimony—the *montjoie*[2] that is the only remaining fragment of those that Philip the Bold erected at every place where he rested when he carried his father's body on his shoulders from Notre Dame in Paris to the royal abbey of Saint Denis. It stands today in the little square of Saint Denis, in the Place de l'Hôtel-de-Ville, on the right hand side looking toward the church.

---

[2] A small shelter, with an altar and a cross. The word was used originally for a cairn of stones heaped up as a sign of victory; a light was usually left burning there at night, and the name was also given to the lamps that flickered before the statuettes placed at street corners or set in a recess in the houses, as is still done in Italian towns. It is well known that the word was for a long time the battle cry of the French.

In the same way as the Christians revered Saladin, the Saracens revered this King who had come twice to fight against them. Even today the site of his tomb near Tunis, Sidi-bou-Saïd—the tomb of the saint—is venerated by the African peoples, and in the same way that Saladin was supposed to have become a Christian, it is said that in that place lie the remains of a great Frankish King who accepted the Muslim faith. These parallel tributes are evidence of the glory that the radiance of these men—a radiance both heroic and saintly—won for them among the enemy.

PART FIVE

THE END OF THE WORLD

CHAPTER XVI

THE LAST ACT

The last years in the existence of Frankish Syria form a kind of preface to the events that were to take place later in the West. All the elements that in France in the fourteenth and fifteenth centuries were to mark the breakdown of a society and the near collapse of a kingdom can already be discerned there. External war was certainly one of these factors, but even more important were internal divisions, and that deep-seated disorder that was undermining French knighthood—a taste for display and for needless gallantry, a fundamental frivolity, in short, that was the exact negation of the chivalrous ideal. Robert of Artois at Mansourah provided the first example of the aberrations that were gradually to prove as deadly to the whole of medieval society as they had been to the Crusade of Saint Louis.

Saint Louis' stay in Syria had restored the unity, and particularly the moral unity, of the Christians, but, to maintain it, nothing less than the presence of a saint was required. Two years after he left, street fighting broke out between the Genoese and Venetian merchants. The episode was called the War of Saint Sabas, because possession of the church of that name, situated between districts belonging to the two nationalities, was its pretext. These rivalries between merchants determined to secure a monopoly for their own goods ended in dividing the Syrian barons into two factions. The Venetians succeeded in attracting to their cause the Ibelin family and the Templars, while the Lord of Tyre, Philip of Montfort, and the Hospitallers upheld the Genoese. Thus for two years Acre was torn by what amounted to a civil war. It was the first war to be fought for economic reasons, and as such it was therefore a forerunner of the war that was to divide Western Christendom for more than a hundred years. Later, the Pisans and the Genoese took part in fresh commercial wars on the seas of Syria and involved in them the lords of Tripoli and those of Gibelet, who were of Genoese ancestry. This state of affairs was strangely mingled with a taste for luxury, a passion for pleasure, that was also characteristic of Western knighthood in its decay. These "Oriental" courts reached the peak of their glory in the festivities and banquets provided for the coronation of King Henry II of Cyprus on August 15, 1286. It was the occasion for brilliant tournaments, as the chronicler Gerard of Montreal tells:

> They held holiday for fifteen days in a part of Acre called the Hospice of the Hospital of Saint John, where there was a very large palace. There had not been such fine festivities for a hundred years, or such rejoicing and such tourneys. They imitated the Round Table and the Queen of Femininity— that is, the knights dressed as ladies and jousted together. Next they pretended to be the young nuns who were with the monks and jousted against each other. And they played at being Lancelot, Tristan, and Palamede, and many other such delectable and pleasant games.

Yet, all the same, the young man who was crowned in the midst of such extravagant tournaments was an epileptic.

On the Muslim side as well, the war took on another aspect as the Mameluke Turks revealed, this time in startling fashion, the bravery that had earned them the admiration even of the Frankish chroniclers since the beginning of the drama. It is true that they were greatly helped by the political mistakes of their adversaries, some of whom had no hesitation in allying themselves with the Mamelukes of Egypt against the Mongols, who were causing an unexpected diversion just at this time. It was thanks to this that in 1260 Sultan Baibars drove Kitbuga's Mongol army, which had entered the country at Aleppo, back into Persia, and was thus able to bring into being the alliance, often attempted but never successful, between Egypt and Muslim Syria.

Sultan Baibars had performed his first feats of arms against Saint Louis at the Battle of Mansourah. This Turk from Russia had been born in the Crimea and possessed a violent disposition. As René Grousset has remarked, "some of the blood in his veins was the same as that which later produced Ivan the Terrible and Peter the Great." He had acquired some Mongol customs, including a taste for *koumis*, the fermented milk of mares, which he drank all the more heavily since, as a strict Muslim, he touched no wine and banned its sale throughout his states. A series of murders had brought him to the throne of Egypt, and now this prodigious soldier led the Mamelukes in an assault on the Frankish fortresses, which fell one after the other. In the three years between 1265 and 1268, Caesarea, Arsuf, Saphet, Jaffa, and Beaufort were forced to surrender to him, and he began the siege of Antioch. This ended with the capitulation of the most beautiful stronghold in northern Syria, the impregnable city that had cost the men of the First Crusade so much in blood and toil.

A man like Baibars could comprehend war only in its most unsparing aspect. His letter to Bohemond VI, the count of Tripoli, reported by several Arab chroniclers, leaves no possible doubt about the way in which he understood its operations:

You cannot have forgotten our last expedition against Tripoli ... how the churches were swept from the face of the earth, how wheels ran over the sites of buildings, how great heaps of corpses were piled like cliffs at the edge of the sea, how men were killed and children taken into slavery, how freemen became bond, how the trees were cut down until only enough remained to provide wood for our engines ... how we pillaged your riches and those of your subjects, including women, children, and beasts of burden; how those of our soldiers who had no family suddenly found themselves possessed of wives and children, how the poor became rich, how the servant became master, and the foot soldier found a horse.

He goes on to describe episodes from the recent siege of Antioch:

Ah! if you had seen your knights crushed beneath the horses' hooves, your city of Antioch laid open to the violence of pillage and a prey for every man, your treasures shared out by the hundredweight, four ladies of the city sold for one gold coin! If you had seen the churches and the crosses overthrown, the leaves of the Holy Gospels scattered, the tombs of the patriarchs broken underfoot! If you had seen your enemies the Muslims trampling over tabernacle and altar, sacrificing the men of religion, deacon, priest, and patriarch! If you had seen your palaces going up in flames, the dead devoured by the fires of this world before being burned in the next, your castles and their dependencies destroyed, the Church of Saint Paul tumbled in ruins from top to bottom!

It is hard to understand why the Franks, faced with an enemy of this caliber, lacked the sense to patch up their discords and halt the mad round of their tournaments. William of Beaujeu, the grand master of the temple, warned them continually, only to be told by some of the barons to "stop playing at bogeyman with all that talk of war". But all the same, he himself took no steps to end the rivalries between the temple and the hospital of Saint John.

It was not until the very last moment, when catastrophe was upon them, that all these scattered forces finally joined together and played their part for the last time in a heroic but useless exploit. On Thursday, April 5, 1291, the Sultan Al-Ashraf, who had just succeeded to the throne of Egypt, began the siege of Acre. It may be recalled that this was a reprisal for an act of savagery committed by newly arrived Italian Crusaders against the unfortunate Syrian merchants who frequented the bazaar of the city. Acre was the last place remaining in the hands of the Franks since the Sultan Qalawun had seized Tripoli on April 26, 1289. The besieging army comprised 60,000 horsemen and 160,000 infantry. Within the town there were 14,000 foot soldiers and only 800 knights. The place sheltered altogether about 35,000 inhabitants.

The vicissitudes of the siege have been reported by an eyewitness, known as the Templar of Tyre, whose story was rewritten about 1325 by a certain Gerard of Montreal:

> The sultan set up his tents and pavilions very close together, and they stretched from Toron toward Samaria, so that the whole plain was covered with them. The sultan's tent, which was called *dehliz*, was pitched higher up, on a little hill, where the Templars had a fine tower with gardens and vineyards.... For eight days they remained before Acre without moving ... and at the end of these eight days they erected and bedded down their siege engines, which were capable of throwing stones weighing a *quintar*.[1]

[1] The *quintar* was an Italian measure, roughly equivalent to 150 pounds.

The sultan had powerful "artillery" at his disposal. He had four huge mangonels and set up one against each of the principal towers of the city. The siege began with the investiture of the one that was called the Accursed Tower.

> They had all their horsemen armed, mounted on armored horses, from one end of the city to the other. . . . In the end they came up to the edge of the moat, each horseman carrying a log on the shoulders of his horse, and they threw them from behind the shelter of their shields and the heap became like a wall, so that no engine could have done anything against it.

The besieged attempted several desperate sorties, particularly when the Accursed Tower collapsed, making a breach in the immense curtain wall. But it was all in vain.

While this was happening, the King of Cyprus, Henry of Lusignan, came ashore in the city. He swiftly summed up the situation and at once sent two messengers to the sultan. The latter awaited them, according to the chroniclers, "in a small pavilion". "Have you brought me the keys of the city?" The messengers tried to make other terms with him, but the sultan would listen to nothing. "Go away, then. I shall not make you any other [proposition]."

So the siege continued.

> The Saracens beside the Tower of the King made little canvas bags filled with sand, and every horseman carried a bag on the shoulders of his beast and threw it down to the Saracens who were stationed there. When night fell, these men took the bags and laid them on the stones, leveling them like a pavement, and the next day, Wednesday, at Vespers they crossed over the bags and captured the aforesaid Tower.

Then followed the entry of the Saracens into the city:

I tell you it was horrible to see, for ladies, townswomen, nuns, and other lesser folk rushed through the streets, their children in their arms, weeping and distraught, and fled to the harbor to save themselves from death. When the Saracens came across them, one would take the mother and the other the child, and they bore them from place to place, and they separated one from the other . . . and often a woman was taken away and her suckling infant was thrown to the ground and trampled to death by the horses. And ladies who were great with child were so stifled in the crowd that they died as they stood, and the life they bore within their bodies died with them. . . . I tell you also that the Saracens set fire to the siege engines and the barriers, so that the flames lit up all the land.

William of Beaujeu, the grand master of the temple, who personified the resistance of the city, died in the midst of the slaughter:

And when he felt himself mortally wounded he made as if to go away, and it was thought that he wished to flee, and his standard bearer . . . came up and went before him, and then all his men followed him. And as he went thus, some twenty Crusaders from the valley of Spoleto came up to him, saying, "Ah! for God's sake, sir, do not leave us, for the city will soon be lost." And he replied in a loud voice, so that all heard him, "Lords, I can do no more, for I am dying. See the wound." And then we saw the arrow piercing his body. And as he spoke, he threw the dart to the ground, and twisted his neck, and began to fall from his horse. But some of his men jumped from their horses and held him up. Then they lifted him down from his horse and laid him on a wide, long shield which they found thrown down there.

Peter of Sevrey, the marshal of the temple, took command after William of Beaujeu's death. To him is due the honor of the last stand in the Templar's ward, where more than ten thousand men and women had taken refuge. The ward was a high, strong tower, "and it was beside the sea, standing as big as a castle . . . and it was so near the sea that the waves broke against it." The knights collected all they could in the way of boats and embarked in them as many of the civil population as they would hold, "and when all these vessels made sail, all at the one time, those Templars who were gathered there shouted with a great cry, and the vessels got under way and went to Cyprus, and the good people who had put themselves under the protection of the temple were saved."

For ten days more the knights held out in the last tower of Acre.

> The temple held out for ten days, and the sultan asked those who were there if they would surrender . . . and they sent to tell him that they would surrender if he would give them safe conduct wherever they wished to go. And the sultan agreed to this and sent to the temple an emir who led four thousand horsemen into the temple. They saw many men and many people, and they wished to take the women who pleased them, to dishonor them. The Christians would not allow this and seized their arms and rushed upon the Saracens and killed and massacred them all, so that none escaped alive, and they made up their minds to defend themselves until death.

They could not, in fact, have had any doubt about the outcome of the battle, which had been launched by that one final gesture of chivalry, made in order to defend the women who had fallen into the hands of the conquerors.

The struggle began again.

> The sultan was extremely angry but showed nothing of it. He sent again saying that he was aware that his men had

been killed as a result of their own folly and insults and that he bore no ill feeling against the Templars for it, and that they could come out with certainty and confidence. The marshal of the temple, who was a straightforward man of great integrity ... accepted the sultan's word and went out toward him, leaving some wounded brothers behind in the tower. As soon as the sultan had the marshal and the Templars in his power he had the brothers and all the men beheaded.

This barbaric act, in defiance of a pledge, was the overture to the third and final episode of the battle:

When those brothers within the tower who were not so sick that they could not help themselves heard that the marshal and the others had been beheaded, they looked to their defenses. Then the Saracens began to mine the tower, and they dug beneath it and shored it up. And those within the tower surrendered, and the Saracens went inside, and there were then so many people within the tower that the props that held it up gave way. And the stones came down, and those brothers of the Temple and the Saracens who were within were killed, and in its fall the tower collapsed upon the street and crushed more than two thousand Turks on horseback.

And in this manner the city of Acre was taken, on Friday, May 18, and the house of the temple fell ten days later, in the way which I have set down.

CHAPTER XVII

THE PLANNER AND THE SAINT

The sculptured doorway of the church of Saint Andrew at Acre was henceforward to adorn the Al-Ashraf mosque, built in Cairo in honor of the conqueror of Acre. The remnants of the population of the kingdom of Jerusalem fled as refugees to Cyprus, where, a hundred years later, Cypriot ladies still wore mourning for the Holy Land. At Constantinople, the Turkish menace grew daily more threatening, while the Greek territories were fought over, piece by piece, by the Franks.

But in Europe there had never before been so much talk of a Crusade. The reconquest of the lost kingdom was, even more persistently than in the past, the object of all discussions, the preoccupation of Kings and peoples alike. For more than two centuries there had been very few princes or barons who had not decided to take the cross, hardly any sovereigns and not a single Pope who had not taken steps to prepare for the reconquest of the Latin kingdoms. In the fourteenth century a certain Philip of Mézières devoted his whole life to a Crusade that never took place, since it ended as soon as it began in the disaster of Nicopolis. Even in the projects of Richelieu dreams of a "Crusade" can be discerned. Plans laid for the "next" Crusade form a whole literature in themselves. It would be tedious to list them all, but some at least are worth recalling, if not for their practical interest, at least for the personalities of their authors.

The Armenian prince Hethoum, known to his contemporaries as Hayton, took orders and spent several years in a Premonstratensian abbey near Poitiers, a fact which serves, incidentally, to demonstrate the real interpenetration of the Eastern and Western worlds at the end of the thirteenth century. In 1307 he wrote a treatise entitled *La Fleur des histoires de la terre d'Orient.* He recommended a Crusade in two phases. A preliminary operation, aimed at clearing the coast of the enemy, with Tripoli and Aleppo as its objectives, should be based on the island of Cyprus and the kingdom of Lesser Armenia. The main expedition (which he called "the General Voyage") could follow one of three routes—that through north Africa toward Egypt and Syria, or that via the Hellespont and Asia Minor, or, finally, the sea route. In the years following, throughout all the numberless crusading projects of the fourteenth century, these three routes were the ones most often recommended.

The same year—the year in which he was taken into custody—James of Molay, the grand master of the temple, had also written a memorandum on the reconquest of the Holy Land. He suggested landing in Armenia. A fleet of ten galleys would sweep the seas to allow the bulk of the expedition, also traveling by sea, to gain a foothold. According to his calculations, a force of twelve to fifteen thousand knights would be required, with ten times as many infantrymen.

It was, however, among the close followers of Philip the Fair that the plans for a Crusade aroused particular interest. The famous jurist Nogaret, the great enemy of the Templars, and the King's right-hand man, drafted one plan, and the lawyer Peter Dubois, at exactly the same time as the two

THE END OF THE WORLD

writers just mentioned, drew up his *De Recuperatione Terrae Sanctae* (Concerning the Recovery of the Holy Land).

None of the concrete detail given by Hethoum or James of Molay can be found in either of these works. Nogaret was concerned almost entirely with the financing of the expedition. He believed that the Templars were responsible for the defeats in the Holy Land (he prepared his accusation along these lines when they were brought to judgment a short time afterward). To his mind the important thing was to confiscate their revenues and to bring together in France those of the other military orders; also a tax should be levied on the possessions of the clergy. Once he had set out these two requirements, he followed them with a few remarks, entirely lacking in practical detail, on the project of reconquest.

Peter Dubois produced a work of very different scope. Modern historians may hesitate to see this lawyer, a native of Coutances, in the active role of royal counselor that was once attributed to him, but it must be admitted that the whole future policy of Philip the Fair is sketched out in the *De Recuperatione*. This may be direct influence or pure chance, but it is nevertheless an interesting fact.

For the lawyer of Coutances, as much as for the keeper of the seals, the main thing was the financing of the expedition, a concern characteristic both of the bourgeois and of the administrator. His plans were far-reaching. It was necessary first of all to abolish the temporal power of the Pope and to confiscate the possessions of unenclosed monasteries. The Templars in particular were aimed at here. The order was to be abolished and its wealth handed over to the King of France. Further, Peter Dubois advocated for the clergy in general certain measures that have been fairly described as "modern" in spirit—they were to be allowed to marry, and schools for girls would take the place of the convents of teaching nuns. The girls would receive a training that would fit them to be the wives of future colonists.

For it was now the intention to establish colonies in the Holy Land. The future colonists were to get an education that would include the Oriental languages and less Latin. As far as the Crusade was concerned, Peter Dubois hardly mentioned technical details—he was, after all, a mere lawyer and had left Coutances, the town of his birth, only to go to Paris for his studies. He could not imagine for the Crusaders any route other than the ancient land route, across the Alps and through Hungary, that Godfrey of Bouillon and his followers had traveled. That, however, did not prevent him from elaborating in his mind the outlines of the future army. He thought of it as a Roman army, divided into centuries and cohorts, and under the command of one man. Nothing could have been in greater contrast to the old concept of feudalism, in which every lord brought his *bataille*, his men at arms, recruited and equipped by himself. Classical Rome, the Rome of the legions, the generals, and the universal empire, haunted the minds of the lawyers and gradually, generation by generation, colored men's thought as well as their customs. Were not the dreams of Peter Dubois brought to life in the person of Napoleon on the day when he stood upon the banks of the Nile?

But if, meanwhile, the projects for Crusades remained somewhat nebulous, they provided the opportunity for this lawyer, who was, like all those of his time, devoted body and soul to the cult of the state, to indulge in grandiose dreams. He imagined a sort of council general of the European peoples gathered together to ensure the peace of Europe—surely a forerunner of the League of Nations and U.N. But this council was to be established under the aegis of the King of France, who was intended for the role of universal monarch and would revive ancient Rome. His brother, Charles of Valois, could marry the heiress of the Latin Emperors of Constantinople; he would be given help to reconquer her domains, and sovereignty over the Latin East would thus complete the domination of Europe, which the King of France would achieve by forcing the Pope to give up to him his temporal power, which he would then administer, bearing the title of senator of Rome. In this way the double empire, that of the East and that of the West, was to be restored. The property of the Church was to be realized, and in return a pension paid to the clergy. Moreover, France, once in possession of the power of the Holy See, would become the natural overlord of those states, such as England, Sicily, Aragon, and distant Hungary, that had committed themselves to the throne of Saint Peter. After this, it would still be necessary to obtain mastery of the Holy Roman Empire and Castile, but that consideration hardly bothered the lawyer, who imagined that it could be achieved by means of a few easily negotiated treaties.

Even if the crusading idea got a little lost among all the others, it still remains true that Peter Dubois' work foreshadows the main lines of the policies of Philip the Fair. The lawyer was certainly actively concerned in them, for at the time of the Templars' arrest he wrote various articles, such as the false petition from the people to the King protesting at the Pope's slowness in proceeding against them. Again, there was his treatise that asserted that the King of France was the true champion of the faith and that developed the idea that the ruler had the right to punish heretics.

In fact in his writings plans for Crusades were little more than a pretext for the elaboration of plans for a universal monarchy along Roman lines.

At the same time that this master planner was spinning a web of bright prospects, soon to be dispelled by harsh reality when France, for a time, became the vassal of England, another man who also had a plan for a Crusade was traveling through Europe.

Raymond Lull was one of the most extraordinary geniuses ever produced by humanity. He was so unusual that even today his reputation is that of a magician or an illuminate, which is far removed from the meaning of the title bestowed on him of *Doctor illuminatus* (the Inspired Doctor). The works that have been attributed to him number 4,000, yet the 328 that are definitely his still represent a surprising achievement. He is known today chiefly as a poet and mystic, but, like that of many contemplatives, particularly in the Middle Ages, his life exhibited a most astonishing activity. He was not concerned with writing alone, but was also in contact with the most important people of the day and traveled incessantly throughout Europe and North Africa.

Yet probably no one suspected the incredible destiny that awaited the young Raymond when as a page at the court of Don James of Majorca he was becoming a proficient horseman and practicing archery with his companions. Certainly no one thought of it when, at the age of twenty-three or twenty-four, he married the lovely and well-born Doña Blanca Picany. Everyday life was for him an affair of display, nobility, and beauty, thrown into relief by the pleasures of the mind (for he was a gifted poet and wrote with facility) and those of the flesh, to which he gave himself with the same ardor that he brought to everything. One story tells of him pursuing a woman with his attentions even into a church. He himself wrote later, "From the age of manhood, when I first became conscious of the vanity of the world, I began to do evil, and I entered into sin, unmindful of the glory of God, pursuing only the way of the flesh."

One day, when he was about thirty, the father of two children by his marriage with Blanca, he was engaged in writing a poem to his current lady love, a beauty a little too virtuous for his liking. He raised his eyes and saw towering on his right a great Christ crowned with thorns, nailed hand and foot to the Cross. Raymond was transfixed with astonishment. After a moment the vision disappeared. But next day, when he returned to the interrupted poem, it came again—a great Christ in agony, bleeding and tormented, like those that the Catalan artists were to be inspired by the devotion of future ages to paint. "Five times Christ crucified appeared to me, that I might be mindful of him and begin to love him."

After the vision had appeared for the fifth time, Raymond spent a whole night weeping and in prayer. In the morning he went to confess himself, heard Mass, and resolved from that moment to consecrate his life to the suffering Christ by going to convert the infidels and to end it in the "crimson robe of martyrdom". He saw quite clearly the general plan of his work, but he hesitated for some time over the choice of method. No one at that time could imagine the infidels being converted by any other means than a Crusade.

> I watch the worldly knights setting off overseas, to the Holy Land, thinking to themselves that they can retake it by force of arms, and in the end they all wear themselves out without achieving their aim. And the thought comes to me that this conquest cannot be accomplished except in the way that you, Lord, with your apostles, accomplished it, that is, through love, prayer, and the shedding of tears. Therefore let holy and religious knights set out, let them fortify themselves with the sign of the Cross, let them be filled with the grace of the

Holy Spirit, let them go to preach the truth of the Passion to the infidels, and let them do for love of you what you did for love of them. And then they may be sure that if they risk martyrdom for love of you, you will grant them in full that which they wish to accomplish for the glory of your name.

Arms could conquer the Holy Land, but to conquer the souls of the infidels different methods were required. It was necessary to preach the truth to them, so that they should know it; it was necessary to preach it to them in their own tongue, so that they should understand it; and so that they should love it, it was necessary to point out to them the way of love "through the laying down of one's own life".

When he had reached this point in his meditations, Raymond offered to God, through prayer, the threefold project that had taken shape in his mind: the writing of books, the founding of colleges to teach Oriental languages, and finally the offering of his own life in confirmation of the doctrine preached by the shedding of blood.

This happened in 1265. From that time on Raymond Lull's life was to take a completely new direction. The mystic began by spending seven months in setting his temporal affairs in order, demonstrating that solid common sense that he was to show all his life. He himself could live henceforth only for God, but he had to provide for the daily life of Blanca, his wife, and Dominic and Madeleine, his two children. So he set aside the money needed for their maintenance. The feast-day of Saint Francis of Assisi, instituted thirty years before, was drawing near. When the day came, Raymond went to church, and in the sermon heard how Francis had espoused Lady Poverty. This struck him so deeply that he decided he himself would espouse Lady Valor. He returned home and distributed to the poor the money that he had set aside for his own use; then, bidding farewell to his wife and children, he left Majorca.

He is to be found next traveling as a pilgrim along the roads of Europe. He certainly visited Montserrat, and perhaps Rocamadour, and even Jerusalem.

In any case, a year or two later, he had returned to Barcelona, where he had a decisive meeting with Saint Raymond of Peñafort.

Saint Raymond was at that time a fine old man of ninety—he was a centenarian before he died—who radiated an amazing efficacity of holiness. He too was both a mystic and a man of action and had in many spheres greatly influenced his own times. This influence had extended from canon law, which he had been the first to codify in a systematic manner, to the most active possible form of charity—the redemption of prisoners by, if necessary, taking their place. This was the aim of the Order of Mercy, which he had founded, together with Saint Peter Nolasco, in 1223, and which, between that date and the time of the French Revolution, achieved the liberation of six hundred thousand captives.[1]

Nowadays those who follow the system of the English week[2] should spare a grateful thought occasionally for Saint Raymond, the patron saint of leisure, who brought it into

[1] H. Daniel-Rops, *Cathedral and Crusade: Studies of the Medieval Church, 1050–1350*, trans. John Warrington (New York: E. P. Dutton, 1957), p. 258.

[2] It might be better to call it the "medieval week", for it had been retained in England, where, generally speaking, the customs of medieval life have been more faithfully preserved than in France, and from there has been brought back to the continent. In the Middle Ages it was the custom to take a holiday on Saturdays and on the days before feastdays, from the time of Vespers, which was between two and four o'clock in the afternoon according to the season of the year.

being. The thirteenth century was brimming with activities that the church feared might become excessive and throw people out of balance by keeping them from the peaceful fulfillment of their Christian duties. It was the influence of Saint Raymond also that led to the disappearance of the custom of trial by battle. He has been called "the confessor of Kings and Popes, the eminent minister of the sacrament of penitence". He was general of the Dominican order and chaplain to Pope Gregory IX: he was also a personal friend of King James I of Majorca and had devoted part of his long life to an attempt to approach Islam by those peaceful means that he advocated in all things. He inspired Saint Thomas to write the *Summa contra Gentiles*, a work on Muslim doctrine. He managed to establish a link of friendship with the sultan of Tunis, and in that town in the year 1256 he personally baptized two thousand Saracens.

It was probably on his advice that Raymond Lull went back to Majorca and began a long period of study. Saint Raymond of Peñafort had emphasized to him the necessity of being well armed spiritually and intellectually so that he could reply to the arguments of the Saracens, while at the same time teaching them by his example. So Raymond Lull threw himself with his usual vigor into the study of Latin and Arabic. A disturbing incident took place at this time. To assist in his study of Arabic, Raymond had bought a Saracen slave, of whom there were a number in Majorca, where the population was half Muslim. He was an educated youth, and Raymond treated him as a friend. After a few months Raymond began to argue with him in order to guide him toward conversion, but he had barely mentioned the name of Christ when the slave began to pour out blasphemies and abuse. Raymond was furious and struck him in the face. They carried on with their work as before, but a few days after the

incident, when they were studying together, the slave snatched
out a dagger that had been hidden under his burnous and
struck several blows at Raymond, who succeeded in freeing
himself and called for help. The slave was overpowered and
imprisoned, but Raymond refused to allow him to be punished by death. The episode threw him into perplexity; he
began to doubt whether, in actual fact, it would be possible
to convert the Muslims by mild and evangelical means. Perhaps after all it might be better to continue the course that
had been followed for two centuries and first conquer their
lands before trying to lead them to Christ.

When he had recovered from his wounds he went to
the prison, still obsessed with the same problem. He found
that the slave had killed himself that very morning. This
was a tragic conclusion. In human terms, there was no
solution.

Raymond had no other recourse than his faith. His whole
life was to be both an act of faith obstinately persevered with
in spite of all setbacks and a battle against the impossible. He
continued his studies for nine years. At the end of that time
he not only had a thorough knowledge of Latin and Arabic,
but had also written two books. One of these, *The Art of
Contemplation* (*Llibre de Contemplació en Déu*), written partly
in Arabic and then translated into Catalan, comprised no less
than seven volumes of 366 chapters (three thousand pages, a
million words). The great passion that dominated the whole
of Raymond Lull's life was there explained in full, and this
one book contained in outline all the ideas that he was afterward to put into practice.

The conversion of the Saracens, at whatever cost, was his
central theme. "Once the Saracens are converted, the conversion of the rest of the world will be but a small matter."
Priests must be sent to them now, not soldiers:

Since, Lord, the Christians are not at peace with the Saracens, they dare not, when they are among them, discuss matters of faith. But if there is peace between them, the Christians will be able to direct the Saracens into the way of truth and to enlighten them, by the grace of the Holy Spirit and the true reasons that are signified in the perfection of its attributes.

He certainly anticipated, at some time, a reconquest by arms of the Holy Land, and even put forward various practical ideas for it. He thought of using Rhodes and Malta as bases and also of completing the reconquest of Spain as a preliminary step, in order to neutralize more easily the coastal districts of North Africa. He advocated above all something that no one else in his day had considered: the dispatch of a corps of doctors, medical orderlies, and technicians, who would be able to serve the native population as well as the army itself, whose strength was all too frequently sapped more by the rigors of the climate than by battle.

Yet this account of an armed Crusade, quite different though it was from those that had so far taken place, occupies only a small part of his book. He considered that to cling to the idea of a Crusade was merely to persist in using the answers of a previous age, to apply an outworn formula to a problem that was being continually renewed. Instead, events ought always to find Christians in the state of preparedness recommended by their Master: "Like unto men that wait", "let your loins be girded about and your lamps burning". The peaceful Crusade, "not by the sword but by the sermon", was the new idea which he developed with fiery logic and a clear-cut sense of concrete realities.

The Pope and the bishops would need to send a great number of priests to the infidels, even if the parishes of the West had to go short, for "one must shout louder to those

who are far off than to those who are nearby". These priests
would need instruction in the faith of the Saracens, a subject
on which Lull makes some penetrating remarks: "The Saracens seek truth through the senses, according to nature;
they must learn to seek it intellectually and spiritually, with
intellectual and spiritual eyes, making use of the mirror of
understanding, according to the course of uncreated nature."

The priests should not be afraid to enter into discussion
with them. The timidity that held back some of them was an
inconceivable lack of faith:

> How can a Catholic fear an argument with an unbeliever?
> For inasmuch as you by your glory have overthrown the er-
> ror and falsity of demons ... it would be a small thing for
> you to confound the false opinions and the errors of unbe-
> lievers. . . . These timid Christians, who hesitate to join bat-
> tle with the enemy, have lost the perfect confidence in the
> aid and power of God that they ought to have.

From the practical point of view, a sum of money would
have to be set aside from the income of the Church and put
permanently at the disposal of the men sent out to the infidels. It would also be necessary to choose a cardinal to be
responsible for each area where the gospel was to be preached.

When in 1622 Pope Gregory XV, by his Bull *Inscrutabili
Divinae*, set up the Sacred Congregation of Propaganda, he
turned the vow of the Inspired Doctor into a reality. The
vast missionary organization that in the seventeenth century
began to carry the gospel to every part of the known world
sprang from the seed sown at the end of the thirteenth century when Raymond Lull made a gift of himself in the extravagant gamble to which he was committed.

However, some of his other projects did not take so long
to accomplish. Since the early days of his conversion he had

had it in mind to make use of his friendship with Don James to attain his end. On the accession of James II of Majorca in 1276, Raymond was at Montpellier, where, with royal assistance, he founded the college of Miramar. Here thirteen friars, destined for the mission to Islam, were to receive special training and, in particular, to study Arabic. The King donated five hundred florins a year for the upkeep of the foundation, which continued in being until 1282.

Meanwhile Raymond, having completed his studies, had returned for a time to the life of a contemplative. On Mount Randa in Majorca is still pointed out a grotto where the holy man is supposed to have lived as a hermit. An oddly twisted variety of mastic tree, different from others in the district, grows there. Tradition has it that it springs from a thicket where, after a night of ecstatic contemplation, Arabic, Greek, Hebrew, and Chaldean characters were shaped in the curls of the moss: it is *mata escrita*.

At the time when the establishment of the first college brought one of his vows to fulfillment, Raymond was busy finding an administrator for the property which he had left for his wife. This act signified that from henceforward he intended to consecrate himself irrevocably to the great plan he had derived from the vision of Christ crucified. In 1277 he journeyed to Rome to obtain from the Sovereign Pontiff permission to establish other colleges like Miramar. It was too late to gain audience with John XXI, who would probably have listened to him, for the Crusade had been the main preoccupation of this Pope, who had even attempted to establish friendly relations with Abaga, the Mongol khan. But perhaps Raymond Lull was not entirely ignorant of the decision of the next Pope, Nicholas III, to send five Franciscans under the direction of Gerard de Prato to preach in Persia and China.

It was a time when a great deal of attention was being given to the "Tartars", whose invasion threatened the Muslim world and thus created a diversion which was in the Westerners' favor. Saint Louis had sent the Franciscan William of Rubruck to them as an ambassador. Better than anyone, Raymond understood the benefit which would result from their conversion, and he wrote *Le Livre du Tartare et du Chrétien*: "What a terrible thing it will be if the Mongols embrace the faith of the Saracens or the Jews!"

It was also during this period that he wrote his masterpieces: *Plant de la Nostra Dona Santa Maria*, in which, recalling his achievements as a courtly poet, he addresses his "sounds of love" to the Virgin; *Blanquerna*, in which there are many autobiographical passages; *Felix*; and above all the unforgettable *Libro de Amigo y Amado*.

We see him next returning to visit the Pope. Then, furnished with a letter from Honorius IV, he journeyed to Paris and tried to revive his project for a school of Oriental languages, and to interest the chancellor of the university on its behalf. He even obtained an interview with Philip the Fair. It must have been an odd tête-à-tête, this conversation between the ardent Catalan and the icy monarch, a man whose mystery has not really been penetrated by any historian. Raymond Lull, who expressed himself so freely in his writing, never mentioned the interview.

A new hope came with the accession of Nicholas IV in 1287, for he was the first Franciscan to become Pope. Raymond had always felt himself attracted to the sons of Saint Francis and had recently been present at their chapter general at Montpellier, at which he had been able to put forward his ideas to a sympathetic audience. Nicholas IV seems, in fact, to have received him well. He was the Pope who later sent to China John of Monte Corvino, the first mis-

sionary to the Far East and the first archbishop of Pekin (Bei-
jing). He also suggested uniting into one order the Hospitallers
and the Templars, whose endless quarrels were a great danger at such a critical period in the history of the Holy Land.
But the proposal came too late. In 1291 heroic Acre was
besieged, and the two military orders, united at last in face
of disaster, fought side by side to the death.

Faced with such hopeless ruin in temporal affairs, Raymond Lull decided to move on to another sphere of activity.
He went to Genoa and came to an agreement with the master of a galley sailing to the Barbary Coast. Then something
happened that shows how human frailty could still get the
better even of such a man as this. Just as the sail was being
raised Raymond was suddenly overwhelmed with doubts.
He dashed off the galley onto firm land when the sailors
were in the very act of loosing off. But the vessel had barely
got under way before remorse followed hard on doubt. He
realized that it was fear that had held him back—and fear is
a negation of faith; regret that he had given way to it was so
violent that he became ill. Certainly once he had recovered,
he thought only of setting out once more. It was at this time,
before his embarkation for Tunis, that he assumed the habit
of a tertiary of Saint Francis.

When he arrived he began to preach in Arabic with that
same fire which he had brought previously to the public dis-
putations to which he had invited Muslims and Jews toward
the end of his time of study in Majorca. This same fire
achieved the same success. So great was his success that the
Khadi came to hear of it, and he was thrown into prison. He
was dragged before the local council and condemned to death.
However, his sentence was commuted to exile, perhaps
through the intervention of the many Genoese merchants
who frequented the town, or perhaps because it was feared

that the execution of a man of noble birth would bring reprisals. The fact remains that he was taken back to a Genoese *nef* that was anchored in the port. As he went he was
pelted with a shower of stones by a crowd that had been
stirred up against him. Once aboard, the first thing he did
was to hide in order to try and make his way secretly back to
land. By doing this he helped to cause trouble for an Italian
merchant who resembled him slightly. This man was seized
by the populace and had great difficulty in proving his identity and getting away from them. Raymond understood that
any attempts to preach would now be useless; he resigned
himself to going back to Naples and decided to travel from
there to Rome.

But he was certain that he would come back.

Rome offered him nothing but disappointments. The Papacy had now involved itself in that long period of troubles,
exile, and decadence that would not come to an end until
after the Great Schism. In *Lo Desconhort*, written in 1295,
Raymond gave free rein to the rancor and bitterness he felt
at the sight of Pope Boniface VIII more concerned with his
war against the King of France than with the Crusade and
the conversion of Islam.

But a great hope dawned for him when the news reached
Majorca that the Tartar khan was conquering Syria. He set
sail at once for Cyprus, but on his arrival he learned that the
news was false. However, he found that the atmosphere there
was favorable for preaching, if not for a Crusade. Many Muslims lived on the island, and he carried on discussions with
them as he had done in Majorca, until one day a mysterious
attempt was made to poison him. When he recovered from
this he left Cyprus, stayed for a while in Rome, then went
on to Naples and Lesser Armenia, returning to Majorca before making various other journeys to Paris and Montpellier.

In 1307 he reverted to his plan for setting sail to North Africa. On this occasion he disembarked at Bougie, but when he applied to the Khadi for permission to preach in public, he was immediately seized, roughly treated, and flung into prison. During this captivity he had frequent opportunity to discuss religion with an educated Moor named Amar. In the end they came to an unusual agreement: Amar was to write a book to which Raymond would reply. This was an unexpected chance for that ardent preacher, but the duel of words was not allowed to go forward. The King of Bougie was told of the suggestion, forbade any further talks, and was glad to rid himself of Raymond by putting him aboard a Christian ship. He had to content himself later on with writing his own part of the projected book: *La Disputation entre Raymond le Chrétien et Amar le Sarrasin*. It was in fact much later that this was written, for his ship was wrecked in sight of Pisa. Raymond, one of the few survivors, was rescued by the people living on the coast and taken to the monastery of Saint Dominic, where he spent some time recovering and planning further travels. These took him again to Paris and Montpellier, and finally to Vienna, where he was able to take part in the Council of 1312 and put forward his views on the Crusade. At this Council it was at last decided to set up schools of Oriental languages—a project which had become almost an obsession with him. Chairs of Hebrew, Arabic, and Chaldean were to be founded at Rome and at Oxford, Bologna, Paris, and Salamanca, the principal universities of Europe.

The following year, back in Majorca, Raymond made his will. His life was now near its end. He was eighty years old, a handsome, white-haired old man, when he embarked once more for the Barbary Coast. He was provided with a letter from King James to the sultan of Tunis, and thanks to this he was allowed to preach and was able to convert several of the more highly educated Arabs. But this no longer satisfied him. What he had come there to seek was no longer preaching or discussion, but that "crimson robe" in which he desired to meet his Redeemer. One day, almost in secret, he left Tunis and went to Bejaïa. There he was immediately recognized by the crowd and stoned to death. Two Genoese merchants, Esteva Colom and Luis de Pastorga, came running up too late to save him and were able to do no more than bear away his body, which was at once accorded the veneration due to a saint.

During the course of his long tormented life, Raymond Lull did at least achieve general acceptance of the great purpose that he bore within him: the transformation of Crusades into missions. At a time when the whole of Europe was holding fast to the old formula of reconquest by armed might, he, at the cost of his life, had demonstrated a different way, one which in succeeding centuries was to change the life of the Church in all her aspects.

In the course of his Eastern adventure feudal man was swept much further on than he had expected, and forced to transcend himself, and thereby to reveal his essential nature, in encounters, at first violent and then more temperate, with foreign worlds. In this context he gives the impression of being untroubled by anxiety, of living in a dynamic and generous atmosphere which his descendants were never to find again, in Europe at any rate. He knew how to pay dearly with his own person; he was passionate, but not sordid; exuberant, and able to weep like a child; violent, but capable, when the fit had passed, of regretting his fault and of paying for it if necessary with the gift of his own life; a sinner, but conscious of his sins and thus capable of repentance. With all his faults and his brutalities, and his sometimes cynical ambitions, he persisted nevertheless in regarding as supreme the ideals of chivalry and in reserving his admiration for the man whom he knew to be "valiant and generous".

When we come face to face with this great living person, this being who asserted and realized to the full his own potential, we see him, as he stood at the crossroads between two ages, already taking the shape of an administrator, of a thinker in his study, and sketching the distinction between two types of men. Peter Dubois and Raymond Lull were both equally representative of their times, even though they represented two different achievements. At the end of the age of feudalism the distance separating the mystic and the practical man was growing greater. At the zenith of that period these two had been one. Gradually the practical man was to turn into an office worker and substitute for spiritual life abstract speculations and theoretical views to which he would later attempt to make reality conform. Rationalists of this sort, lawyers, politicians, or theorists of any kind easily lose touch with concrete realities, even when the object of their planning is of a purely material order. On the other hand, those who were animated by supernatural mysticism were to live in increasing separation from the life of secular cities, and their accomplishments were to lie on the fringe of normal activities.

From these parallel evolutions more than one misapprehension was to spring within Christendom, as it began to split apart and every Christian nation strained to exert its individuality against its neighbors, as thinkers began to elaborate systems and not syntheses, as every fresh movement tried to destroy the ones that had gone before. The early crusading impulse had been possible only because of the intimate union, in each individual, as in the whole of Christendom, between the spirit and the practical means, between what Saint Augustine had called the earthly city and the City of God.

BIBLIOGRAPHY

As well as the books mentioned in the Introduction, the following are recommended:

Anonymous. *Gesta Francorum et aliorum Hierosolimitanorum.*
_____. Ed. L. Bréhier (with French translation). *Histoire Anonyme de la première Croisade.* Paris, 1924.
_____. Ed. R. Hill (with English translation). *The Deeds of the Franks,* and Other Pilgrims in Jerusalem. London, New York: T. Nelson, 1962.
Alphandery, P., and A. Dupront. *La Chrétienté et l'Idée de Croisade.* Paris, 1954.
Bréhier, L. *L'Église et l'Orient au Moyen Age.* Paris: Lecoffe, J. Gabalda, 1921.
Cahen, C. *La Syrie du Nord à l'époque des Croisades.* Paris, 1940.
Deschamps, P. *Les Châteaux des Croisés en Terre sainte.* Paris, 1934.
Fedden, R. *Crusaders' Castles.* London, 1950.
Grousset, R. *Histoire de Croisades et du Royaume franc de Jérusalem.* 3 vols. Paris, 1934–36.
Grousset, R. *L'Epopée des Croisades.* Paris, 1939.
Hill, J. H., and L. L. Hill. *Raymond IV de Saint-Gilles.* Toulouse, 1959.
History of the Crusades. Ed. K. M. Setton. University of Pennsylvania.
Longnan, J. *Les Français d' outre-mer au Moyen Age.* Paris, 1929.
_____. *L'Empire latin de Constantinople.* Paris, 1949.

354

Mayer, H. E. *Bibliographie zur Geschichte der Kreuzzüge.* Hanover, 1960.

Pernoud, Régine. *Women in the Days of Cathedrals.* San Francisco: Ignatius Press, 1998.

Richard, J. *Le Royaume latin de Jérusalem.* Paris, 1953.

Rousset, P. *Les Origines et les Caractères de la première Croisade.* Neuchâtel, 1945.

Runciman, Steven. *A History of the Crusades.* 3 vol. Cambridge, Eng.: University Press, 1951–1954.

Smail, R. C. *Crusading Warfare, 1097–1193.* Cambridge, Eng.: University Press, 1956.

Stevenson, William Barron. *The Crusaders in the East.* Cambridge, Eng.: University Press, 1907.

Cahen, Richard and Runciman give detailed notes on the sources and the bibliography of the history of the Crusades.